WHICH? WAY TO SAVE TAX 1996–7

WHICH? WAY TO SAVE TAX 1996–7

WHICH? BOOKS

CONSUMERS' ASSOCIATION

Which? Books are commissioned and researched by
Consumers' Association, and published by
Which? Ltd
2 Marylebone Road, London NW1 4DF

Distributed by The Penguin Group:
Penguin Books Ltd, 27 Wrights Lane, London W8 5TZ

Editor: Anthony Bailey

Acknowledgements to:
Eve Filmer, Teresa Fritz, Jonquil Lowe, Veronica McGrath,
Virginia Wallis

Typographic design by Paul Saunders
Cover design by Steve Ridgeway

First edition August 1992
Second edition April 1994
Third edition April 1995
Fourth edition April 1996

British Library Cataloguing in Publication Data
Which? Way to Save Tax 1996–7
A catalogue record for this book is available from the
British Library

ISBN 0 85202 635 8

Typeset by Litho Link, Welshpool, Powys, Wales
Printed and bound in Great Britain by Clays Ltd,
Bungay, Suffolk

CONTENTS

Addresses and telephone numbers for those organisations marked with an asterisk (*) can be found in the address section at the back of the book.

INTRODUCTION

A new era has begun in the tax affairs of the 9 million or so people who are sent a tax return each year. As a result, it has become more important than ever to know how the tax system works. This book explains the rules and shows how you can legitimately use them to your advantage.

In the main, if you are an employee who pays basic-rate tax through the Pay-As-You-Earn (PAYE) system and your tax affairs are fairly straightforward, you are unlikely to be asked to complete a tax return. That does not mean that you are paying the right amount of tax. Mistakes are made. Furthermore, there may be allowances you can claim or rules you don't know about which could benefit you. A report commissioned by IFA Promotion estimates that £5.5 billion each year is paid in tax unnecessarily because people are not making use of legitimate tax breaks.

It is the people who do fill in a tax return who will be affected by the changes. A completely re-designed tax return will be sent out in April 1997, to accommodate the new system known as self-assessment. These first new-style tax returns will relate to the 1996–7 tax year beginning on 6 April 1996. Self-assessment means that you will be given the opportunity to work out your own tax bill. This could be quite a daunting prospect. If the professionals can get it wrong, so can you. In addition, you could incur a range of new penalties if, for instance, you fail to keep to all the deadlines in the new timetable. It is vital to get to grips with the tax system now: don't wait until April 1997. There are strict rules on keeping records to support the information you send to your tax inspector and they take effect from April 1996. Failure to keep documents could result in penalties.

But if all this sounds daunting, it need not be. For example, if you get your tax return back by 30 September each year, you can ask your tax office to work out your bill – but you will still need to make sure you send in all the right information. And if you decide to 'self-calculate' your own bill (for which the deadline is 31 January each year) it can be a relatively painless procedure if you know exactly what you are doing. That is where this book will help.

KEY FIGURES FOR THE 1996–7 TAX YEAR

Allowances	
Personal allowance	£3,765
Married couple's allowance	£1,790*
Personal allowance (age 65–74)	£4,910
Married couple's allowance (age 65–74)	£3,115*
Personal allowance (age 75+)	£5,090
Married couple's allowance (age 75+)	£3,155*
Income limit for age-related allowances	£15,200
Additional personal allowance	£1,790*
Widow's bereavement allowance	£1,790*
Blind person's allowance	£1,250

*You save 15p in tax for every £1 of allowance.

Income (and capital gains) tax rates		
first £3,900	20p**	
next £21,600	25p	
over £25,500	40p	
Capital gains tax		
annual exemption		£6,300
Inheritance tax		
exempt amount		£200,000
Pension contributions		
earnings cap		£82,200
Mortgage interest relief		
interest on first £30,000 of loan		15 per cent

**Unless you are a higher-rate taxpayer, most taxable income from savings will be taxed at 20p – see p. 23.

1 GETTING TO GRIPS WITH TAX

- Maintain good records – it is more important now than ever if you want to avoid stiff penalties.
- Keep your tax bill down – 52 ways to save tax.
- Check previous year's tax bills – you might still be able to claim a rebate.

Successive chancellors have tinkered with the tax system in order to close loopholes, get rid of complexities and make life easier for both the Inland Revenue and the taxpayer. This year sees the biggest shake-up: self-assessment, which came into force on 6 April 1996. We deal with self-assessment in more detail in Chapter 4, but broadly it will mean new forms, new obligations, new time limits – and new penalties. The people most affected by this change will be the 9 million or so taxpayers who regularly fill in a tax return. Now more than ever, it is important to understand how the tax system works and to make sure you are paying the right amount of tax, which is where this book will help. You may have limited understanding of tax, or you may be someone who gives advice to others. The first thing is to decide what you want the book to do for you. So where do you fit in?

Beginners

The best starting-place is Chapter 2, *How your income tax bill is worked out*. This gives a step-by-step guide through the basics of the income tax system. Once you've mastered this chapter, the rest of the chapters on income tax should fall into place.

General readers

If you're reading for interest, or if you want to sharpen up your knowledge of tax, the whole book is your oyster. Each chapter looks at tax from a different angle. So if you're particularly interested in knowing how getting married (or divorced) can affect your tax bill, you could go straight to Chapter 5, *Tax and families*. Or if you are not sure how your investments are taxed, go to Chapter 13, *Investments*, which looks at investments in general, and includes details of schemes like personal equity plans (PEPs), which have special tax perks.

Planning ahead

One of the major worries for many people is how to pass their money on to their children. Chapter 18, *Inheritance tax*, gives practical advice.

Checking a specific point

Start with the *Index*, which should give you quick guidance to the right place. Wherever there's space, we've given *examples* to illustrate what we say in the text. And we give *references* to Finance Acts – so that you can, if you want, give chapter and verse to your tax office, or your tax adviser. See below for the abbreviations we use.

Checking your tax bill over past years

If you're trying to adjust your tax bill from earlier years, Chapter 19, *Tax facts*, has a handy reference section with tax rates for the past six years.

Trouble with the Revenue?

Chapter 3, *Dealing with the Revenue*, gives advice if you are in dispute with the Revenue, and gives details of the penalties you might face.

The taxes covered in this book

Income tax

Income tax takes up most of the book. It's by far the most important tax, not only for the government, for which it brings in more money than anything else, but also for ordinary people. Anyone with more than a very modest wage has to pay income tax. So do many people with no earnings but with money coming in from investments. The main aim of the book is to help you realise:

- what income tax is
- how it affects you
- how you can check your tax bill
- how you can make the most of the rules and pay less tax.

Capital gains tax

You may have to pay capital gains tax if you sell some of your possessions at a profit – or even if you give them away. The rules are complicated, and you're quite likely to find that there's no tax to pay. But it's as well to skim through our explanation in Chapter 15, *Capital gains tax*, to make sure that you're not at risk. And if you *are* at risk, we suggest ways of cutting down tax you have to pay.

Inheritance tax

With inheritance tax there is no tax to pay on what you give away while you are still alive (with a few exceptions), as long as you live for at least seven years after making the gift. Even if you do die within seven years, there may be no tax to pay. Giving away possessions and money while you are alive won't save *you* tax, though it could mean less tax for your heirs: so don't let the idea of saving them tax threaten your own financial security.

Value added tax (VAT)

We don't go into detail, but there is a brief summary of VAT rules in Chapter 11, *Working for yourself*.

National Insurance

Although this is not called a tax, it is money that has to be paid to the government, and what you have to pay varies with your income. We give some National Insurance details in Chapter 11, *Working for yourself*, and Chapter 17, *Building up a pension*.

References throughout the book

Here's an explanation of what the letters and figures mean:

FA	Finance Act
ICTA	Income and Corporation Taxes Act 1988
TMA	Taxes Management Act 1970
TCGA	Taxation of Chargeable Gains Act 1992
CAA	Capital Allowances Act 1990
IHTA	Inheritance Tax Act 1984
s	Section
Sch	Schedule
IR	Inland Revenue leaflet
ESC	Extra-statutory concession
SI	Statutory Instrument
SP	Inland Revenue Statement of Practice

Schedules come at the end of Finance Acts. Lists of Inland Revenue leaflets and of extra-statutory concessions are in Chapter 19, *Tax facts* (p. 372). In addition, some *Tax cases* are mentioned – see below.

Here are some examples:

FA 1989 s8	Finance Act 1989, Section 8
ICTA 1988 s168 (8–20)	Income and Corporation Taxes Act 1988, Section 168, subsections 8–20
TCGA Sch 1 para 2	Taxation of Chargeable Gains Act 1992 Schedule 1, paragraph 2
SI 1975/610	Statutory Instrument number 610 of 1975
IR 6	Inland Revenue leaflet 6
SP 14/80	Inland Revenue Statement of Practice number 14 of 1980
SAT2 (1995)	Self-Assessment Technical of 1995

Sometimes you'll see several references together. Where this happens, and the references are to different topics, we put the topic (in brackets) after the reference:

ESC A27 (interest relief); TCGA s223; ESC D3, D4 (capital gains).

Where to find the sources

Inland Revenue leaflets are free from tax offices or tax enquiry centres (for exceptions, see p. 374). Tax cases and statutes should be in central reference libraries.

We give references to tax cases when the outcome of the case has an important effect on tax rules. Tax cases may be reported in more than one publication. References in this book are to *Tax cases* (TC) and to the *All England Law Reports* (All ER). So, for example, *1976 1 All ER p272* means that the case is found on page 272 of volume 1 of the 1976 All England Law Reports.

Tax advice

There are three rules to follow if you want to keep your tax bill as low as possible:

- **keep in control** If you let your tax affairs get out of hand, you'll store up trouble and expense.
- **make the right choices** In planning your life, the choices you make can drastically affect your tax bill. Of the 52 choices listed on p. 18, any one might affect you.
- **act in time** Many of the choices you make have time limits attached to them.

Keep in control

You have always been obliged to notify the Revenue if you have earnings or gains which should be taxed and which the Revenue does not already know about. What's new under self-assessment is that you must notify the Revenue within six months of the end of the tax year in which you received the income or made the gain. So if you have new income or gains in the 1996–7 tax year, you must tell the Revenue by 5 October 1997. And you must then file a completed tax return and pay the tax due by 31 January following the end of the tax year (for the 1996–7 tax year, this means that tax must be paid by 31 January 1998). If you don't, you will pay a penalty.

Self-assessment also brings with it a legal requirement to keep records in support of information you give on your tax return. If you have been lax about keeping track of who you worked for and what you were paid, and have not kept receipts for expenses or assets that you bought and sold, start keeping track now. If you don't, you could face a penalty of up to £3,000 for each failure to keep an adequate record.

Maintaining control and keeping the Revenue informed

is not just a question of avoiding penalties. If you don't tell the Revenue about changes in your personal circumstances, you could be paying too much tax because you're not claiming an allowance that you're entitled to or because your income has dropped. If you already receive a tax return each year, you get the chance to give the Revenue the necessary information. But now that the form has been re-designed, you will need to check that you get the parts (or 'Schedules') which apply to you – see p. 73. If you don't get a tax return, it is up to you to keep the Revenue informed of any change in your circumstances or financial affairs which could affect your tax position.

To sum up:

1 Keep clear records of income you get, and of any expenses you can set against your income. And keep your records up to date.

2 Keep the Revenue informed of what's going on. Tell them if there's any change in your circumstances – for example:

- you get married
- you separate or get divorced
- you become unemployed, or retire
- you gain or lose a source of income
- you start or stop making a payment which qualifies for tax relief
- you change from being an employee to being self-employed.

3 Check your tax. Even though self-assessment means that you can calculate your own tax bill if you want to, it will still be the Revenue's job to send out your tax code (if you're an employee or receiving a pension) and to tell you how much tax it would like you to pay in advance (if you are self-employed). Whenever you get a tax statement, or a PAYE Coding Notice, check to see that the figures are correct, and write to your tax office at once if you don't think they are.

Make the right choices

Here are 52 ways to pay less tax – one for every week of the year. See how many of them apply to you now, or might apply in the future. Making the right choice can reduce the amount of tax you have to pay.

Your family

1 Are you married? Make sure you get the married couple's allowance (p. 82).

2 Unmarried with children? You should claim the additional personal allowance (p. 98).

3 If you are married, does one of you own all the investments? Husbands and wives are taxed separately and there could be less tax to pay if you shared out the spoils differently – for instance, if only one of you is a higher-rate taxpayer (p. 87).

4 Paying maintenance under the old tax rules? You *might* save tax by opting for the maintenance deduction instead (p. 92).

5 Does your child use his or her tax allowance? Any child, no matter how young, can have an income of £3,765 without paying tax (p. 100).

6 Recently widowed? Make sure you claim all your allowances (p. 89).

7 Married this year? In this year only, the husband can choose not to take the married couple's allowance – it could save tax (p. 83).

In a job?

8 Can you get any fringe benefits? Many perks are taxed at much less than their value to you (p. 155).

9 Can you set any expenses against tax? See the table on p. 132 onwards.

10 Approaching retirement? It may be worthwhile making additional voluntary contributions to your pension scheme (p. 320).

11 Not in a pension scheme? You can get tax relief (at your top rate) on premiums paid into a personal pension plan (p. 322).

12 A student? If you have vacation earnings, signing a form can save you the bother of paying tax now and claiming it back later (p. 101).

In business?

13 Self-employed? You may be able to save tax by employing your husband or wife (p. 206).

14 Loans for your business? See if they qualify for tax relief (p. 30).

15 Entitled to capital allowances? It may pay you to claim less than you're able to, and to roll on the balance to succeeding years (p. 198).

16 Business losses? You have three choices of how to deal with them – and the choice you make can affect your tax bill and your cash-in-hand (p. 202).

17 Losses in a new business? You can get tax relief by setting them against other income or capital gains (p. 203).

18 Should you register for VAT? See p. 207 for the answer.

19 Are you claiming all your expenses? See the table on p. 193.

On a low income?

20 Not a taxpayer? If you don't pay tax, and you've got money to invest, you should register as a non-taxpayer if you're putting it in a bank or building society account (p. 246).

21 Tax to claim back? Make your claim as soon as possible (p. 60). And if you'll be claiming tax back each year, arrange with the Revenue to get it paid in instalments (p. 109).

Elderly?

22 Approaching 65? You may be able to claim some allowances for the whole of the tax year in which you (or your wife) reaches 65: you don't have to wait for your 65th birthday (p. 103).

23 Not getting full age-related allowances? Consider switching to investments where the return is tax-free (p. 242). Beware of cashing in a life insurance policy where the return is taxable (p. 266).

24 Need more income? One solution might be to buy an annuity (p. 110). Or consider a home income plan (p. 114).

25 Can you make use of your husband's pension contributions? A married woman can get a state retirement pension based on her husband's contributions. It's worth doing so if this would be higher than the pension you would have got on your own contributions. The extra is counted as the wife's income, so there could be less tax to pay if the wife hasn't fully used her personal allowance (p. 107).

26 Retiring from a business? You may be able to claim retirement relief from capital gains tax (p. 292).

27 Coming up to retirement – and with a personal pension plan? You may be able to get yourself a larger pension and cut your recent tax bills (p. 330). If you haven't got a personal pension plan, see whether you should take one out.

Investments and life insurance

28 Buying British government stocks? If you buy them through the National Savings Stock register, income is paid to you without tax being deducted (p. 247) and the costs of the transaction can be lower.

29 Have you made use of the annual capital gains tax exemption? Investing for capital gains, rather than income, may give you a better after-tax return (p. 284).

30 A large amount to invest, and worried about inheritance tax? Consider investing in certain types of property (p. 349).

31 Getting tax relief on a pre-March 1984 life insurance policy? Beware of extending the policy, or of altering it to increase the benefits. You may lose your tax relief (p. 271).

32 Self-employed, or in a job but not in an employer's pension scheme? You can get tax relief on a life insurance policy (p. 272).

33 Willing to take a risk? The enterprise investment scheme gives you tax relief on your investments (p. 249).

34 Life insurance for your family? Cut your inheritance tax bill by making sure the proceeds aren't added to your estate (p. 274).

35 Made a loss when you sold some shares? Keep a record of any losses when you dispose of something. You may be able to use the loss to cut down any capital gains tax you have to pay (p. 285).

You and your home

36 Thinking of buying? There's tax relief available on your mortgage (p. 214).

37 A home to let? If you're borrowing to buy the home, you can get tax relief on the interest you pay (p. 232). For the expenses you can claim, see p. 230.

38 Selling your house and garden separately? Sell the garden first (p. 223).

39 Working at home? See p. 225 for expenses you can claim.

40 More than one home? Be careful about which home you choose as your 'main home' for capital gains tax purposes (p. 219).

41 A home with your job and another which you own? Make sure that the home you own is free from capital gains tax (p. 227).

42 Moving house? You can get tax relief on two loans at once (p. 215).

43 Moving house when you marry? You may be able to get tax relief on three loans (p. 87).

44 Buying a home for around £60,000? Juggling with the price could save over £600 in stamp duty (p. 307).

Passing your money on

45 Can 'estate freezing' save you tax? See p. 352.

46 Made a will yet? Make sure you word it correctly; otherwise, your spouse could be left short (p. 354).

47 Married with valuable property which one of you owns exclusively? Sharing some of it between you can cut down your inheritance tax bill (p. 353).

48 High income, and young children? Consider an accumulation and maintenance trust (p. 357).

49 Inheritance tax to be paid by your beneficiaries when you die? Making regular gifts out of income can get rid of a lot of the value of your estate. And you can give away at least £3,000 a year tax-free (p. 344).

50 A beneficiary under a will? You may be able to pay any inheritance tax by instalments (p. 361).

Charities

51 Giving to charity? Your gift could be worth a lot more if you make use of the tax breaks (p. 32).

52 Can you have your charitable donations deducted straight from your pay? If not, you should ask your employer to set up a payroll-giving scheme (p. 32).

Act in time

Tax rules are hedged round with time limits. They can be as short as 30 days and as long as six years. We start by explaining how far back you can go to claim personal allowances or tax relief that you've missed. You'll find details of the various time limits throughout this book.

The normal rule

You may have forgotten to claim personal allowances in past years. Or, more likely, you may have forgotten to claim tax relief on, for example, a loan which qualifies for tax relief. Is it too late to make a claim? How far back can you go?

The answer is that you can go back six tax years into the past, i.e. you can claim tax relief, or allowances, for the six tax years before the current tax year.

Tax years run from 6 April in one year to 5 April in the next. So if you act *before* 6 April 1997, you can go back six tax years before the 1996–7 tax year – which takes you to the 1990–1 tax year. (See below for later tax years.)

Note that the six-year rule is changing in 1996–7. For claims relating to the 1996–7 tax year you will have two months less in which to act – i.e., if in the tax year 2002–3 you realise that you forgot to claim an allowance in the 1996–7 tax year, you will have five years ten months (or until 31 January 2003) in which to make your claim.

How much can you claim?

The *allowances* you can claim are the amounts which applied in the relevant tax year; the figures are on p. 366.

Together with any extra tax relief you can claim, these will (in normal cases) reduce your taxable income for the relevant tax year. Your tax bill for that tax year will be recalculated, using the tax rates that applied at the time; the rates are on p. 364.

EXAMPLE

Charles Fox looks through his tax bills for previous years. In the 1990–1 tax year, his taxable income was £11,392, and his tax bill was £2,848.

Charles realises that he forgot to claim the additional personal allowance which he was entitled to for that year. In the 1990–1 tax year, this allowance was £1,720 (see p. 366). So Charles can subtract £1,720 from his taxable income, leaving him with a taxable income of £9,672. Tax (at 1990–1 rates) on that amount was £2,418.

So Charles can claim back the difference between £2,418 and the £2,848 he paid – £430.

The six-year rule

Act before 6 April 1997 for the 1990–1 tax year

Act before 6 April 1998 for the 1991–2 tax year

Act before 6 April 1999 for the 1992–3 tax year

Act before 6 April 2000 for the 1993–4 tax year

Act before 6 April 2001 for the 1994–5 tax year

Act before 6 April 2002 for the 1995–6 tax year

Act before 31 January 2003 for the 1996–7 tax year

Tax advice – where to find it

No one person – and no one book – can answer every tax problem. In the following paragraphs, we suggest sources of advice which, depending on your circumstances, you might find useful.

Start with this book
It's the obvious starting place. With over 400 pages of information and advice, it covers the great majority of tax situations.

Use Inland Revenue leaflets
These vary considerably in the amount of detail they give. Some are easy to read but quite sketchy. Others are labyrinthine. The majority provide relatively straightforward information, often with worked examples. Not all leaflets are up to date – though sometimes there are supplements, which should be given to you with the main leaflet. All leaflets are free, from tax offices and tax enquiry centres. We list them on p. 372.

Go to tax enquiry centres
These Inland Revenue advice centres may be nearer (and more convenient) than your own tax office. They should be able to sort out most problems.

Use the **Which? Tax-Saving Guide**
This is the best short guide to the tax system, and takes you step by step through filling in your tax return. It's published in March each year.

Try **Simon's Taxes**
This is a nine-volume looseleaf tax encyclopaedia, certainly not worth buying unless you're a tax professional. But it's the best place to consult statutes. One of the problems for the ordinary person is that Finance Acts very often make changes to sections in earlier Acts, so you need to find a version of the earlier Acts which contains all the changes. *Simon's Taxes* (Volumes G and H) do just that. Your local library might have a copy; otherwise, try a reference library or university library.

Get professional help
Only if your tax affairs are complicated, or you're making a will, will you need a professional to handle your tax affairs. If you're setting up a trust, or engaging in detailed inheritance tax planning, you'll need a professional adviser – a taxation consultant, accountant or solicitor. The level of competence and expertise varies enormously, and there's no easy way to find someone who's good. Try asking friends, or your employer.

2 HOW YOUR INCOME TAX BILL IS WORKED OUT

- The last of the old-style notices of assessment will be sent out in 1996. They are notoriously difficult to understand, but it is well worth trying to decipher them and to check they are accurate – tax inspectors do make mistakes.
- Discover three ways to make your donations to charity go further (see p. 32).
- For new tax breaks for those seeking work see p. 33.

This book deals with three main taxes: income tax, to which most of this book is devoted; capital gains tax, which is explained in Chapter 15; and inheritance tax, described in Chapter 18. This chapter deals only with income tax and takes you through the stages involved in working out your income tax bill. Use it to get an overall picture of how all the elements of the income tax system come together, and to find out where in the rest of the book you'll be able to check up on the particular details which affect your individual circumstances.

It is important to remember that income tax is an annual tax. Although the principles of the tax system don't really change, what you have to pay tax on, and the amount of tax you have to pay, varies from year to year (depending on changes announced in the Budget). Your annual tax bill is generally based on the income you receive in a *tax year* and calculated according to the rules (and rates) which apply to that tax year.

A tax year runs from 6 April in one year to 5 April in the next. This book describes the tax rules for the tax year running from 6 April 1996 to 5 April 1997 – in other words, the 1996–7 tax year. If you want to check your tax bill for a different tax year, Chapter 19 gives a summary of tax rates and allowances for the last six years.

How to work out your income tax bill

You don't pay income tax on all the money you have coming in; instead you pay it on the part of that money which the Inland Revenue calls *taxable income*. The following steps outline how you arrive at your own figure for taxable income:

- start with the money you have coming in during a tax year but don't include income from savings (see below for the explanation)
- subtract the money which doesn't count as income, or which counts as tax-free income (p. 26) to arrive at your income for tax purposes
- subtract payments you make on which you get full *tax relief* which are called *outgoings* (see p. 28, but see below for what to do with outgoings on which tax relief is restricted) to arrive at your *total income* (p. 33)
- subtract your full *personal allowances* (see p. 34, but see below for where to include *fixed-relief allowances*) to arrive at your *taxable income*
- add your 'gross' taxable income from savings (see below).

Your taxable income is the amount on which you will have to pay tax. This is then sliced into tax bands, each band attracting a different rate of tax. In the 1996–7 tax year, you pay tax at:

- the *lower rate* of 20 per cent on the first £3,900 of your taxable income
- the *basic rate* of 24 per cent on the next slice of £21,600
- if your taxable income from other sources *plus* your taxable income from savings is less than £25,500, your savings income is taxed at the lower rate of 20 per cent
- the *higher rate* of 40 per cent on any taxable income over £25,500.

If your taxable income from *savings* takes you over £25,500 once it is added to your income from other sources, the amount which takes your total taxable income up to the limit is taxed at 20 per cent, and the remainder at 40 per cent. If your taxable income (excluding savings) is over the

£25,500 limit, all your income from savings will be taxed at 40 per cent. To determine your final tax bill, add up the amounts of tax due on each slice of your taxable income. Doing these sums will give you your final tax bill *unless*:

- you are entitled to one of the *fixed-relief allowances* (see p. 34)
- you can deduct an outgoing on which tax relief is restricted (see pp. 29, 30, 31) and you have not already received tax relief at source. Multiply the amount of the outgoing and/or allowance by the rate of tax relief – e.g. 15 per cent – and then deduct the result from the tax bill you've already worked out.

EXAMPLE 1

Horace Walpole received £25,000 in the 1996–7 tax year. But he doesn't pay income tax on all of this. First, he takes away sums which aren't income: £300 he inherited and £1,550 of capital gains from selling shares at a profit. Then he knocks off his tax-free income: £50 from a National Savings Ordinary account. He then deducts taxable income from savings – this will be added back later in the calculations. The next things to go are his outgoings on which he gets full tax relief: £1,000 in contributions to his employer's pension scheme. Lastly he takes away his personal allowance of £3,765.

That leaves him £18,335. Tax at 20 per cent on the first £3,900 is £780. Tax on the rest at 24 per cent comes to £3,464.40. That's £4,244.40 tax in total. However, Horace is married and can claim the married couple's allowance of £1,790, on which relief is fixed at 15 per cent. This knocks £268.50 (15 per cent of £1,790) off his tax bill, bringing it down to £3,975.90. However, he has not yet taken into account the £500 (grossed-up) interest he received from his savings on which he will pay tax at 20 per cent because his taxable income from other sources added to his (gross) income from savings is less than £25,500. The £100 of tax on his savings brings his final tax bill to £4,075.90.

money	**£25,000**
subtract things which aren't income	
– inheritance	£300
– capital gains on shares	£1,550
income	**£23,150**
subtract tax-free income	
– NS Ordinary account interest	£50
income for tax purposes	**£23,100**
subtract outgoings which qualify for tax relief	
– contributions to pension scheme	£1,000
total income	**£22,100**
subtract personal allowance	£3,765
taxable income	**£18,335**
tax 20 per cent of £3,900	£780
24 per cent of £14,435	£3,464.40
total tax before fixed-relief allowances	**£4,244.40**
subtract 15 per cent of fixed-relief allowance	£268.50
plus tax at 20 per cent of £500	£100
final tax bill	**£4,075.90**

Your income for tax purposes

As you have already seen, not all of the money you have coming in counts as income for the purposes of working out your income tax bill (though some money may be subject to other forms of tax). Some income is tax-free, and can also be disregarded.

Items which aren't income

- gifts and presents
- money you borrow
- money you inherit, though there may be inheritance tax
- profits (gains) you make when you sell something for more than you bought it (though you may have to pay capital gains tax), unless you did this as a business venture or as part of your business

- betting winnings – unless you bet (e.g. on horses) for a living
- lottery winnings
- premium bond prizes.

Tax-free income from investments

- first £70 interest from a National Savings Ordinary account
- proceeds from National Savings Certificates (or, in most cases, from Ulster Savings Certificates if you live in Northern Ireland)
- interest from National Savings Children's Bonus Bonds
- part of the income from annuities except annuities you *have* to buy – see p. 111
- proceeds from Save-As-You-Earn contracts
- proceeds from a regular-premium investment-type life insurance policy (if held for 10 years or three-quarters of its term – whichever is shorter)
- most proceeds from a personal equity plan (PEP) – see p. 252
- proceeds from a qualifying tax-exempt special savings account (TESSA) – see p. 254
- proceeds from some friendly society savings schemes – see p. 250.

Tax-free income from the state or local authorities

- many social security benefits – see p. 117
- a few special pensions (including the £10 Christmas bonus)
- council tax, housing benefit and rent rebates
- grants for improving or insulating your home
- most grants or scholarships for education
- some work-incentive schemes piloted by the government
- the Jobfinders' Grant – note that you can reclaim tax you may have paid on this grant back to April 1995.

Tax-free income from jobs

- some earnings from working abroad – see p. 173
- some fringe benefits – see p. 154
- in many cases, up to a total of £30,000 in redundancy pay, pay in lieu of notice, etc. when you leave a job – see p. 149

- gifts which are genuine personal gifts, i.e. not those given to you because you're an employee
- certain profit-related pay – see p. 130.

Miscellaneous tax-free income

- certain maintenance payments you receive (see p. 94)
- income from a covenant
- income from family income benefit life insurance policies
- the income from a permanent health insurance policy
- interest from a delayed settlement of damages for personal injury or death
- strike and unemployment pay from a trade union
- interest on a tax rebate
- compensation for mis-sold personal pensions paid into a tax-approved pension scheme
- cash lump sums awarded by a court or out-of-court settlements in respect of mis-sold personal pensions.

Income which is taxable

Once you have disregarded money which doesn't count as income for tax purposes and income which is tax free, you are left with income which *is* taxable. But remember that you still won't pay tax on all of this because of outgoings and allowances. The main sources of income which is taxable are:

- earnings (and some fringe benefits) from your job with an employer – see p. 129
- any spare-time earnings – see p. 151
- profits you make from running a business – see p. 191
- earnings and fees for work you do on a freelance or self-employed basis – see p. 181
- some social security benefits – see p. 117
- pensions (including the state pension) see p. 106
- rent from letting property – see p. 228
- some maintenance payments you receive – see p. 94
- interest from bank, building society and other savings accounts – see p. 246
- dividends from shares – see p. 253
- distributions from unit trusts – see p. 255.

Outgoings

From a tax point of view, your outgoings are the amounts of money that you spend on which you get tax relief. There are three main types of outgoing:

Outgoings on which you receive full tax relief Where tax relief is given at your highest rate of tax. These outgoings can be deducted from your income for tax purposes to arrive at your total income – see p. 33.

Outgoings on which tax relief is restricted Where the tax relief is set at the same level for all levels of taxpayer, and limited to a fixed percentage.

Expenses These are outgoings which can be deducted only from the income to which they relate – e.g. if you run a business, you deduct your business expenses only from the money the business made, and not from any other source of income. (However, a loss may be claimed against total income; for how to deal with losses, see p. 202.)

Whatever the type of outgoing, how you actually get the tax relief varies:

Tax relief at source You get the tax relief by making lower payments. With outgoings with restricted relief, there will be no need for your tax bill to change if all the relief is given at source. This is also true of outgoings on which you receive full tax relief at source – unless you are a higher-rate taxpayer. If you are, you will get basic-rate relief, not higher-rate relief, at source. To get the extra relief you're due, you'll need to give details on your annual tax return and make the necessary adjustments to your tax bill.

Claiming tax relief If you don't get tax relief at source, you will have to claim relief on your outgoings by giving details on your annual tax return. If you pay tax through Pay-As-You-Earn (PAYE) – see p. 136 – the Revenue may alter your tax code to take your outgoings into account.

The main outgoings on which you get tax relief are summarised below together with the pages and chapters where you will find more detailed information. Unless stated otherwise, you will need to claim the relief on these outgoings by filling in a tax return.

EXAMPLE 2

Arnold Brown is self-employed, and in the 1996–7 tax year makes payments into a personal pension plan of £1,500. Because these payments qualify for full tax relief, he pays tax on £1,500 less of his income. As his income is well over the lower-rate band, he would have paid tax at the basic rate of 24 per cent on the £1,500, so he pays £360 less tax than he otherwise would.

Interest on loans for your home

You get tax relief on the interest you pay on the first £30,000 of loans to buy your only or main home. In the 1996–7 tax year it is restricted to 15 per cent. If more than one of you shares a property, then you don't get relief on more than the first £30,000 of loans on the property as a whole, unless the loan was taken out before 1 August 1988, when each person (or each married couple) had their own £30,000 limit.

Loans taken out before 6 April 1988 to improve a main home, or to buy homes for dependent relatives or a former wife or husband, also qualify for 15 per cent tax relief.

In most cases, you get tax relief at source by making lower payments to the lender (the mortgage interest relief at source, or MIRAS, system). Otherwise, write to your tax office and get the relief by paying less tax through PAYE, or by getting a tax rebate or a lower tax bill.

More details See p. 214.

Interest on loans for property you let

Any amount of loans to buy or improve the property count for full tax relief. The interest can be deducted as an allowable business expense from your letting income.

More details See p. 231.

Interest on a loan to buy an annuity

You get tax relief of 24 per cent on the interest for up to £30,000 of loans to buy an annuity if you are 65 or over and the loan is secured against your only or main home. This is in addition to any tax relief you can get on mortgages to buy the home. Relief is given at source: you make lower payments to the lender.

More details See p. 114.

Interest on loans to pay inheritance tax

You get tax relief for up to 12 months on the interest you pay on a loan to pay inheritance tax when someone dies, provided you actually pay the tax before probate is granted or letters of administration are received.

More details See p. 360.

Interest on other loans

You can get tax relief on the interest you pay on loans for a variety of purposes connected with business:

- contributing capital to, or buying a stake in, a partnership (but not a limited one)
- buying a stake in, or lending to, a 'close' company (e.g. a family one)
- buying a stake in an employee-controlled company or industrial co-operative which employs you more or less full-time
- buying machinery or plant (e.g. a car or typewriter) for use in your job or in your partnership, provided capital allowances can be claimed for it. There's no relief on interest payable more than three years after the end of the tax year in which you took out the loan.

You must use the money borrowed for one of these purposes within a 'reasonable' time (usually six months) before or after taking out the loan. The loan must not have to be paid back within 12 months of being taken out, unless the interest is paid in the UK to a bank, stockbroker or discount house. You will lose relief on this type of loan if you recover capital from the business (e.g. you sell some shares) without using the proceeds to pay off your loan. Overdrafts and credit cards don't qualify.

These outgoings apply to individuals: *businesses* (including the self-employed and partnerships) can claim interest paid on loans, overdrafts and credit card debts for most business purposes as an allowable business expense.

More details See p. 192 for allowable business expenses.

Expenses in your employment

You get tax relief on money you spend *wholly, exclusively and necessarily* in carrying out the duties of your employment. This is interpreted very strictly.

More details See p. 130.

Maintenance payments

You get tax relief, restricted to 15 per cent in the 1996–7 tax year, on maintenance payments you're legally obliged to make. For payments under an order applied for before 15 March 1988 (and in place by 30 June 1988), relief is limited to the amount you actually paid in the 1988–9 tax year and which qualified for relief. For orders applied for after 15 March 1988 (or not in place until after 30 June 1988) relief is limited to 15 per cent of payments up to £1,790 in the 1996–7 tax year.

More details See p. 91.

Pension payments

You get tax relief on contributions to employers' pension schemes or personal pension plans, and additional voluntary contributions (AVCs) to either an employer's scheme or a separate free-standing scheme.

There are limits on the amounts of contributions that qualify for relief in any one year between 15 per cent and 40 per cent of your earnings or profits depending on the type of scheme or plan you're in and your age. But you may be able to claim tax relief on extra contributions if you didn't pay the maximum allowed in previous years.

With employers' schemes (including AVCs) you get the relief automatically by paying less tax through PAYE.

With free-standing AVCs, or personal plans taken out by employees after 1 July 1988, you get basic-rate relief at source by making lower payments. If you pay higher-rate tax, you'll need to claim your extra relief by filling in a tax return.

With personal plans taken out by the self-employed (or employees before 1 July 1988) you do not get tax relief at source. Instead, you pay the full premium and will need to claim tax relief on your tax return.

More details See Chapter 17.

Covenant payments

You get full tax relief on payments you make under deeds of covenant to charities. The covenant must be capable of lasting for more than three years.

You give yourself basic-rate tax relief by subtracting an amount equivalent to the basic-rate tax on the payments before making them. The charity can reclaim basic-rate tax from the Revenue. For example, if you want a charity to be £100 a year better off, you need give them only £100 less basic-rate tax at 24 per cent, i.e. £76. The charity will be able to claim a tax repayment of £24 (24 per cent of the gross equivalent – see p. 37 – of the £76 they get from you).

If you pay higher-rate tax, you will have to claim the higher-rate relief you are due on covenants you make to charities.

Covenants to individuals don't qualify for tax relief.

Payroll giving

Payroll-giving schemes are run by your employer. If your employer has such a scheme, you can get tax relief on payments through it to charities of up to £1,200 a year. You get tax relief (at your highest rate) automatically because your donations are taken from your gross pay before the deduction of tax is worked out.

Gift aid

You can get tax relief on single donations (i.e. other than covenants) made to charities after 1 October 1990. Each donation has to be for at least £250 to qualify, but there's no maximum. The relief applies only to genuine gifts (i.e. where you don't get any benefits in return) and only to gifts of money. Gifts which have already qualified for tax relief (e.g. covenant payments or payroll-giving deductions) don't qualify either, nor do bequests made on death.

You will need to claim relief through your tax return. But note that the lower limit of £250 is *net* of basic-rate tax (i.e. you can't give the charity £250 less 24 per cent tax).

Private medical insurance

You can get relief, restricted to the basic rate, on some private medical insurance policies you take out for anyone (including yourself) who's 60 or over. There are restrictions on the types of policy that are acceptable, e.g. only conventional policies are covered, and any cash benefit for policyholders while they are in-patients must be limited to £5 a day.

You get basic-rate relief at source by making lower payments to the insurer. Since 6 April 1994, premiums for private medical insurance have no longer counted as an outgoing when you work out your total income for age-related allowances – see p. 105.

More details See p. 109.

Vocational training

In the 1996–7 tax year, you can claim tax relief on study and examination fees for your own 'qualifying' training. To qualify, the training must lead to National Vocational Qualifications or Scottish Vocational Qualifications up to level 5. From 5 May 1996, people over 30 will also be able to get relief on a 'qualifying' course of vocational training. For course fees to qualify for tax relief, the course must be full-time, last more than four weeks but no more than a year and be 'wholly aimed at learning or practising knowledge or skills for gainful employment'.

You will get basic-rate relief by paying lower fees, so you will benefit even if you are not a taxpayer. Higher-rate taxpayers can claim higher-rate relief.

Total income

In most cases, the important figure being worked towards to in this chapter is *taxable income* – broadly speaking, the money you receive less everything you can find that you don't have to pay tax on. But in a few cases, the important figure for tax purposes is *total income*. This is the figure you arrive at after deducting your outgoings from your income for tax purposes but before subtracting allowances.

The total income figure is, most importantly, used in working out whether older people are entitled to the full age-related allowances or only reduced allowances – see

p. 103. It's also the figure used when working out whether you are entitled to tax relief on life insurance policies taken out before 14 March 1984.

Taking account of allowances

Subtracting allowances from your income is the last step in arriving at your taxable income. Like outgoings, you subtract them from your income for tax purposes to reduce the amount of income on which you have to pay tax. Unlike outgoings, which depend on you actually spending money on specific things, everyone gets a basic personal allowance. The other allowances you can deduct from your income depend on your individual circumstances. There are now three main types of allowance:

- **Full allowances** These will give you tax relief at your highest rate of tax. Provided you are entitled to them, you can deduct them from your total income to arrive at your taxable income.
- **Fixed-relief allowances** The relief you get is restricted to 15 per cent of the allowance (including age-related married couple's allowances, see below) to which you are entitled. See p. 25 for where to include these allowances when working out your tax bill.
- **Age-related allowances** These are, in effect, means-tested allowances for people aged 65 or over. In the tax year that you reach 65, your personal allowance and married couple's allowance (but see *fixed-relief allowances* above) are increased, provided your total income (i.e. your income for tax purposes after deducting certain outgoings) is below £15,200. If your income is above this level, the amount of the allowance you will get is limited. However, the allowance is never reduced below the level of the allowance you would get if you were under 65.

The tables opposite give details of the allowances which you can use to reduce your tax bill in the 1996–7 tax year. If you want to check your allowances for earlier tax years, see Chapter 19.

Full allowances for the 1996–7 tax year

Allowance	How much	Details
personal allowance	£3,765	everyone gets this allowance – but see table of age-related allowances if you will reach 65 in the 1996–7 tax year
blind person's allowance	£1,250	this allowance is given to people who are registered as blind with a local authority in England and Wales. In Scotland and Northern Ireland (where there is no register), the equivalent requirement is that a person must be unable to perform any work for which eyesight is essential. A concession means that you may get the allowance backdated by a year when you first claim – see p. 384

Fixed-relief allowances for the 1996–7 tax year
Relief on the following allowances is fixed at 15 per cent in the 1996–7 tax year which means that the value of each allowance is a reduction of £268.50 in your tax bill.

Allowance	How much	Details
married couple's allowance	15% of £1,790	this allowance is automatically given to the husband (on top of his personal allowance), but husband and wife can choose to share the allowance. If you marry after 5 May 1996, you get a reduced amount. See p. 82 for more details
additional personal allowance	15% of £1,790	this allowance is for single and separated people (and some others) who have responsibility for a child. See p. 98 for more details

widow's bereavement allowance	15% of £1,790	this allowance is given to a widow in the tax year her husband dies and (unless she remarries) the following tax year. See p. 89 for more details

Age-related allowances for the 1996–7 tax year
If you have reached 65 in the 1996–7 tax year, you can claim the full amount of the allowance given in the table unless your total income is over £15,200. If it is, the allowance will be reduced by £1 for every £2 you are over the limit.

Allowance	How much	Details
personal allowance:		
(1) aged 65 to 74 at any time in the tax year	£4,910	even if you are over the total income limit of £15,200, these allowances will never be reduced to below the level of the basic personal allowance of
(2) aged 75+ at any time in the tax year	£5,090	£3,765 in the 1996–7 tax year

Fixed-relief age-related allowances

Allowance	How much	Details
(1) Either partner aged 65 to 74 in the tax year	15% of £3,115	you get this allowance on top of your personal allowance if you are married. If you get a reduced amount of this allowance (because your total income is over the £15,200 limit), relief is fixed at 15 per cent of the reduced amount of the allowance.
(2) either partner aged 75+ in the tax year	15% of £3,155	However, the relief will never be reduced to below the level of the basic married couple's allowance of 15% of £1,790 in the 1996–7 tax year. And note that if you are over the limit, it is your age-related *personal* allowance which is reduced first. For more details, see Chapter 6

Gross and net – what they mean

Throughout this book, you'll come across references to *gross payments* and *net payments*, and to *gross income* and *net income*. Here we tell you:

- the difference between gross and net
- how to get from gross to net (or from net to gross).

The net amount

The *net* amount of any income you get, or payment you make, is the amount *after* tax has been deducted or tax relief allowed for. The net amount is typically what you receive if you get income where tax is deducted at source, or what you pay if tax relief is given at source. You can't work out the gross amount of any income or outgoings unless you know the net amount.

If you know the gross amount of your income or outgoings, but you want to know what you'll actually get after tax, or how much you will pay once tax relief has been allowed for, you can calculate the net amount by multiplying the gross amount by:

- 0.85 for tax or tax relief at 15 per cent
- 0.8 for tax or tax relief at 20 per cent
- 0.76 for tax or tax relief at 24 per cent
- 0.6 for tax or tax relief at 40 per cent.

EXAMPLE 3

Bert Williams has been quoted a before-tax return of £200 on a new investment account. But as he's a higher-rate taxpayer, he knows that the net return won't look as attractive once he's deducted the 40 per cent tax that he'll have to pay. To calculate the net (after tax) return, he multiplies the gross (or before-tax) return by 0.6 which gives him £120.

The gross amount

The *gross* amount of any income you receive or payment – i.e. outgoing – you make is the amount *before* tax has been deducted (in the case of income) or before tax relief has been allowed for (in the case of outgoings). You will need to know the gross figures for your income and outgoings if:

- you want to work out your annual tax bill (as in the Example on p. 24)
- you need to work out your total income for the purposes of calculating age-related allowances – see p. 103
- you are asked to give gross figures on your annual tax return and you know only the net amounts.

To work out the gross amount, you need to know the net amount of the payment or income and the rate of the tax relief that has been given, or the tax that has been deducted. If the rate is 15 per cent, you divide the net amount by 0.85 to get the gross figure. If the rate is 20 per cent, you divide the net amount by 0.8 to get the gross figure. If the rate is 24 per cent, you divide the net amount by 0.76 to get the gross figure. (If you don't have a calculator, you may find it easier to divide by 85, 80 or 76 and then multiply by 100.)

EXAMPLE 4

Percy Spencer turned 65 this tax year, and wants to work out his total income to find out how much age-related personal allowance he'll get. To do this he needs to calculate the gross amounts of his income and outgoings.

Percy knows what the gross amount of his pension is, but he needs to add the interest he gets from his building society account. His passbook shows only the net amount of interest he has received – i.e. the amount after deducting tax at 20 per cent. The net amount is £160 so he divides this by 0.8 to give the gross amount of £200.

Tax Schedules

Tax Schedules go back to the earliest days of income tax and are a way of dividing income up into different types. For example, earnings from your job are taxed under Schedule E, whereas earnings from being self-employed are taxed under Schedule D.

Why are Schedules important?

Schedules affect the *expenses* you can deduct from your income before tax is worked out and also when the tax has to be paid. However, with the introduction of self-assessment, all income will be taxed on a current-year basis – i.e. your tax bill for the 1996–7 tax year is based on the income due to you in that tax year. Before self-assessment, some income was taxed on a preceding-year basis, which meant that your tax bill for 1995–6, for example, was based on the income you were due in the previous tax year. Special transitional rules will apply for income which used to be taxed on a preceding-year basis to move to the current-year basis. What has not changed is the fact that different Schedules have different rules about the expenses you can claim. They also distinguish investment income from earned income. The distinction can be important. For instance, you can't claim tax relief on pension contributions based on investment income.

Cases

Some of the Schedules are divided up into Cases. Traditionally, Cases are given Roman numerals – Case I, Case II, Case III, Case IV, Case V and Case VI.

Rules about expenses can differ from Case to Case. For example, Schedule D Case I income has fairly generous rules, whereas Schedule D Case III is the meanest.

Working through the Schedules

Schedule A

Schedule A deals with the rules for taxing investment income, including all income from land and property.

Expenses you can claim

Although income from property is taxed as investment income, you will pay tax as though the income is profits from a business. You will be able to deduct expenses incurred in the business of letting property. For the expenses you can claim when running a business, see p. 192.

Schedule C

Schedule C, which was abolished on 1 April 1996, used to cover investment income in the form of interest paid in the UK on some government securities (UK government and foreign governments). This is now dealt with under Schedule D.

Schedule D Case I, Schedule D Case II

Case I and Case II of Schedule D deal with the tax rules for earned income from self-employment. If the profits are from a trade (e.g. window-cleaner, shopkeeper, manufacturer), you're taxed under Case I. If the profits are from a profession (e.g. barrister, architect, accountant), you're taxed under Case II. The tax rules in each case are virtually identical.

Expenses you can claim

You can claim any expense incurred *wholly and exclusively* for your trade or business. This definition is more generous than for people who are employed – see p. 192.

Schedule D Case III

Case III income is investment income. The main items are interest (e.g. interest from National Savings accounts, interest from loans), income from annuities and income from government securities (including those which used to be taxed under Schedule C). Other things taxed under this Case are annual payments (e.g. maintenance payments).

Expenses you can claim

There are no expenses you can claim. Case III income is often referred to as *pure profit income* – i.e. it's assumed that you don't have any expenses.

Schedule D Case IV, Schedule D Case V

Case IV and Case V income is investment income (unless it comes from carrying on a business). These are both concerned with income from abroad. Case IV covers income from foreign securities, including securities which used to be covered by Schedule C. Case V covers most other types of income from abroad – e.g. rents, dividends, pensions, trading profits, maintenance payments. Broadly speaking, if you're not domiciled in the UK, or (for UK or Irish citizens) you're not ordinarily resident in the UK, you're taxed only on money which comes in to the UK. Otherwise, you're taxed on the lot – whether or not it reaches the UK. If the money comes from a pension, one-tenth of the income normally escapes UK tax.

Note that changes to the rules dealing with income from

property outside the UK will mean that you will be allowed to deduct expenses from that income – see p. 235.

Expenses you can claim

If the money comes from a trade or profession, tax is charged on your taxable profits – so you can subtract the usual expenses in working these out. Otherwise, there are normally none.

Schedule D Case VI

Case VI income is investment income (and *post-cessation* receipts). Case VI is a rag-bag of odd bits of income which don't fit in anywhere else. Examples are income from occasional freelance work; post-cessation receipts – i.e. after a business or partnership ends; income from investing in plays – unless you do this for a living.

Expenses you can claim

There's nothing in the tax acts about exactly what you can claim, but you have to pay tax on 'profits or gains'. So expenses necessarily incurred in making those profits are deducted when working out how much income is taxed. Losses can be set against other Case VI income for the same (or a following) tax year, but not against income from other Schedules or Cases.

Schedule E

Schedule E income is earned income and it covers:

- income from your employment – e.g. wages, expense allowances, tips, fringe benefits (if they're taxable)
- pensions from employers
- taxable social security benefits
- freelance earnings under a contract of employment. This can be a grey area, but if, for example, you're a teacher, and receive some money for marking examination scripts the Revenue will normally tax this extra income under Schedule E.

Schedule E is divided into three cases, of which Case I is by far the most important. Broadly, Case I catches income from employment if the employee is resident and ordinarily resident in the UK (see p. 173); Case II applies to people who normally live and work abroad, but who have some earnings arising in the UK; Case III applies to income remitted to the UK (by people resident in the UK) earned in employment abroad.

Expenses you can claim
The rules are harsher than for self-employed people: you can claim only expenses which are *wholly, exclusively and necessarily* incurred in the performance of the duties of your employment. For example, you could spend money on something which was entirely for use in your job, but unless it was *necessary* you wouldn't be able to claim it against tax (see p. 130).

Schedule F

Schedule F income is investment income in the form of dividends from companies resident in the UK, and distributions from unit trusts resident in the UK.

Expenses you can claim
There are no expenses you can claim.

Your tax bill

From the start of the 1996–7 tax year – i.e. 6 April 1996 – the responsibility for working out how much tax you owe or assessing your tax liability has shifted from the Revenue to you the taxpayer. Instead of the Revenue telling you how much tax you owe, you can (with or without the Revenue's help in doing the sums – see p. 73) tell the Revenue. However, you will not see the full effects of the new system until the end of the 1996–7 tax year – i.e. 5 April 1997 – after which the new self-assessment tax forms will be sent out. If you filled in a tax return for the 1995–6 tax year, the Revenue will tell you how much tax you owe by using a notice of assessment.

If most of your income came from earnings and pensions, you'll be sent a Schedule E notice of assessment and statement of tax unpaid or overpaid. Small amounts of investment income or freelance earnings taxed under Schedule D and property income taxed under Schedule A may also be shown on this notice. But if you had substantial amounts of these, you'll get a separate Schedule A and D notice of assessment.

If you paid tax under PAYE and your affairs were

straightforward, you may not be sent a notice of assessment – though you can ask for one if you wish. This isn't always a good idea, as you might then be asked to pay small amounts of tax unpaid because of roundings in the PAYE system.

If you are refused a notice, it may be because this underpaid tax cancels out the overpayment you're claiming.

Although this book deals in the main with the 1996–7 tax year, here we give guidance on what to do if you receive an assessment for the 1995–6 tax year, with worked examples of Schedule D and Schedule E notice of assessments. Note that these examples use the rules for the 1995–6 tax year.

Appealing against a notice of assessment

If you get a notice of assessment, check it at once. If you think any of the figures on it are wrong, you must normally appeal within 30 days of the date on it. If it's a Schedule A or D assessment, you must still pay all the tax demanded by the date given, unless you also apply for a postponement of part or all of the tax. See p. 62 for details.

How to read a Schedule A or D notice of assessment for the 1995–6 tax year

You'll get one of these assessments if you let property or work for yourself (full-time or spare-time), or have investment income not on your Schedule E notice of assessment. Here we describe Jenny Burns' notice of assessment for 1995–6, shown on pages 44 and 45. The items in **bold** are all mentioned on the actual form.

In her accounting year which ended in the 1994–5 tax year, Jenny Burns made a profit of £17,200 from her shop, Jenny's Joke Shop, after deducting all her allowable business expenses. As well as this earned income she also gets money from investments which are not taxed before she receives them: the tax on these is handled in a different way, so the notice of assessment splits the figures into two columns, one for each type.

The **Source(s) of income** section shows her earned profit in the first column. In the second column are shown **Property rents** she gets from unfurnished lettings of £5,675 in the 1995–6 tax year and untaxed **Investment income** of £1,740 that she received in the 1994–5 tax year.

In her business, Jenny claims **Capital allowances** of

District reference

000 000000 0

Inland Revenue
Income Tax

Income Tax (Schedule A or Schedule D) and
Class 4 National Insurance Contributions
YEAR ENDING 5 APRIL 1996

Date of issue
3 NOV 1996

Ms J BURNS
14 TWINTREES AVENUE
SWINSIDE SW30 0SF

Dear Madam,

This notice is addressed to you personally as required by law but if you have a professional adviser or agent it is desirable that you let him see this Notice of Assessment IMMEDIATELY.
If you do not agree with the assessment you should appeal in writing WITHIN 30 DAYS from the date of issue above.
If you also consider that the amount charged is excessive you may apply to postpone some or all of the tax etc. (see form 64D enclosed).

Yours faithfully
MR J. WILTSHIRE
HM INSPECTOR OF TAXES
BRIDGENORTH
WALKER HOUSE
CONISTON DRIVE
BRIDGENORTH
SHROPSHIRE BR3 7TQ

Notice to pay:
Please pay the amount shown on the attached payslip, to
IR Accounts Office, Cumbernauld, Glasgow G70 5TR

How to pay: See back of payslip.

AMOUNT PAYABLE	1st INST	2nd INST
TAX	2440.25	1707.50
NATIONAL INSURANCE	318.28	318.28
TOTAL	2758.53	2025.78
PAYABLE 1 JAN 1997	2758.53	
PAYABLE 1 JUL 1997		2025.78

300 (CODA)

NOTICE OF ASSESSMENT 1995/96		*Assessment number*
Source(s) of income	**£**	**Unearned Income**
JENNY'S JOKE SHOP	**17200**	
Property rents		**5675**
Investment income		**1740**
TRADING DEDUCTIONS		
Capital Allowances	**1840**	
TOTAL CHARGEABLE	**15360**	**7415**
Allowances		
Personal pension	1700	
PERSONAL ALLOWANCE		3525
Class 4 NIC relief		319
TOTALS	1700	3844
Net chargeable to tax	13660	3571
TAX CHARGEABLE		
Lower rate @ 20% on £3,200		640
Basic rate @ 25% on £14,031	3415	92.75
Net tax payable	3415	732.75
CLASS 4 NATIONAL INSURANCE PAYABLE		
Profit	15360	
Lower limit	6640	
Charged at 7.30% on	8720	
AMOUNT PAYABLE	636.56	

Notes

£1,840, making the **TOTAL CHARGEABLE** for the business £15,360; and for unearned income, £7,415.

Jenny can claim a number of **Allowances** (this section includes both allowances and outgoings). She paid £1,700 into a **personal pension** plan, which she can set only against her earned income, i.e. business profits. But her other allowances can be set against either earned or unearned income. And, as she'll have to pay the tax on her unearned income in one lump at the beginning of 1996 (rather than in the two instalments she can pay her earned income tax bill), it makes sense for these all to be set off against her unearned income.

She has a **PERSONAL** allowance of £3,525; **Class 4 NIC relief** (see below) of £319. The next row of figures in the assessment gives the **TOTAL** of these allowances; and these are subtracted from the **TOTAL CHARGEABLE** to give the **Net chargeable to tax** figures: for the business, £13,660; and for unearned income, £3,571.

These two figures are added together: £17,231 – not enough to pay higher-rate tax on. So the first £3,200 of unearned income is charged at the lower rate of 20 per cent with the balance of £14,031 charged at the basic rate of 25 per cent; and the tax payable on the two types of income is shown separately: for the business, £3,415; and for unearned income, £640 (at the lower rate) and £92.75 (at the basic rate). The **Net tax payable** row shows the totals of tax payable at lower and basic rate.

The next section works out **CLASS 4 NATIONAL INSURANCE PAYABLE** (see p. 206 for details). From Jenny's business **Profit** of £15,360 is subtracted the **Lower limit** of £6,640 to give the per cent **Charged at 7.3 on** figure of £8,720, and an **AMOUNT PAYABLE** of £636.56. She gets tax relief on half of this amount: £318.28, or £319 rounded up to the next pound, as shown in the Allowances section of the notice. The bottom part of the form is the **Notice to pay**, together with a payslip. Jenny will have to pay in two instalments. In the **1st INST** is:

- all the unearned income tax of £732.75 plus half the earned income tax of £3,415, a total **TAX** of £2,440.25
- half the Class 4 due of £636.56: **NATIONAL INSURANCE** of £318.28, making a **TOTAL** of £2,758.53. This is **PAYABLE 1 JAN 1997**.

The **2nd INST** is made up of the other half of the earned income tax, plus remaining Class 4. This **TOTAL** of

£2,025.78 is **PAYABLE 1 JUL 1997**. The payment form is for the first instalment; Jenny will receive a second one for the second instalment before the beginning of July.

How to read a Schedule E notice of assessment for the 1995–6 tax year

You're likely to get a Schedule E notice of assessment if you're an employee who pays tax at the higher rate of 40 per cent or you have income from investments on which higher-rate tax is due. Here we describe the notice of assessment for William Orange, which is shown on pp. 48–9. The items in bold are all mentioned on the actual form.

1 Income from employments, pensions, benefits, etc., and Deductions

This section has three columns:

- **Deductions** shows allowable expenses of employment – William paid £440 in expenses which the Revenue has accepted were 'wholly, exclusively, and necessarily' incurred in carrying out his duties.
- **Income** shows earned income such as wages, salary, perks, pensions and so on. William earned £28,170 from **ROYAL CITRUS FRUIT**, plus £4,310 in **BENEFITS IN KIND**.
- **Tax Deducted or Refunded** shows tax already paid on earned income, e.g. through PAYE, or (if there's an **R** in front of the figure) refunded.

TOTALS gives the sum so far of the three columns above. The **Amount of assessment** box shows the net income after subtracting the **Deductions** total: £32,580 for William.

2 Allowances, etc.

This section first deducts your allowances, and any outgoings you are entitled to for which you have not had tax relief and on which tax relief is not restricted, from your income calculated so far. William has his own **PERSONAL ALLOWANCE** of £3,525. Since this is his only allowance given in full, his **Total Allowances** is £3,525.

The section then adds in income you have which is taxable but which hasn't been taxed yet. The **Less allowed elsewhere** figure of £1,850 shows that William has untaxed

Please use both lines of this reference if you write or call – it will help to avoid delay

Inland Revenue
Income Tax - Schedule E

YEAR ENDED 5 APRIL 1996
NOTICE OF ASSESSMENT AND STATEMENT OF TAX UNPAID OR OVERPAID FOR 1995–96

246 / 1RCFI				
OR	12	34	56	A

MR WILLIAM ORANGE
CLEMENT HOUSE
1 TANGERINE ST
LONDON SE11 0NB

Date of issue

26 JUN 1996

Dear Sir,

This Notice of Assessment is addressed to you personally as required by law, but if you have a professional adviser or agent it is advisable that you let him see it IMMEDIATELY.

If you think the assessment is wrong you should appeal to me IN WRITING, WITHIN 30 DAYS from the date of issue of the Assessment Notice. You should say what you think is wrong with the assessment and, if necessary, let me have the correct details or state the date by which I may expect to receive them.

The enclosed notes give general guidance, and advice on appeals, and tell you how to check this Notice.

If you require any further information please do not hesitate to contact me.

Yours faithfully

MR J WILTSHIRE
HM INSPECTOR OF TAXES
BRIDGENORTH
WALKER HOUSE
CONISTON DRIVE
BRIDGENORTH
SHROPSHIRE BR3 7TQ

5 Explanation

THE FIGURE FOR 'ADJUSTMENTS' IS MADE UP OF THE FOLLOWING:

MARRIED ALLOWANCE	1720 @ 15%	258.00
LOAN INTEREST	520 @ 15%	78.00
	TOTAL	336.00
MAXIMUM OF BASIC RATE		21100
ADD FURTHER RELIEF DUE FOR:-		
1) PERSONAL PENSION CONTRIBUTION: PPR		1500
2) CHARITABLE PAYMENTS UNDER DEED OF COVENANT		400
TOTAL CHARGE @ 25%		23000

P70(T)

NOTICE OF ASSESSMENT 1995/96

1 Income from employments pensions benefits etc and Deductions

	Deductions £	Income(R = Refund) £	Tax Deducted or Refunded £	See note
ROYAL CITRUS FRUIT		28710	9145.00	
BENEFITS IN KIND		4310		5
EXPENSES	440			7
TOTALS	440	33020	9245.78	
Less Total Deductions		440		
Amount of assessment		32580		

2 Allowances etc

Personal	3525
TOTAL ALLOWANCES	3525
Less allowed elsewhere	1850
Allowed in this assessment	1675

3 Amount chargeable to tax 30905

Chargeable at:	
Lower rate at 20% on £2200	440.00
Basic rate at 25% on £22900	5725.00
Higher rate(s) on £5805	2322.00
Total tax due	8487.00
Less adjustments (see Section 5)	336.00
Tax Assessed for 1995–96	8151.00
Less tax deducted	9145.00
Net tax overpaid at 5 April 1996	994.00

4 Allocation of allowances and rates of tax

Allowances		Rates of Tax		
Allowed elsewhere:		20%	25%	40%
UNTAXED INTEREST	350			
FURNISHED LETTINGS	1500			
BSI RECEIVED	0	0	100	
DIVIDENDS ON SHARES	0	1000	0	
Elsewhere total(s)	1850	1000	100	
This assessment	1675	2200	22900	5805
TOTALS	3525	3200	23000	5805

income of this amount (it is described in detail in section 4) which is counted in by reducing his total allowances from £3,525 to £1,675 – the **Allowed in this assessment** figure.

3 Amount chargeable to tax
This box shows the amount of your income on which you have to pay tax – £30,905 for William. It's arrived at by deducting **Allowed in this assessment** from **Amount of assessment**.

The next part of this section calculates how much tax is payable on this amount: the first part at the **Lower rate** of 20 per cent; the next £22,900 at the **Basic rate** of 25 per cent; the rest, if any, at the **Higher rate** of 40 per cent. Note that the amounts on which you pay lower and basic-rate tax are different from the standard bands of £3,200 and £21,100. This is because, as explained in sections 4 and 5, these bands have been personalised. The total tax so far is shown under **Total tax due**, but this is then reduced by the **adjustments** shown in section 5 which are William's fixed relief allowances and outgoings. This gives the **Tax assessed for 1995–96** of £8,151 which is the amount of tax William should have paid this tax year. Since he has already paid £9,145 in tax through PAYE he is due a rebate of £994. This is the amount of tax he has paid less the tax he *should* have paid, and is shown under **Net tax overpaid at 5 April 1996**. There may be a cheque with the assessment, or it may come separately. If the figure showed **Net tax underpaid**, the extra tax would have been collected either by adjusting William's PAYE code or, especially if the amount was large, by requesting him to pay the Revenue within 14 days.

4 Allocation of allowances and rates of tax
This somewhat misleading section has more to do with calculating what extra tax you owe than with what allowances you are due.

The items listed in the **Allowed elsewhere** column are amounts of income which were not included in section 1. If the income hasn't yet been taxed, it's listed in the **Allowances** column; if it's an income you receive after lower-rate tax has been deducted, the grossed-up amount (see p. 37) is listed in the **20%** column. If basic-rate tax has been deducted, the 'grossed-up' amount is listed in the **25%** column.

William has received **UNTAXED INTEREST** of £350

from his National Savings Investment account; and £1,500 from **FURNISHED LETTINGS** of a home he rents. He received £800 in **DIVIDENDS** payments – but that's after tax, so the before-tax equivalent of £1,000 is shown in the **20%** column. His building society interest of £75 is shown alongside **BSI RECEIVED** in the **25%** column as the before-tax equivalent of £100.

The **Elsewhere total(s)** give the totals of the incomes on which William has paid no tax (£1,850) and on which he's already settled his lower-rate tax bill (£1,000) and his basic-rate tax bill (£100 before tax).

The figures in the **This assessment** and in the **TOTALS** lines show you how much of your income is free of tax (i.e. your allowances) and how much will be taxed at 20, 25 and 40 per cent. However, neither of these last two figures is actually calculated in either section 3 or section 4: that's done in section 5.

5 Explanation

In the same way that section 4 slips in information on tax you owe under the heading of Allowances, section 5 tells you how much relief will be deducted from your tax bill for your fixed-relief allowances and outgoings (see section 3); how your personalised tax bands have been arrived at; and how your basic-rate band is amended to take account of any extra relief you are due (if you are a higher-rate taxpayer) on outgoings where you have received basic-rate tax relief at source. William is married and so will receive the married couple's allowance for which tax relief is fixed at 15 per cent. Also shown here is the 15 per cent relief he gets on a loan which is not in MIRAS.

William's basic-rate band of £21,100 is then personalised to take account of the outgoings on which higher-rate relief is due (though he's already had basic-rate relief at source). To allow for the extra relief due, the gross amount of these payments is added to the basic-rate band. This means that an equivalent amount of your income is taxed at the basic rate, rather than at the higher rate.

William pays £1,125 in personal pension plan contributions after basic-rate relief. These **PENSION CONTRIBUTIONS** gross up to £1,500. He has **CHARITABLE PAYMENTS UNDER DEED OF COVENANT** of £300 (£400 grossed up) as well. By adding these grossed-up sums to the basic-rate band, it reduces the amount of his income he has to pay higher-rate tax on by the same amount, and so automatically gives him the higher-rate relief to which he's entitled. The **NEW BASIC RATE BAND** shows his personalised basic-rate tax band of £23,000.

William then goes back to section 4 where his basic-rate tax band is amended to arrive at the figures which will be used to calculate his total tax bill. Where section 5 adjusts the bands upwards, section 4 will adjust them downwards to collect the higher-rate tax due on income where only lower-rate and basic-rate tax have so far been paid. The new basic-rate tax band from section 5 is shown under the **25%** column on the **TOTALS** line of section 4. The **This assessment** line shows how the normal lower-rate band of £3,200 is reduced to £2,200 to take account of the £1,000 of dividends on which William has paid tax at 20 per cent; and the new basic-rate band is reduced to £22,900 to take account of the £100 of building society interest on which basic-rate tax has been paid.

The figures under the **rates of tax** columns on the **This assessment** line should add up to £30,905 which is the **amount chargeable to tax** figure given in section 3. This means that the figure for tax at 40 per cent will be £5,805 – i.e. £30,905 less the adjusted figures of £2,200 and £22,900.

3 *DEALING WITH THE REVENUE*

- Learn how to handle the Revenue and you will have a better chance of getting a swifter and more satisfactory resolution of problems.
- If you can't get satisfaction, you may have to lodge a formal appeal – but watch out for the time limits or you might lose your chance to appeal.

If the words 'Inland Revenue' conjure up images of pinstriped suits, black briefcases and incomprehensible forms, it's likely that you haven't had much contact with the Revenue recently. In the past few years, the Revenue has been making a concerted effort to improve the way it treats taxpayers and deals with their affairs through a ten-year 'Change Programme' due to be completed in 2002. The core of this programme is the change to self-assessment, but it also covers streamlining and simplification of Revenue working methods and procedures; reorganisation of the office structure; and greater use of information technology. In addition, a major rewrite of tax legislation has been proposed to cut down on misunderstandings and misinterpretations of tax law.

Despite all these good intentions, however, you may meet the odd problem. This chapter concentrates largely on the existing system. Many of the details will change once the new system of self-assessment (see Chapter 4) takes over. The chapter starts with how to find your tax office, then looks at giving the Revenue information: which forms you have to fill in and then how to check the forms which tell you how much tax you have to pay. If you think you have paid too much (or too little) tax, you'll find advice on getting problems sorted out. Finally, if your relationship with your tax office breaks down, there's information on how to appeal.

Finding your tax office

The tax office which deals with your tax affairs is not necessarily the one closest to where you live. It depends on your circumstances:

- **Employees** As a general rule, your tax office will be the one which deals with the area where you work, or, more particularly, the place from which you are paid. But there are exceptions. Pay-As-You-Earn (PAYE) for all employees in Scotland is handled by one office in Scotland. If you are a government employee – e.g. civil servant or member of HM forces – your affairs will be dealt with by one of the Public Department's offices in Cardiff. If you work for a large national organisation, or in London, or in another large city or town, your office may not be local. Your employer will be able to tell you the name and address of your tax office. If you change your job, your tax office may also change.
- **Self-employed** If you are in business on your own, or in partnership, your tax office is usually the one nearest your place of business.
- **Income mainly from pension or investments** If you are getting a pension from a former employer, your tax affairs may well be dealt with by the tax office dealing with the area in which the pension fund paying your pension has its office. But if the pension from your former employer is fairly small, or your only pension is a state pension, your affairs will be dealt with by the tax office for the area in which you live.
- **Unemployed** You stay with the tax office of your last employer.
- **Special cases** If you have to fill in a tax return in your capacity as trustee, the tax office will be one of the few that deal with the affairs of trusts and settlements.

Paying tax

Your tax office is concerned with assessing how much tax you should pay, not with chasing you for payment. Tax collection is the responsibility of the collector of taxes. You'll deal with either a local collection office or one of the two central accounts offices, depending on the address on your tax bill. However, once the new system of self-assessment (see p. 71) is in place, both assessment and collection will be dealt with by the same tax office.

General enquiries

If you just want to make a general enquiry or you want to get hold of one of the free Revenue leaflets, you don't need to go to your own tax office. Instead, you can phone any tax office or a tax enquiry centre. Find them in the phone book under *Inland Revenue*. If your enquiry is specific to your particular tax affairs, it's always best to write to your own tax office.

The Taxpayer's Charter

This states clearly that taxpayers are entitled to expect the Inland Revenue:

to be fair The Revenue should treat everyone with equal fairness and impartiality and you should be expected to pay only what is due under the law.

to be helpful All Revenue staff should be courteous, and assist you in getting your taxes right, by providing clear information to help you understand your rights and obligations.

to be efficient The Revenue should be prompt, accurate, and keep your affairs confidential. Information obtained from you should be used only as allowed by the law. It should also strive to keep both your expenses and those of the tax office down.

to be accountable Standards, and how well the Revenue lives up to those standards, should be made public.

to be open to criticism Taxpayers should be told how to complain, and be able to have their tax affairs looked at again. An appeal can be made either to an independent tribunal or your MP can refer you to the Parliamentary Commissioner for Administration.

In return, you the taxpayer have an obligation to be honest, to give the Revenue accurate information, and to pay your tax on time.

Copies of the charter are available from local tax and VAT offices.

Giving and getting information

One of your obligations as a taxpayer is to give the Revenue accurate information. To help you do this, the Revenue issues various forms. The main one that you'll have to deal with is likely to be the tax return (though you won't necessarily get one of these every year). Once you've given the Revenue the information it needs to calculate your tax bill, you're likely (though not bound) to receive a PAYE Coding Notice (see below) if you're an employee and you pay tax through PAYE. In certain circumstances – e.g. you're self-employed, you owe tax or you're due a rebate – you will also get a *notice of assessment* (see p. 42) which tells you how your annual tax bill has been calculated.

Once self-assessment starts (see p. 71) your own tax return will replace the notice of assessment.

Tax forms

Your tax return, 1995–6

Here are details of the pre-self-assessment tax returns (see p. 71), the last of which will relate to the 1995–6 tax year and will be sent out in April 1996. There are several different types of tax return, designed for different types of taxpayer.

- **Employees** If you are an employee you'll get form 11P. But if your affairs are not complicated and you earn at a rate of less than £8,500 a year, you'll get the simpler form P1.
- **Self-employed** If you are in business on your own, or in partnership, or your main sources of income are chargeable to tax under Schedule D, you'll get form 11.
- **Partnerships** If you are self-employed and in partnership, you'll get form 1 on which to give details of the partnership income for the tax year and how that partnership income has been shared out between the partners. It is sent out in addition to form 11, which will be sent to individual partners.
- **Trustees and personal representatives** Form 1 is also issued to the personal representatives of someone who has died, so that they can report the income arising during the period of administration of the estate. Form 1 goes to trustees of a settlement too. But form 1 asks only for information about sources of income which have not had tax deducted before payment, so further forms are issued to trustees, which ask for information about income which has been paid after deduction of tax, including dividends from UK companies.

Whichever tax return you get, your obligations as a taxpayer remain the same. All tax returns have space for you to give details of your income, to deduct your outgoings and expenses, and to claim your personal allowances. And they all come with a set of explanatory notes which tell you what you need to fill in and when you may need to approach your tax office for more information before giving your details.

The tax return is designed to cover every eventuality, so don't be put off by its length. It's unlikely that you'll have to fill in all of it. If you are sent a tax return, you are required by law to fill it in and send it back within 30 days of receiving it – though in practice, you have until the end of October in the year you receive it before the Revenue will penalise you with interest on any tax you owe. If you are self-employed, it's best to get your tax return back to your tax office within the 30-day limit so that an assessment can be issued in good time. Don't forget to take a copy before you send it back.

Claims for rebates

If you regularly reclaim tax – e.g. because your income has tax deducted from it but the income is less than your outgoings and allowances – you will probably be sent tax claim form R40. This is like a tax return but is sent to people who claim a repayment of tax each year. This form is usually sent at the same time as you receive a cheque for the previous year's repayment of tax, unlike tax returns which are sent out after the end of the tax year in April.

PAYE Coding Notice

If you pay tax under PAYE – e.g. you are an employee, or you get a pension from a former employer – you may receive a *PAYE Coding Notice*. This is basically the Revenue's way of telling you which allowances and outgoings you're getting, and how much untaxed income they think you're receiving – i.e. what has gone into working out your tax code. It determines how much tax you pay under PAYE. See Chapter 8 for how your PAYE code is worked out.

The notice makes it easy to see which allowances you're getting since they are shown by their names (see p. 35 for a full list). If an allowance you can claim doesn't appear on the notice you receive, you're not getting it and you should write to your tax office pointing this out. You should also check that all your outgoings are included – but note that if tax relief is given at source and the relief is restricted, you won't see them on your notice. However, outgoings where relief is not restricted should appear on your notice if you are a higher-rate taxpayer, to take account of the extra tax relief due to you.

If you think that any of the figures on your notice are wrong, write to your tax office telling them why. If you need more information on the notice you receive, and you haven't already got it, ask your tax office to send you leaflet *P3(T) PAYE: Understanding Your Tax Code.*

Your notice of assessment 1995–6

If the amount of tax you've paid is either more or less than the amount of tax that you owe, you are likely to receive a notice of assessment which explains how this has been calculated. You'll find examples of the two main types of notice of assessment on p. 44 and p. 48. The entries which appear on the notice of assessment should match the figures which you gave on your tax return. If they don't, tell your tax office which figures are wrong within 30 days of the date on the assessment.

If you get a notice of assessment, but you haven't yet filled in a tax return, there are likely to be a lot of estimated figures (marked 'E'). You should send the correct information back to the tax office within 30 days. It is essential that you appeal against the assessment within 30 days if you think it is wrong. At the same time you should apply for a postponement of the tax if you think it is more than you should pay. You may then get a revised assessment showing the figures changed in the light of the information you sent in.

Correspondence and disputes

This section is about writing – and talking – to the Revenue and solving problems that way. For the more formal procedures of an *appeal*, see p. 62.

Your move . . .

There may well be times when it's your responsibility to write to your tax office. If you become entitled to a new allowance or, for example, get a taxable benefit such as a company car you should write a brief letter giving all the relevant information. If a man gets married and wants to claim the extra allowance due, the tax office will need to know the wife's name and maiden name, date of marriage, and the name of her employer; her tax office and National Insurance number would also be helpful.

When writing to your tax office quote your reference number. This will be shown on any PAYE Coding Notice, notice of assessment or tax return which you have received. Your National Insurance number is important, as this is used for all employees as the tax reference.

Certain matters are given priority, e.g. repayments. So if you consider that you are entitled to a repayment, write *repayment claim* (preferably in red) at the top of your letter. Your claim is then more likely to get priority. In fact, as a general rule, it's helpful to head your letter with a brief reference to the subject of your letter.

. . . and theirs

After you have sent in your tax return, the tax office may write to you and ask for further information about the income shown or expenses claimed. Letters may now be signed by a tax inspector, so it will be clear to whom a reply should be sent (but not all are signed by an inspector.)

Problem-solving

When replying to any letters from your tax office, give the information requested if this is possible (and try to see the request as reasonable).

If you are convinced that the inspector is being unreasonable in a request for further information, a telephone conversation or meeting may succeed in sorting things out. A meeting should present no problem if your tax office is a local one. But if it's not, you can arrange with the local tax office for your file to be passed to them for a short period so that you can discuss your affairs with a local inspector.

If (in your view) the person you are dealing with continues to be unreasonable, remind him or her of the requirements of the Taxpayer's Charter. If this step fails, you could write a personal letter to the district inspector, whose name will appear at the head of any letter you receive, on your tax return and on any notice of assessment. Ask for a review of all the correspondence; you should summarise the main points in your argument again. The district inspector should reply personally, and will either agree with you or set out fully the reasons why your argument is not accepted.

If you are still unable to get any satisfaction from your tax office, write to the regional controller who deals with your tax office (names and addresses of regional controllers can be got from any tax office). Mark your letter for his or her personal attention, set out concisely and clearly your grounds for complaint against your tax office and ask for an investigation. If you still have no joy, you can refer your complaint to the Adjudicator's Office*. The adjudicator will be able to look at your case impartially while still having access to all the files. Alternatively, you could try your MP, who may refer your case to the Parliamentary Commissioner for Administration.

Claiming tax back

It's quite common for people to pay too much tax. For example, because:

- too much tax has been deducted under PAYE (see p. 136)
- you've paid too much tax on income you've received (see below)
- you've paid too much tax in previous years – e.g. you've forgotten to claim an allowance or an outgoing. If this has happened in your case, you can claim back the tax overpaid in the six tax years before the tax year you're now in. So if you claim before 6 April 1997, you can recover tax overpaid as far back as 6 April 1990.

What to do

- Write to your tax office, saying why you're making a claim, and (if you know) how much you're claiming.
- If you're sending back a tax return at the same time, write *repayment claim* at the top (preferably in red).

If you are due a rebate, you may be entitled to some interest – called a *repayment supplement*. But the rebate doesn't start to earn interest until 12 months after the end of the tax year for which it is due, or until the end of the tax year in which you actually paid too much tax, whichever is

later. If the rebate due is less than £50, it won't be paid until the end of the tax year.
ICTA 1988 s824

Mistakes by the Revenue

The staff in your tax office are not infallible, and mistakes do occur. It is therefore important to check all correspondence received from your tax office, such as a notice of assessment or PAYE Coding Notice.

If the Revenue demands tax you owe due to a mistake on their part from tax years further back than the previous one, you may not have to pay all (or any) of the tax you owe. But this will apply only if you've taken reasonable care to keep your tax affairs in order and up to date, and if it was reasonable for you to believe you didn't owe any tax.

You may have to pay only a percentage of the tax owed (see below) depending on your gross income in the tax year that you receive the *amended* assessment.

£15,500 or less	none
£15,501–£18,000	25%
£18,001–£22,000	50%
£22,001–£26,000	75%
£26,001–£40,000	90%
£40,000 or more	all

ESC A19

Mistakes by you

You may discover that a mistake in past tax returns meant that you paid more tax than was actually due. If this has happened, it is possible to make a claim to have the appropriate assessment corrected and any tax you have overpaid repaid to you. The time limit for such a claim is six years from the end of the tax year in which the assessment giving rise to the overcharge was made. But you cannot get a repayment of tax overcharged as a result of an assessment determined by the commissioners in the absence of the appropriate accounts or tax return (see *Appeals* below). Nor can you claim tax back if your tax return was completed on the basis of the law as it was then understood to be, which has since been changed following a decision in a case before the Courts.
TMA 1970 s33

Appeals

When you are sent any kind of tax assessment, it is important that you check it straight away. You are allowed 30 days from the date of the assessment in which to appeal against a notice of assessment if you consider it is incorrect. If you do not appeal within this period, the assessment becomes *final and conclusive* and cannot be altered unless you discover a mistake or omission in your return. The appeal, which must be in writing, is sent to the inspector who issued the notice of assessment, and must state the grounds of the appeal. Your tax office will send you, with the notice of assessment, a pink appeal form which you can use to make your appeal. Although you could write your appeal in a letter, it helps your tax office if you use the appeal form provided, perhaps accompanied by a letter if appropriate.

If you are unable to appeal within the 30 days allowed – e.g. you are away on holiday or business or in hospital when the notice of assessment is issued – send in your appeal as soon as you can, with an explanation for the delay, and the inspector will probably accept your appeal. If the inspector is reluctant to accept a late appeal, you may request that your application for a late appeal be heard by the general commissioners – see p. 63.

You also have to ask to be allowed to postpone payment of the tax you think excessive (you can do it on the same pink form). You have the same 30 days in which to do this, unless there's a genuine change in your circumstances which makes you think you've been overcharged (for instance, further work on your accounts reveals an error). If you do not apply for postponement, the whole of the tax charged on the assessment will be payable by the normal due date, and the collector of taxes will keep chasing you until it is paid.

If you make an application to postpone part of the tax charged and this is accepted by the inspector, the tax not postponed becomes payable 30 days after the inspector's agreement to your application if this is later than the normal due date.

If you do not pay the tax agreed as payable by the time it is due, the collector of taxes can charge you interest from the due date until the date of payment. Your tax office will tell you the rate at which interest will be charged. If you are self-employed or run a business, note that the interest on overdue tax is not allowable as a business expense.

Settling the appeal

The vast majority of appeals against assessments are settled by agreement with the inspector. It is quite likely, therefore, that after discussion or correspondence with your tax office you will reach an agreement on the correct amount of income chargeable, or the correct amount of relief or deduction due, and the inspector will then revise the assessment in line with the figures agreed. Any further tax as a result of the issue of that revised assessment is due for payment 30 days after the issue of the revised assessment, or the normal due date if later.

Any further tax found to be due following the issue of a revised assessment may attract interest. The rules about the charging of interest are fairly complicated; but, broadly speaking, if the notice of assessment has been issued at the correct time, i.e. before the normal due dates for payment, interest will start no later than six months after the normal due date (for Schedule D assessments, it will always be 1 July following the year of assessment). If the assessment is issued late, i.e. more than six months after the normal due date, interest will start from 30 days after the date of issue of the notice of assessment.
TMA 1970 s31, s46, s49, s55, s86

Appeals before the commissioners

If you are unable to reach agreement with the inspector, two possible courses of action are open to you. You can give up, i.e. accept the inspector's point of view and pay the tax due on the basis of his or her figures, or you can ask for your appeal to be heard before the commissioners, who are independent of the Inland Revenue.

You appeal to the *general commissioners* or the *special commissioners*. The special commissioners are tax experts. The general commissioners are unpaid local people who hear appeals in your area; they aren't usually tax experts, but have a paid clerk to advise them on legal matters.

In some cases you have no choice about whether to go to the general commissioners or the special commissioners. For example, the special commissioners must consider your appeal in certain specified (and usually complex) circumstances, or if you're claiming because you made a mistake filling in the income sections of your tax return and the inspector has refused your claim.

If, on the other hand, your appeal is about your PAYE code, or you're claiming tax back because you've failed to claim a personal allowance, the general commissioners must deal with it.

Other appeals normally go automatically to the general commissioners, too. But if your appeal depends on some fine point of law (as opposed to a matter of fact, or common sense) you can elect to have your appeal heard by the special commissioners. You must make this choice within 30 days of the date of the notice of assessment. The general commissioners have the power to direct that your election be disregarded.
TMA 1970 s31, s33, s46

At the commissioners' hearing . . .

Taking an appeal before the commissioners will certainly be time-consuming, and may be expensive if you engage someone to appear on your behalf. You can appear on your own behalf, and the commissioners are required to hear any barrister, solicitor or qualified accountant who appears for you.

The preparation and presentation of your case before the commissioners is extremely important. As appellant, it is up to you to prove your case – not for the Revenue to disprove it. Although the proceedings before the commissioners are not as formal as in a court of law, the normal rules of evidence will apply. You, as appellant, will open the proceedings and put your case. The inspector then responds by putting the view of the Revenue; you then have a final opportunity to stress the important points in your own case and deal with any points raised by the inspector which you had not previously covered. Any witnesses produced by either you or the inspector may be cross-examined; and the commissioners can summon anybody to appear before them.

When preparing your case, bear in mind that the commissioners will know nothing about you or your affairs until the day of the appeal hearing. So introduce yourself, and the facts of the matter under dispute, as clearly and briefly as you can. If you want to show documents in support of your case, make sure you have enough copies for the commissioners (there are usually three of them at a general commissioners' hearing) and the clerk. The inspector will probably have copies already, but have extra copies just in case. You may want to refer to previously decided tax cases: the clerk will almost certainly have copies of these available, but it would be as well to take copies of these, too.

It may be possible, before the hearing and in conjunction with the inspector, to prepare an agreed statement of facts, supported by appropriate documents, which can be presented to the commissioners. This will save time on the day of the hearing. However, it will still be necessary to explain the facts to the commissioners and provide the commissioners and clerk with a copy of the agreed statement of facts and documents.

It is a good idea to have your own presentation typed out in full, with copies for the commissioners and clerk. Take the commissioners carefully through the arguments, both for and against your case. Do not ignore the points you know the inspector will make. If you deal with these points at the same time as you deal with your own, you are likely to strengthen your own case while at the same time reducing the impact of what the inspector will say later. You will also give the impression of being a reasonable person – there will almost certainly be something in the inspector's argument, and it is just as well if you are seen to recognise this.

If, in spite of all your efforts, the commissioners decide in favour of the inspector, and you don't agree, you must immediately register your dissatisfaction with the decision. If you don't do this immediately, you lose the right to take the case further. Do this verbally at the end of the hearing, or (if the decision is communicated by letter) by an immediate written reply. You may then, by giving notice in writing to the clerk within 30 days, require the commissioners to state and sign a case for the opinion of the High Court (see below). You must also pay the fee of £25.
TMA 1970 s50, s56; FA 1984 Sch 22

. . . and after

The tax payable as a result of the decision of the commissioners must be paid, regardless of any request for the opinion of the High Court.

The decision of the commissioners on a question of fact (for instance, what your business takings were) is final and can be overturned only if the decision was one that no reasonable body of commissioners could have reached on hearing the evidence.

Otherwise, an appeal against the decision of the commissioners can be made only on a point of law. The appeal is normally to the High Court, then to the Court of Appeal and ultimately to the House of Lords. But certain appeals against the decision of the special commissioners may be referred direct to the Court of Appeal, missing out the High Court. Some appeals may skip even the Court of Appeal and go straight to the House of Lords. In Scotland, the equivalent of the High Court is the Court of Session, and an appeal from the Court of Session is direct to the House of Lords.

The taking of an appeal through the procedure outlined above can be very expensive. At the commissioners' hearing each party pays its own costs. However, if you or the Revenue are found to have behaved unreasonably in pursuing your case, costs can be awarded. In the later stages of appeal it is usual for the costs of both sides to be awarded against the unsuccessful litigant. You could be faced with a bill running to many thousands of pounds, so think very carefully before you start on this road. If you feel that your case has been mishandled – that you've suffered maladministration, bias, or delay, for example – your MP can refer your case to the Parliamentary Commissioner for Administration, also known as the Parliamentary Ombudsman.

TMA 1970 s50, s56

Investigations

The Revenue may start an investigation, or enquiry, into your affairs. These fall broadly into three categories:

- an enquiry into an omission of a source, or sources, of income from your tax return, or an understatement of the income declared
- an enquiry into your business accounts
- a more serious investigation into your affairs when the Revenue suspects fraud.

An investigation into the last category may well be conducted by one of the Inland Revenue Enquiry Branch Offices and not your local tax office. If you find that the Enquiry Branch is investigating your affairs, you would be well advised to seek professional advice.

The Revenue receives information from a variety of sources. For example, banks are required to make a return of interest credited to their customers of more than £500 in one year (for building societies, the figure is £1,400). Information such as this is compared with the taxpayer's return, and if the income is not shown, the inspector will write to the taxpayer suggesting that the tax return submitted is incomplete and ask him or her to reconsider the entries made. If you receive such a letter, go over your tax return carefully (you should always keep a copy of what you fill in). If you find that you have omitted something from your tax return, make a full report of all income omitted for all years concerned as soon as possible.

If the amount of tax is not substantial, it should be possible to agree a settlement fairly quickly. But be prepared to pay, in addition to the amount of tax which is due on the income or capital gain previously omitted from your tax return:

- an amount of interest at the appropriate rate, calculated from the date the tax ought to have been paid, assuming it had been declared at the proper time
- a penalty – see below.
  TMA 1970 s88, s95

Penalties 1995–6

If you have underpaid tax, you can be liable for a penalty of up to 100 per cent of the tax due. In practice, it would be this great only in the worst cases of fraud, followed by obstruction in the investigation.

The inspector uses a rough 'tariff' scale to reduce the 100 per cent figure, according to the circumstances of the case. This could be:

- up to 30 per cent for making a full disclosure of your true situation
- up to 40 per cent for full co-operation in the investigation: answering questions honestly; attending interviews; supplying information fully; paying tax on account as soon as it's possible to estimate what you owe
- up to 40 per cent for size and gravity. If your failure to pay the correct tax is due to a mistake rather than a deliberate attempt to hide income, you'll get a bigger discount for gravity.

How many 'Brownie points' you'll earn for each of these factors depends on the inspector's assessment. It's up to you to persuade the inspector that you're worthy of bigger discounts.

The offer in settlement

At the end of the enquiry the inspector will ask you to sign a *certificate of full disclosure*. The declarations previously signed on your tax return are now held to be incorrect, and this new certificate confirms that, taking into account the income disclosed in the enquiry, you have now made a full return of all your income for the years covered by the enquiry. The inspector will also ask you to make a formal offer in settlement of the tax lost, interest and penalties, and will normally suggest the amount of the offer which he or she considers the Board of Inland Revenue will accept. By deducting the tax and interest from the amount of the offer suggested by the inspector, you can calculate the amount of penalty suggested. If you feel this is unreasonable, it is open to you to make a reduced offer in settlement. This will be considered by the Revenue head office, in the light of the recommendation of the local inspector, and may well be accepted if reasonable. Once the offer has been accepted, the tax is payable direct to the collector, within a period agreed in advance with the inspector, and no formal assessments will be made.

Offers in settlement can include provisions for the charging of interest if the amount due under the settlement is not paid by the agreed date.
SP6/86

Enquiry into your business accounts

Business accounts are sometimes selected for detailed investigation, but only if the inspector suspects the figures are not correct. Inspectors look for inconsistencies: profits lower than for similar businesses; expenses higher than seems justifiable; savings larger than the business profits could generate; or information from other sources (for instance your bank, on interest paid to you) that's different from what you've told the Revenue.

The first you'll know about it may be when the inspector writes and asks some detailed questions about your accounts. If you have an accountant acting on your behalf, and in particular in the preparation of your accounts, the inspector will probably first direct these questions to your accountant. It is possible that the enquiry will be settled by correspondence, but it is more usual for the inspector to request an interview with you, and your accountant if you have one.

The interview with the inspector

This can be a daunting experience, particularly for first-timers. The inspector will want to establish why the pattern of your business is different from others of the same type (there may be perfectly good reasons for this, of course), and will also want to ensure that any adjustments made for tax purposes – e.g. private use of a car – have been worked out correctly. So you'll be asked a lot of searching questions about your business: how you run it, how frequently you make up your books, how purchases and sales are recorded, how frequently you bank your takings, whether you bank all your takings and pay for all purchases by cheque, or whether you keep cash to pay for purchases or wages. It is usual to try to establish an approximate total for your living expenses, including such items as the cost of clothes, holidays, entertainment, general household expenses, and so on, to see if the money you have drawn from your bank is adequate. From this information, the inspector will form a view about the accuracy of your accounts and the need to continue the enquiry. If your explanations are satisfactory, and if your business accounts reflect all your takings and only business expenses, this will probably be the end of the enquiry. The inspector may suggest some adjustments to the private proportion of any expenses, but these are likely to be minor.

If, however, the inspector is not satisfied with your explanations, or the money you have drawn out does not reflect accurately your total living expenses, he or she will seek to increase your profit for tax purposes to reflect the adjustments considered necessary. If the adjustment is of a fairly minor amount, the inspector may not suggest any adjustments to previous years' accounts. But if the adjustment for the current year is more substantial, the inspector may well seek to adjust the profits for previous years, too.

The inspector will make full notes of the interview, and will forward copies to you or your accountant for approval. It is important to review these notes carefully and report any inaccuracies you find to the inspector immediately, so that corrections can be made and the revised notes agreed between you. This can be important if you fail to reach agreement with the inspector and the matter has to be taken before the commissioners, when the notes of the meeting will probably be introduced as evidence.

Settling the enquiry

If you are able to agree with the inspector the amount of any adjustment to your business profits for tax purposes, the enquiry can be settled. If the adjustments are fairly minor, the inspector will probably simply revise the assessments and you will be asked to pay the tax to the collector in the usual way. If, however, the adjustments are more substantial and cover a number of years, the inspector will probably seek a settlement on the lines described on pp. 67–8, to include interest and penalties.

4 *PREPARING FOR SELF-ASSESSMENT*

- Find out sooner rather than later about the big changes already taking place in the tax system – or you could fall foul of the new rules and end up paying interest, surcharges and penalties.

Major changes to the UK tax system were introduced in the 1994 and 1995 Finance Acts. The new system of self-assessment is at the heart of the changes. It means that you will be able to work out your own tax bill. A new type of tax return will be issued in April 1997, designed specifically for self-assessment. It will relate to the 1996–7 tax year – and taxpayers will need to prepare for self-assessment long before April 1997. This chapter outlines what it could mean to you.

Self-assessment will make the biggest difference to the 9 million people who are sent tax returns each year. If your affairs are straightforward and all the tax you owe is collected at source – e.g. through Pay-As-You-Earn (PAYE) – self-assessment may not have much impact. However, if you are self-employed, in a business partnership, a company director, a higher-rate taxpayer or have several sources of income and/or capital gains, you will see a major difference in the way your tax affairs are dealt with. Self-assessment will affect your dealings with the Inland Revenue in terms of:

- your new obligations
- the forms that you will have to check or fill in
- new procedures for checking your self-assessment
- new deadlines for assessing and paying your taxes
- what happens if you don't pay your tax on time
- getting problems sorted out
- what to do if you want to complain
- what you can appeal against and how to do it.

Your obligations as a taxpayer are to be honest, to give accurate information and to pay your tax on time. These obligations will come into sharper focus under self-assessment. If you *don't* receive a tax return you are required to notify the Revenue of income or capital gains they don't know about within six months of the end of the tax year in which you make the income or gain. That's a tighter timetable than under the old rules, under which you had 12 months. You are also legally obliged to keep records in support of information you give on your tax return. Failure to meet these obligations will result in penalties in the form of interest on tax paid late; surcharges for continued late payment; and penalties (some automatic) for not supplying information requested by the Revenue – e.g. failing to file your tax return on time or to keep records.

Keeping records

From 6 April 1996, you are legally obliged to keep records in support of the information you give on your tax return – e.g. bank statements, tax credits for share dividends, business accounts. This applies to all taxpayers. Any taxpayer could find a tax return landing on their doormat, even if they have not received one in the past. If you choose to work out your own tax, you will also need to keep a copy of the *working sheets* of your calculations (which is part of the tax return guide – see below). If you run a business, you have to keep all records (not just your business records) for five years after the filing date for a particular tax year. If you don't run a business, records have to be kept for at least one year from the date you file your return (though it could be slightly longer if you filed your return late). These time limits are extended if there is an enquiry, in which case records have to kept until the enquiry is complete.

The new tax return

You will be sent a tax return to fill in if the Revenue thinks that you have income and/or capital gains which should be taxed. The first self-assessment returns will be sent out in April 1997 – i.e. after the end of the 1996–7 tax year. In preparation for self-assessment, the tax return and its guidance notes have been completely re-designed, and pilot exercises with taxpayers in various parts of the country are being undertaken to make sure that the new tax return will be easy to fill in. At the time this book went to press, the new forms were still under review. However, it is likely that the new tax return will be made up of a short tax form which everyone has to fill in plus *Schedules* dealing with different types of income. You will also get a tax return guide which will give guidance on how to fill in your tax return. It will include a working sheet for you to calculate your tax bill (if you want to do this yourself).

What to do when you get your tax return

When you get the new tax return, it will be your responsibility to make sure that you have all the bits you need. Everybody who is sent a tax return will get the basic tax form but you may also need to fill in one or more Schedules. These will deal with different types of income or gains. So if you have income from letting property, for example, you will need to fill in the basic tax form and the Schedule dealing with income from land and property in the UK. Someone receiving a pension or social security will need to complete the Schedule covering pensions and social security benefits. There will be another Schedule for savings and investments. In total there may be as many as 7 Schedules.

The idea is that the new tax return should be more tailored to an individual taxpayer's circumstances. You should receive only the Schedules appropriate to the particular type of income you receive (or capital gains you make). But if you don't automatically get the Schedule you need, you must ask for it – the tax return guide will explain which Schedules deal with what. As well as checking that you have the right Schedules, it will be worth skimming through the tax form and the tax return guide to see if you want any *help sheets* or Revenue leaflets. If there's anything you are not sure about, ask your tax office.

Once you've got all the information you need from the Revenue and you've gathered together all your own records of your income, gains and outgoings, fill in the tax return.

Working out the tax bill

The new tax return will contain a section which asks you to calculate the tax due. There will be full instructions on how to do this. However, this is not compulsory. The Revenue will still do these calculations for you provided you send the return back by 30 September following the end of the tax year. Otherwise, the deadline for sending the return back will be 31 January.

You can in fact still ask the Revenue to calculate your tax bills even if you send in your tax return after 30 September. But the Revenue won't guarantee to have worked out the amount of tax due by 31 January, the date by which tax has to be paid. As a result, you may have to pay a surcharge for late payment of tax.

The 31 January 1998 *filing date* (for 1996–7 tax returns) is also the deadline for paying tax, so you will be able to send in your payment along with your return. Tax due will be income tax, capital gains tax and (if you are self-employed) Class 4 National Insurance not yet paid for the 1996–7 tax year. In addition, under the new system some tax payers will have to pay half the income tax and National Insurance for the 1997–8 tax year *on account* (i.e. in advance) by the same date – see below.

If you owe tax of £1,000 or less and you want the amount to be collected through PAYE (rather than paying it in a lump sum), you must send your tax return back to your tax office by 30 September 1997 (for 1996–7 tax returns).

If you don't file a return, the Revenue will have to make an estimate of the tax it thinks you owe and the tax it thinks you should pay on account, and may issue a *determination*. This determination will be treated as your self-assessment until you send in your completed tax return. The figures you supply on your completed tax return will automatically replace the estimated figures in the determination.

Payments on account

Under self-assessment some people will have to pay tax on account. The amount you will have to pay will never be more than the previous year's bill for income tax and Class 4 National Insurance less tax deducted at source (e.g. through PAYE or tax credits on share dividends). So if your tax and NI bill for the 1996–7 tax year was £9,150, and £2,095 of this tax was deducted at source, the amount you have to pay on account for the 1997–8 tax year will be £7,055 (i.e. £9,150 minus £2,095). Half of this *relevant amount* is payable on 31 January 1998 (the filing date for your 1996–7 tax return), the rest on 31 July 1998.

If your tax bill for the 1997–8 turns out to be more than what you paid on account, you make up the difference (or make a *balancing payment*) when you file your 1997–8 tax return. If your 1997–8 tax bill is less than the amount you paid on account, you can deduct the amount you have overpaid from the next payment on account.

Because your payments on account are based on your assessment for the previous tax year, you may end up overpaying tax. If you know that your income is going to fall, you can ask for your payments on account to be reduced. To make a claim to reduce your payments on account, do so in writing (by letter, on a claim form or on your tax return) before the first payment on account is due – i.e. before 31 January of the tax year in question.

Your written claim should give your reasons for believing that your payments on account will result in an overpayment of tax – e.g. you're going off travelling for six months and you won't be earning during that time. The claim should state that it is your belief that either you won't be liable to tax or your tax liability will be covered by tax deducted at source and that as a consequence the tax you will end up owing will be less than the payments on account. If you make such a claim, it can't be rejected but it's likely that the Revenue will look very carefully at your tax return to check that there isn't a significant difference between the amount of income tax due and the amount paid as reduced payments on account. Penalties exist to deter gross or persistent abuse.

Checking your self-assessment

Although technically it's up to you to tell the Revenue how much tax you owe (or are owed), in practice, the Revenue will have a large part to play in making sure you get it right. Your completed tax return will be subject to two checks. The first check (the initial processing of the return) will simply be to ensure that your return is legible, that the sums are right (if you have worked out your own tax bill) and that the figures you have provided are correct in themselves. This first check will happen shortly after you file your return. If there are any mistakes, your tax office will let you know and will ask you to correct your self-assessment.

The second check is a more in-depth one to make sure that the information you have provided on your return is complete and accurate and consistent with information from other sources – e.g. your employer or your bank. This second check may give rise to an *enquiry* into your tax return (see below).

Amending your assessment

You may need to amend your assessment if you send back your tax return and then discover that you have made a mistake. You may also be asked to amend your assessment by the Revenue as the result of an enquiry (see below). In the case of amendments you want to make yourself, you have 12 months from the 31 January filing date in which to do so.

The exception to the 12-month rule is where you realise that you have paid too much tax in the past because of a mistake you made on a tax return for an earlier tax year. In the 1996–7 tax year it is possible to ask for assessments back to the 1990–1 tax year to be corrected and the overpaid tax repaid to you. This might apply to you if, for example, you forgot to claim an allowance to which you were entitled.

Tax statements

To help you to keep track of how much tax you've paid and to remind you that tax is due (as well as other key deadlines), the Revenue will send regular tax statements. As this book went to press, the precise format and frequency of these statements had not been decided, but they may look something like a credit card bill with a tear-off payment slip at the bottom. Interest you owe (or are owed) and any penalty payments will also be shown on them.

Enquiries into your tax return

The Revenue will have the right to make enquiries into the completeness and accuracy of any tax return. You cannot appeal against an enquiry being held, though you can appeal if you think it has gone on for too long or without good reason. It is proposed that enquiries will be made into tax returns selected at random and where the Revenue suspects that something is wrong. Whatever the reason for selecting a tax return, the enquiry process will be the same.

First you will receive a written notice than an enquiry is

going to take place. If you don't receive such a notice within a year of filing your return, you can assume that no enquiry will take place. Note that the time limits are longer if you file your return late or make an amendment to it: the time limit will be the quarter date (31 January, 30 April, 31 July, 31 October) after the anniversary of the date you file or amend your return – e.g. if you send your return back on 28 February 1998, the Revenue will have until 30 April 1999 to enquire into it.

You may also receive a notice asking you to produce documents, accounts or other written particulars. You must produce whatever is asked for within 30 days of receiving the request. If you need more time or if the document requested doesn't exist, contact your tax office as soon as possible. The Revenue should request only information that is relevant to determining whether or not your return is complete or the information you have given is correct. If you don't think that the request is reasonably relevant to determining whether your return is complete and correct, you can appeal. You can also appeal if you haven't been given a minimum of 30 days in which to produce the papers requested.

Once the enquiry is complete you should receive written notice that this is the case. If everything on your tax return is in order, that's the end of the matter. However, it may be that the Revenue believes that your self-assessment should be amended, in which case you will have 30 days in which to do so in the light of the Revenue's conclusions. If you fail to amend your assessment or if you amend it incorrectly, the Revenue then has 30 days in which to amend your assessment in the way that it concludes will make it correct. If you don't agree with what it has done you have 30 days in which to appeal.

If the amendment to your assessment made by Revenue results in a higher tax bill than your original self-assessment, you will have 30 days from the date of the amendment to pay the additional tax you owe.

Discovery assessments

Before self-assessment, it was up to the Revenue to tell taxpayers how much tax they owed, which it did by issuing notices of assessment. Under the new system of self-assessment, the only assessments which the Revenue will issue will be *discovery assessments.* Unless you are guilty of serious negligence or fraud, it is unlikely that you will get one of these. If you do, you would be well advised to seek professional help.

Interest charges, surcharges and penalties

As well as new forms, new deadlines and new procedures for checking up on you, the new system of self-assessment has brought with it a streamlined approach to interest owed by or to you and new penalties – some automatic – for failing to abide by Revenue rules.

Late tax returns

If you miss the 31 January deadline for sending back your tax return, or if you send your tax return back incomplete – e.g. you have not filled in all the Schedules you need to – you will have to pay an automatic penalty of £100. A further £100 penalty will have to be paid if you haven't sent back your return within six months of the 31 January filing date. However, these automatic penalties cannot be more than the tax that is due for the year.

Note that the Revenue can apply to the general or special commissioners to impose a daily penalty of up to £60 a day, but this is likely to happen only if it believes that you owe a substantial amount of tax.

Inadequate record-keeping

The Revenue can charge a penalty of up to £3,000 for each failure to keep adequate records in support of information provided on your tax return.

Tax paid late

If you don't pay your tax on time, you will have to pay interest from the date the tax was due to the date you make payment. If the tax due on 31 January has not been paid by 28 February in the same year, you will have to pay a surcharge of 5 per cent of the tax due. If you still have not paid the tax you owe by 31 July, there will be another 5 per cent surcharge to pay.

Failure to produce records

If you fail to produce documents requested by the Revenue in the course of an enquiry, you will have to pay a fixed initial penalty of £50. If you still fail to produce the document requested, a daily penalty of £30 can be imposed, though this could rise to £150 if formal penalty proceedings are held to determine the level of the penalty.

Note that you cannot be penalised for failing to produce a document which does not exist – though you may have to pay a penalty for failing to keep adequate records.

Late payment of surcharges and penalties

Interest will also have to be paid on surcharges and penalties which are unpaid 30 days from the date of the written notice telling you that they are going to be imposed. You also have 30 days in which to appeal against the imposition of a surcharge or penalty.

Interest on overpaid tax

If you have paid too much tax, the Revenue will repay it with interest. The interest will be calculated from the later of the date you made the overpayment or the date that tax was due, to the date the repayment is made. So if you overpaid tax on 28 January (in time for the 31 January deadline), interest on the tax being repaid would be calculated from 31 January.

Appeals

Under the old system, the Revenue told you how much tax you owed by issuing a notice of assessment. If you didn't agree with it, you had to appeal in writing within 30 days of its issue. Although the only assessments issued by the Revenue now will be discovery assessments (see p. 77), there may still be occasions where you need to appeal because the Revenue has taken action which you don't agree with.

The new rules governing self-assessment make very clear what you can and can't appeal against. For example, you can't appeal against an enquiry into your tax affairs but you can appeal against:

- the imposition of surcharges and penalties
- a request for documents under an enquiry
- an enquiry that you think has gone on too long and hasn't got anywhere
- a Revenue amendment to your assessment if you don't agree with it.

If you want to appeal, your first stop should be your tax inspector, and you should have reasonable grounds for appealing. If, for example, you have been surcharged for late payment of tax, you have grounds for appeal if you can show that you actually paid your tax on time. The vast majority of appeals should be able to be settled after discussions with your tax office. However, if you can't reach agreement, you have a choice: you can either give up or ask for your appeal to be heard before the commissioners, who are independent of the Inland Revenue. For how the appeals system works, see p. 62.

Getting problems sorted out

The move to self-assessment represents a big change for both taxpayers and the Revenue and it is inevitable that there will be some problems in making the transition from one system to another. You should be able to keep problems to a minimum by giving honest and accurate information, keeping records and paying your tax on time. To avoid creating problems, ask the Revenue for help if there is anything you are not sure about. At the time this book went to press, a special tax-return helpline was planned which should be widely advertised in the media.

5 *TAX AND FAMILIES*

- In some circumstances, men are better off not making a claim for the married couple's allowance in the year of marriage – see p. 83.
- It can be tax-efficient for the wife to claim the married couple's allowance – see p. 83.
- A newly married couple may qualify for mortgage tax relief on three separate loans – see p. 87.
- Are your children paying too much tax? See p. 99.

Everyone, however young (or old), is potentially a taxpayer. In this chapter we explain the income tax rules that affect married couples (both during and after the marriage), couples living together, children and students. If you're approaching 65, you'll find more information in Chapter 6, *When you are older*.

Tax and marriage

Since 6 April 1990 a husband and wife have been taxed independently of each other. They are each:

- taxed on their own income, both earned and investment income
- given their own tax-free allowances
- given their own tax bands – in 1996–7 this means that a husband and wife can each have £3,900 of taxable income taxed at the lower rate of 20 per cent and £21,600 taxed at the basic rate of 24 per cent
- responsible for their own tax affairs – dealing with the Inland Revenue, paying their own tax and receiving any tax rebate due.

When you get married

After marriage you each continue to get your own personal allowances. In addition, the husband or wife can claim a married couple's allowance. The allowance is £1,790 in the 1996–7 tax year, but the tax saving will be only £268.50 as relief is restricted to 15 per cent, and is not at your highest tax rate. You may get a higher married couple's allowance if either partner is 65 or older during the tax year – see p. 103.

In the year in which you get married, you can claim the full married couple's allowance if the marriage takes place before 6 May. If the wedding is on or after that date, your married couple's allowance for that year will be reduced by one-twelfth for each complete month after 6 April that you remain single. The chart below shows the amount by which your tax bill will be reduced, with the actual allowance in brackets.

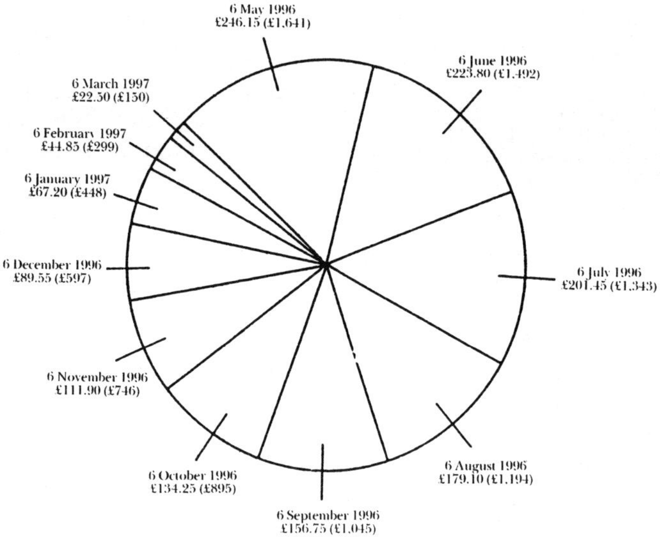

So if, for example, you get married on 10 September 1996, you have been single for five complete months of the tax year and so get seven-twelfths of the married couple's allowance for the 1996–7 tax year, that is £1,045, a tax-saving of £156.75.

ICTA 1988 s257 s257A

Additional personal allowance when you marry

The additional personal allowance can be claimed by a lone parent (whether man or woman) who has a dependent child or by somebody looking after a child at their own expense, and is equal to the married couple's allowance (£1,790 in the 1996–7 tax year).

If a man is claiming an additional personal allowance before he gets married, he can choose to keep it for the tax year in which he gets married instead of claiming the married couple's allowance. It may be worth doing this as you will get the whole additional personal allowance, whereas if you claimed the married couple's allowance this could be reduced, depending on the date of the marriage. Note, however, that the additional personal allowance cannot be transferred to the wife.

A woman who is claiming the additional personal allowance before getting married can continue to claim it for the remainder of the tax year in which she marries.

After the year of the marriage neither husband nor wife can claim the additional personal allowance unless the wife is totally incapacitated for the whole of the tax year. In this case the husband can claim the additional personal allowance in addition to the married couple's allowance. For full details of this allowance, see p. 98.

ICTA 1988 s259, s261

How to claim the married couple's allowance

Tell your tax office that you want to claim the married couple's allowance as soon as possible after the wedding. If you pay tax under Pay-As-You-Earn (PAYE), use form 11PA, which you can get from any tax office. The married couple's allowance will be given to the husband unless you notify the Revenue that it should be given to the wife or shared equally between you. If you decide the wife should get half or all of the allowance jointly inform the inspector of taxes *before* the start of the tax year on 6 April and must complete form 18. This could be beneficial if the wife is paid under PAYE but the husband is self-employed, as the tax saving is made earlier. If the husband's total income (see p. 33) is likely to be less than his allowances, half or all of the allowance should go to the wife if she is a taxpayer. The election remains in force until you inform the inspector otherwise. A wife can claim half the allowance without her husband's consent, following the same timetable.

ICTA 1988 s257

Transferring the blind person's allowance

You can transfer the blind person's allowance between husband and wife (and *vice versa*) if the person who gets the allowance is unable to make use of some (or all) of it (see p. 35 for details of who can claim this allowance).

The Revenue will send you form 575 to complete and will then estimate the amount of allowance to be transferred. This will then be given to the other spouse on a provisional basis.

After the end of the tax year, the Revenue will check its estimate. If it was too low, a rebate of tax already paid will be sent to the spouse to whom the allowance was transferred. If the estimate was too high, that spouse will owe some tax which will be collected the following year through the PAYE code or by altering the tax assessment.
ICTA 1988 s265

Transferring the personal allowance

Before the start of the 1990–1 tax year, a husband whose income was less than his allowances could set his unused personal allowance against his wife's income, but since the 1990–1 tax year married women have been taxed independently of their husbands, and neither the husband nor wife can transfer any unused portion of their personal allowance to their spouse (only the married couple's allowance may be transferred to the wife). However, special rules can still be applied where a husband's income was lower than his personal allowance in 1990–1. These rules mean that a husband can transfer some of his unused personal allowance to his wife – the amount transferred is known as the *transitional allowance*.

To benefit from the transitional allowance rules in the 1996–7 tax year you need to have been eligible for transitional allowance in 1990–1 and every tax year since.

Working out transitional allowance for 1990–1

Slightly different rules apply depending on whether you were married before or during the 1989–90 tax year and what other allowances you were getting before the wedding. But the principle is similar in all cases and the end result is that the total allowances given to a couple in 1990–1 are the same as those in 1989–90. To claim transitional allowance in 1990–1 all the following must apply:

- the husband's income for 1990–1 must have been below his personal allowance, i.e. less than £3,005
- the couple must have been married and living together since the 1989–90 tax year
- the couple must not have elected to have the wife's earned income taxed separately from her husband's income in 1989–90.

To work out the transitional allowance for 1990–1:

Step 1 Add up the couple's allowances for 1989–90.
Step 2 Deduct the wife's personal allowance and the married couple's allowance given to her for 1990–1.
Step 3 Deduct the husband's taxable income for 1990–1.

The answer gives the amount of transitional allowance given to the wife in 1990–1. If the husband had no earnings, the maximum transitional allowance for a couple not eligible for the higher age-related personal allowances was £2,435 in 1990–1.

EXAMPLE 1

Janice and Ian Edwards have three young children and they decided in 1989 that Ian should run the house and look after the children while Janice worked full time. Ian worked in the local pub a couple of nights a week earning about £22 a week.

Step 1 In 1989–90 Ian and Janice's total allowances were the married man's allowance (£4,375) and the wife's earned income allowance (£2,785). The total is **£7,160**.

Step 2 Janice's allowances in 1990–1 were her personal allowance (£3,005) and the married couple's allowance (£1,720), a total of £4,725. Deducting this from the total in Step 1 gives **£2,435**.

Step 3 Ian's earnings in 1990–1 were £1,056. Deducting this amount from the figure in Step 2 gives **£1,379**. This is the amount of Ian's personal allowance that is transferred to Janice as a transitional allowance.

In later years
The amount of allowance that can be transferred in later years is the smaller of:

- the amount of the husband's personal allowance which he can't use himself, *or*
- the amount of allowance transferred from husband to wife the previous year *less* any increase in her personal allowance.

Each tax year a husband can continue to give the unused part of his allowance until it is reduced to nil by the increases in allowance or earnings, or until the marriage ends. The maximum amount of transitional allowance for a couple not eligible for the higher age-related personal allowances was £2,145 in 1991–2, £1,995 in 1992–3, 1993–4 and 1994–5, £1,915 in 1995–6 and £1,675 in 1996–7.

EXAMPLE 2

In 1991-2, the basic personal allowance went up to £3,295, the married couple's allowance stayed the same and Ian's earnings rose to £1,600 (see Example 1 above). The transitional allowance was the lower of:

- Ian's unused allowance, £3,295 – £1,600 = **£1,695** or
- the transitional allowance in 1990-1 of £1,379 less the increase of £290 in Janice's personal allowance: £1,379 – £290 = **£1,089**. The transitional allowance was £1,089.

In 1992-3, the basic personal allowance went up to £3,445, the married couple's allowance stayed the same and Ian's earnings rose to £1,900. The transitional allowance was the lower of:

- Ian's unused allowance, £3,445 – £1,900 = **£1,545** or
- the transitional allowance in 1991-2 of £1,089 less the increase of £150 in Janice's personal allowance: £1,089 – £150 = **£939**. The transitional allowance was £939.

In 1993-4 and 1994-5 personal and married couple's allowances stayed the same. In 1993-4 Ian's earnings rose to £2,100 so his unused allowance went down to £1,345, and the transitional allowance remained at the previous year's level, £939.

But in 1994-5 Ian earned £2,600. His unused allowance was £845, less than the previous year's £939 transitional allowance. So £845 was the transitional allowance for Janice in 1994-5.

In 1995–6, Ian's earnings fell to £2,400. The allowance transferred the previous year (£845) less the £80 increase in Janice's personal allowance gives £765. This is less than £1,125 – Ian's unused personal allowance of £3,525 – £2,400. So Janice gets £765 transitional allowance in 1995–6.

In 1996–7, Ian returned to full-time work and earned £17,000. Since Ian is now using all his personal allowance, there will be no transitional allowance for Janice in 1996–7. There will not be any transitional allowance in any subsequent tax year either, even if Ian gives up his new job, since you can never claim a higher transitional allowance in one tax year than you claimed in the previous tax year.

ICTA 1988 s257, s257B, s257D, s259, s261, s265

Joint investments

If you have investments or savings in joint names, any income you get will be treated automatically as if it were paid to you in equal shares, and each of you will be responsible for paying tax due on your share.

But if you own the investments in unequal shares, the income can be taxed accordingly. For the Revenue to do this you have to make a joint written declaration on form 17 setting out in what proportions the investment, and consequently the income, are shared between you. This declaration will take effect from the date it is received by the Revenue.

A note of warning: you can't simply choose the proportions that are most convenient for you. You can make a declaration only according to your actual shares of the property and income. Of course, if you decide to split the investments into separate accounts in sole names and the other partner has no control or interest in either the investment or the income, then the income will belong to the partner whose account it is in, and will be taxed accordingly.
ICTA 1988 s282, s282A, s282B

What happens to your mortgage(s) when you marry?

If you and your husband or wife each had a mortgage which qualified for tax relief before you married and you were not living together, and you intend to sell both homes, you can:

- continue to get the tax relief on the old homes for up to twelve months *and*
- jointly get tax relief on up to £30,000 of loans to buy your new home.

Alternatively, if you decide to live in one of your existing homes and sell the other you can:

- continue to get tax relief on the home you're selling for up to 12 months *and*
- continue to get tax relief, as before, on the home in which you live.

If you were living together before you married and qualified for mortgage interest relief on up to £60,000 on a joint mortgage (because you exchanged contracts before 1 August 1988), you will not get any tax relief on the amount of loan over £30,000 from the date you get married.

Who gets the tax relief on a mortgage?

If you have a joint mortgage the relief is normally split evenly between you. If it is not, it is given to the person in whose name the mortgage is. But if you are a married couple, you can choose the proportions in which you get relief, even if the mortgage is in only one name, by making an *allocation of interest election*.

In most cases, if your loan gets mortgage interest relief at source (MIRAS), making an election will have no effect on the total tax relief you receive as a couple. But if your loan is outside MIRAS and one of you is not a taxpayer, an election could be beneficial. Your tax office can advise you.

To make an election, complete form 15 (1990), signed by both of you, and send it to the Revenue no later than 12 months after the end of the tax year to which you want it to apply. The election will remain in force until you inform the Revenue otherwise and complete the necessary forms.
SP10/1980; ICTA 1988; s354, s355, s356A

Covenants to charity

Money given to charity under a deed of covenant qualifies for tax relief at your highest rate of tax so long as the covenant is capable of lasting more than three years. So if you covenant to give a charity an amount which will cost you £76 a year after taking basic-rate tax into account, you pay £76 to the charity. The charity can claim the basic-rate tax of £24 from the Revenue, boosting the value of your donation to £100.

If you're a higher-rate taxpayer, tell your tax office about the covenant on your tax return. You will get higher-rate tax relief, usually through your PAYE code or your tax assessment.

If your top rate of tax is 20 per cent you still deduct basic-rate tax of 24 per cent from your donation. But you are liable to pay the Revenue the difference between the basic-rate tax and the lower rate of tax.

If you are a non-taxpayer you would have to pay the Revenue all the 24 per cent tax claimed by the charity. So there would be no tax advantage in having a covenant. It's simpler just to give donations to charity. You could, though, get your husband or wife to make a covenant to charity if he or she pays tax.

Death of a spouse

In the tax year in which your husband or wife dies, these rules apply:

- **After the death of the wife**, the husband continues, for the rest of the tax year, to get the married couple's allowance (less any part that his wife used against her income) in addition to his personal allowance to set against his own income. He can't, for that year, get the additional personal allowance unless his wife was totally incapacitated and he has a dependent child.

  In the following years, until the husband remarries, he gets the personal allowance, and, if he has a 'qualifying' child living with him he can claim the additional personal allowance (see p. 98). If the husband remarries within the same tax year as his wife has died, he *doesn't* get the reduced married couple's allowance (see p. 82) – he continues to get the full amount.
- **After the death of the husband**, the wife gets any of the married couple's allowance which her husband had not used against his income up to the date of his death plus the widow's bereavement allowance (see below) plus the additional personal allowance if she has a dependent child living with her after her husband's death – and, of

course, her personal allowance. In subsequent years, she gets the personal allowance and any other allowances to which she is entitled.

Widow's bereavement allowance

This can be claimed by a widow in the tax year of her husband's death, and in the following tax year, unless she remarries before that year begins. The allowance is £1,790 in the 1996–7 tax year, no matter when in the year her husband dies. Relief is restricted to 15 per cent, a tax saving of £268.50.
ICTA1988 s262; IR91

> **If your spouse leaves any money** when he or she dies, see *Inheritance tax*, p. 342, for the tax rules.

Separation and divorce

After separation or divorce, the same income may have to support two households instead of one, so it's vital that you plan your finances carefully. This section shows you how to keep as much money as possible for yourself, your spouse (or ex-spouse) and your children, and how to keep the Revenue's share to a minimum.

Typically, separation or divorce will involve one or both of these:

- the payment of maintenance
- two homes instead of one.

It's important that husband and wife decide *together* the most tax-efficient way of paying maintenance, and the best solution to the housing problem.

The end of the marriage
Your marriage can end by *divorce*, or (for tax purposes) by *separation*. The Revenue treats you as separated if:

- there's a *deed of separation*, or
- there's a *decree of judicial separation*, or
- the separation is likely to be *permanent*.
  ICTA1988 s282

If you separate, tell your tax office straight away. Even if you weren't paying tax before, get in touch with the local tax office – you may have dealings with them later. You can find the address in the phone book under *Inland Revenue*.

Maintenance – if you pay it

Maintenance payments are regular payments made out of your income to maintain your divorced or separated spouse, or your children, or both. There are two types of maintenance payments:

- **enforceable payments** – ones you're legally obliged to make, e.g. under a legally binding written agreement, or a court order, or (since April 1993) as assessed by the Child Support Agency
- **voluntary payments** – those you can't be made to pay.

You don't get tax relief on any voluntary payments you make.

If you make enforceable maintenance payments, the rules on tax relief vary depending on whom the maintenance is paid to and when the legally binding agreement was made. But even if you pay under a court order certain payments won't qualify for tax relief:

- payments for which you already get tax relief in some other way, e.g. mortgage payments
- payments made under most foreign court orders or agreements – but payments made (since April 1992) under a European Union country court order or agreement, or (since January 1994) under a European Economic Area country court order or agreement, do count for tax relief
- capital payments or lump sums, even if they are paid in instalments.

Agreements made after 15 March 1988

Maintenance paid to your ex-husband or ex-wife You can get tax relief on enforceable payments up to the *maintenance deduction* limit of £1,790 in 1996–7 (i.e. on an amount equal to the married couple's allowance). In the 1996–7 tax year, relief is restricted to 15 per cent, a maximum tax-saving of £268.50. All periodical payments and any bills you pay on behalf of your spouse count towards this, if they are covered by a court order or other legally binding agreement. But tax relief stops if your ex-husband or ex-wife remarries.

Maintenance paid to children You can't get tax relief for these payments if they are made direct to a child and count as a child's own income. (If the wording of the court order says that the money is paid to your ex-spouse for the children, then tax relief is available within the limit shown above.)

Agreements made before 15 March 1988 (in place by 30 June 1988)

Maintenance paid to your ex-husband or ex-wife The tax relief you can get on enforceable payments is limited to the amount of maintenance payments you paid which qualified for tax relief in the 1988–9 tax year. This is the case even if your payments have subsequently increased. In 1996–7, relief on the first £1,790 of maintenance you pay is restricted to 15 per cent; on the rest you'll get relief at your highest rate of tax.

Maintenance paid to children The tax relief you get is limited to the amount of maintenance you paid which qualified for tax relief in 1988–9.

Tax relief – a choice to make

If you pay maintenance only to an ex-husband or ex-wife and have increased the amount since April 1989, your tax relief will not have been increased to take this extra into account. So if you are still paying less than the maximum maintenance deduction (£1,790 in 1996–7) you would get more relief by claiming the maintenance deduction. But if you are also getting tax relief on payments made direct to a child, you will lose all the tax relief on these payments.

If the amount of maintenance on which you can get relief is more than £1,790 in 1996–7, you should not elect to receive the maintenance deduction as it will have the effect of reducing your tax relief.

EXAMPLE 3

Harriet and Charles have been divorced since 1987. When they divorced, Charles was ordered to pay £20 a week maintenance to Harriet and £10 a week to each of their two children who live with her. In 1988–9 he paid £1,040 to Harriet and £520 to each of the children.

Harriet and Charles have now agreed that she should receive an extra £520 a year maintenance and a new court order is being drawn up. Charles wonders what the situation regarding tax relief is.

As the initial court order was made before the rules changed in 1988, the amount of tax relief that Charles can claim in 1996–7 is limited to the amount he received in the 1988–9 tax year, i.e. £1,040 for the payments to Harriet and another £1,040 for the payments to the children. He won't be able to claim extra tax relief just because he has increased payments.

If Charles elected to claim the maintenance deduction when he increased the maintenance he pays, he would get an extra £520 tax relief for the increase in payments to Harriet; but he will lose the £1,040 relief he gets for payments made to the children.

Charles decides to stick to the old arrangements for tax relief as the total relief he gets will be higher than if he switched.

EXAMPLE 4

Marion and Eric divorced in 1987 when their children had grown up. Eric is unable to work through illness and Marion pays him maintenance under a court order. She's been paying £25 a week for the last few years, but has increased it to £35 since the start of the 1996–7 tax year.

In the 1988–9 tax year Marion paid £1,300 in maintenance and received this amount of tax relief. In 1996–7 the total of payments made will be increased to £1,820.

Marion elects to claim a maintenance deduction of £1,790. The amount of tax relief being claimed increases by £490. With 15 per cent relief, that's an extra tax saving of £73.50, compared with relief on just £1,300.

How to make the choice

You need to complete form 142 and return it to the Revenue within 12 months of the end of the tax year for which you want to claim the maintenance deduction. For the 1996–7 tax year you have until 5 April 1998 to decide. You also have to write to the person to whom you make the payments to let him or her know that you have made the switch.

Once you have made an election, you cannot withdraw it, so make sure that you will be better off by making it.

How to make the payments
Payments should be paid in full, without deducting any tax. You will get tax relief through an adjustment to your PAYE code (see p. 138) or it will be shown on your tax assessment (see p. 42) so that you get a lower tax bill.

The only exception to this rule has been payments to children who reached 21 before 6 April 1994 made under court orders which were unchanged since 15 March 1988. The payments were made with basic-rate tax deducted. However, from 1996–7 such payments will have no effect for tax so should be paid in full.

Maintenance – if you receive it

Whether you have to pay tax on any maintenance you get depends on whether it's voluntary or enforceable and when the agreement was made.

If you receive *voluntary* maintenance, i.e. the person making payments can't be made to pay up, you don't have to pay tax on what you get.

If you receive *enforceable* maintenance, i.e. it's paid under a court order or other legally binding agreement:

- if the agreement was made after 15 March 1988 (or if it was applied for before then but wasn't in place by 30 June 1988), what you receive is tax-free income
- if the agreement was made before 15 March 1988 (or it was applied for before that date and was in place by 30 June 1988) and you're a divorced or separated spouse, you won't pay tax on the first £1,790 of maintenance you receive in the 1996–7 tax year. Anything over this amount will count as taxable income. But the taxable amount of maintenance is 'pegged' to the amount on which you paid tax in 1988–9. This means that if the amount of maintenance you get increased after 5 April 1989 you won't have to pay tax on the extra you receive. If the person paying maintenance switches to claiming maintenance deduction (see p. 91) you won't be taxed on any maintenance you get.
- if the agreement was made before 15 March 1988 and you're a child receiving maintenance from a parent or step-parent the amount that counts for tax is 'pegged' to

the amount that was taxable in 1988–9. Any increases since then are not taxable. However, you will pay tax only once your taxable income exceeds your personal allowance. If you go on receiving maintenance payments after you turn 21, those payments will be paid gross and are tax-free.
ICTA 1988 s347A, s347B; FA 1988, s38, s39

Maintenance to a partner you weren't married to
You can end up paying maintenance to a former partner even if you were never married to him or her. If you separate after living together, no tax relief will be available on any maintenance payments whether they are enforceable or voluntary. But the income received from such payments will be tax-free to the recipient.

Claiming social security benefits?

Any payments received by you or your children – whether they're voluntary or enforceable – may be taken into account if you claim means-tested benefits, including income support, family credit, disability working allowance, housing or council tax benefit. Check with your local social security office or Citizens Advice Bureau.

Allowances

If you are a married couple, in the tax year you part you'll each get your own personal allowance plus the same amount of married couple's allowance you were receiving at the time you separated. If you have a dependent child living with you, you can also claim the additional personal allowance but will have to deduct from this allowance any of the married couple's allowance you are claiming. If some of the married couple's allowance has been transferred to you because your spouse doesn't have enough income to make full use of it, this will not affect the amount of additional personal allowance you can claim in the year of separation.

In following tax years, both ex-partners will get their own personal allowance plus any other allowances they are entitled to, e.g. additional personal allowance (see p. 98) or blind person's allowance (see p. 35). A husband can continue to claim the married couple's allowance if all the following apply:

- he separated from his wife before 6 April 1990
- he is still married, i.e. is separated but not divorced
- since the separation he has wholly maintained his wife by making voluntary maintenance payments.

ICTA 1988 s257F

Inheritance tax

Gifts between husband and wife don't count for inheritance tax purposes – and this applies even after separation *right up to the moment of divorce* (i.e. when the decree absolute is granted).

After divorce, the following gifts are normally tax-free:

- maintenance for your ex-spouse or children
- transfers made under the divorce settlement
- in some cases, money given to you following a change to an agreement you made on or before your divorce – get professional advice
- gifts which would, in any case, be tax-free, e.g. those made out of your income as part of your normal spending. See *Inheritance Tax*, p. 342, for more details.

What happens to your home?

After separation or divorce, you and your ex-spouse will probably need *two* homes instead of one, which may mean two mortgages. Below, we explain the rules about tax relief on mortgage interest, and show you how to keep your tax bill to a minimum.

The general rules

You get tax relief on the interest you pay on up to £30,000 (in total) of loans to buy your only or main home, at a rate of 15 per cent in 1996–7. Until 6 April 1988 you could also get tax relief on loans for home improvements and for buying a home for a dependent relative or for a former husband or wife, though these all counted towards the overall limit of £30,000. If you took out a loan for one of these purposes before that date you can continue to get tax relief – of 15 per cent in 1996–7.

From the date of separation or divorce (whichever comes first) each of you can get tax relief on interest you pay on a mortgage of up to £30,000, if you live in different homes. So you can each get tax relief if you each take out a mortgage for your own home.

Maximising tax relief

If you are faced with having to pay two mortgages, you need to arrange your affairs so that you get two lots of mortgage relief:

- **If you sell the old home and each buy a new home** you will each get tax relief on up to £30,000 of your mortgage, provided you pay the interest yourself.
- **If one of you stays in the old home** he or she can get tax relief on any increase in the mortgage (up to the limit of £30,000) needed to buy out the other person's share or interest in the home.

If you pay an ex-spouse's mortgage costs

If you are paying your ex-spouse's mortgage costs, it is normally sensible to increase the maintenance you pay to include the mortgage payments but to allow your ex-spouse actually to pay the mortgage and claim tax relief. You can then claim relief on a mortgage of your own.

Raising a lump sum

You might need to raise a lump sum for your ex-spouse – to enable him or her to buy a new home while you stay on in the old one. But if you have to borrow to raise the lump sum, make sure you get tax relief on the interest you pay.

You could raise a lump sum by taking out a mortgage (or a second mortgage) on the old home, and the interest on this loan would qualify for tax relief *provided* it's used to buy out the other person's share and you're within the £30,000 limit. So if, for example, the old home is owned jointly by you and your ex-spouse, you can specify that the lump sum is being used to buy out their share.

Even if the house is in your name only, your ex-spouse may still have an interest in it. For example, the interest could be the right to occupy the home. Make sure that the separation or divorce agreement says that you're buying out this interest – then you'll still get tax relief.

ICTA 1988 s354, s355, s356A

Transferring the home

You don't normally have to pay *capital gains tax* (CGT) if you sell or give away your only or main home – see p. 219. But if you transfer the home to your ex-spouse, things are more complicated.

If you move out and transfer the home to your ex-spouse, you won't have to pay CGT, provided the transfer takes place within three years of the separation. But after three years, part of the gain you make on the transfer *is* a chargeable gain, unless:

- your ex-spouse has lived in the home ever since you moved out, *and*
- you haven't yet chosen another home as your main residence for CGT purposes.

If you stay in the old home and your ex-spouse moves out, you can later transfer it to him or her without having to pay CGT, provided you haven't chosen another home as your main residence.
ICTA 1988 s354–s357, s369; TCGA 1992 s222–223

Capital gains tax

A husband and wife are each allowed to make net taxable gains of £6,300 in the 1996–7 tax year before having to pay CGT. Gifts between husband and wife don't count for CGT purposes – but this doesn't apply if you're divorced or (except in the tax year of separation) if you're separated.
TCGA 1992 s3, s58

Tax if you have children

If you've got children, it may make a difference to *your* tax bill. Here, we deal with things you may need to watch out for.

Additional personal allowance

The additional personal allowance is equal to the basic married couple's allowance – £1,790 in the 1996–7 tax year, with relief limited to 15 per cent. You can claim it (in addition to your personal allowance) if you have a dependent child and:

- you are a single person (whether or not you are living with someone as man and wife)
- you are separated from your husband or wife
- you are a widow or widower
- you married after the start of the tax year and had a child living with you before you got married
- you are a married man whose wife will be totally incapacitated throughout the tax year.

In order to claim additional personal allowance, you must have one or more 'qualifying' children living with you for all or part of the tax year. A qualifying child is one who is under 16 at the start of the tax year, *or* who is in full-time education, *or* who is undergoing full-time training (lasting at least two years) for a trade or profession.

The child must be either:

- your own child, a step-child or a child you have legally adopted before he or she reaches 18
- any other child who is under 18 at the start of the tax year, and whom you maintain at your own expense (a younger brother or sister, say).

If two people can claim the additional personal allowance for the same child (i.e. if the child lives with each of them for part of the year), the allowance is divided between them in agreed proportions. If they can't agree, the allowance is divided in proportion to the time the child spends with each of them during the year.

Note that the amount you can claim doesn't depend on the number of children you're bringing up: the most you can get is £1,790 whether you have one child or ten. And if you're not married but living with someone as man and wife, you can get only one additional personal allowance between you.

ICTA 1988, s259, s260

Your children's income

This section describes how children's income is taxed, and how to make the most of your child's tax-free allowances.

Income

No matter how young your children are, they will be taxed on their earned income just as if they were adults. They will also be taxed on their investment income, unless the investment was given to them by their parents, in which case it may be taxed as the parent's income (see below).

Grants or scholarships to pay for children's education don't count as their income, and so don't affect their tax bill. But if the scholarship is paid by the parent's employer as a perk of the job, the parent may be taxed on it – see the table on p. 161 for details.

ICTA 1988 s331, s663

Allowances

Children can also claim allowances in the same way as adults. All children are entitled to the basic personal allowance (£3,765 in the 1996–7 tax year), which means that they can have income of £3,765 before they have to pay any tax. And if they qualify for any other allowances, this figure will be even higher. For example, a 17-year-old bringing up a younger brother or sister at his or her own expense could claim the additional personal allowance – £1,790 in the 1996–7 tax year.

Children's investment income

Remember that children can have income of at least £3,765 before they have to pay tax. But investment income is often paid after basic-rate tax has been deducted. So if your child gets investment income, and this income (including the gross amounts) is £3,765 or less, any tax deducted can be claimed back from the Revenue. For how to claim tax back, see p. 60. If the income comes from a building society or bank (other than the National Savings Bank) account, you should complete form R85 and hand it in to the institution, in which case tax won't be deducted at source. Tax won't be deducted from the income from National Savings Children's Bonus Bonds.

If *parents* give a child something which produces investment income – e.g. if they open up a National Savings Investment account for their child – the income is usually taxed as the parents' income, unless the child is 18 or over, or married. There are two exceptions to this rule:

- if the income which comes from investments given by the parents is less than £100, or
- if the parents set up an *accumulation trust* for the child and the interest is 'accumulated' (i.e. not spent) until the child reaches 18, or marries.

  ICTA 1988 s64, s234, s468 (investment income); s343 (building society interest); s165, s331 (scholarships); s663–s670 (settlements on children)

How to check your child's tax bill

Write down all the sources of your child's income, the *gross* (i.e. before deduction of tax) amounts and how much tax (if any) has already been deducted. It might help if you fill in a tax return for your child (you can ask your tax office to send you one).

Then write down all your child's outgoings and allowances, to work out the tax-free income he or she is entitled to receive. If the gross income is less than or equal to tax-free income, then your child shouldn't be paying tax, and you can claim back any that has already been deducted.

If the child's gross income is *more* than his or her tax-free income, work out how much tax is due on the difference. If this is less than the amount already deducted, you can claim back the difference.

If you find that your child is due a rebate you can reclaim it using form R40(SP) – obtainable from your tax office. And the child can make his or her own claims if the tax was deducted from income 'within his or her control' – e.g. if tax was deducted from the child's earnings from a holiday job.

Check your children's tax bills every year, and make sure you reclaim any tax overpaid. Don't forget that you can also reclaim any tax owing from the previous six years – see p. 246 for more information.

But note that if your child *owes* any tax, then you, as the parent or guardian, are responsible for paying it out of your own income, if the tax isn't paid from the child's income.

Tax and students

As a student, you may have to pay tax, just like anyone else. But certain things don't normally count as income for tax purposes:

- student grants from a local education authority (LEA)
- parental contributions
- certain non-LEA discretionary grants – e.g. from the DSS
- post-graduate grants from one of the research councils
- most other awards or scholarships – but always check with your tax office.

If you are being sponsored through college (e.g. by a company or by one of the armed forces), or if you are on a sandwich course, the money paid to you to cover the time spent *at college* is usually tax-free – but, again, check with your tax office. The money paid to cover the time you spend *at work*, however, does count as your income for tax purposes.

Any income which isn't tax-free is added together and, if it comes to more than your outgoings and allowances, you'll have to pay tax on the excess.
ICTA 1988 s331; SP4/86; IR 60

Vacation jobs

Earnings from vacation jobs count as income. But you and your employer can fill in a form to say that your total earnings, plus all your other income for the year, won't exceed the personal allowance – and then tax won't be deducted under PAYE. You can get the form (called **P38(S)**) from tax offices.

6 *When You are Older*

- You may need to select your investments carefully, or you could lose age-related tax allowances – see p. 105.
- If too much tax is deducted at source from your investment income, you may not have to wait until the end of the tax year to reclaim it back – see p. 109.
- You pay less tax on an annuity bought with your own money (as opposed to one bought with a personal pension plan) – see p. 111.

Older people are liable to tax on their income in the same way as anyone else. But many people over 64 pay less tax than a younger person receiving the same income. In this chapter we look at special age-related allowances. We also look at other aspects of income tax which are likely to be of special concern to older or retired people.

Higher personal and married couple's allowances

If you were 64 or over before the start of the tax year, i.e. you will be 65 at some time during the tax year, you qualify for an increased personal allowance (depending on your 'total income' – see overleaf). This higher personal allowance is up to £4,910 for the 1996–7 tax year, compared with the basic personal allowance of £3,765. So if you pay basic-rate tax on up to £1,145 less of your income, you can make a saving of up to £274.80 (24 per cent of £1,145). If you were 74 or over before the start of the tax year, the maximum allowance goes up to £5,090 – a further saving of up to £43.20.

Similarly, the married couple's allowance, with relief restricted to 15 per cent in the 1996–7 tax year, can go up to £3,115 if either partner was 64 before the start of the tax year, and £3,155 if either became 74 before the start of the tax year.

You won't get the full amount of the extra allowances if your total income is above a certain amount – £15,200 in the 1996–7 tax year. The extra allowance will be reduced by £1 for every £2 by which your total income exceeds this limit. Husband and wife each have a total income limit of £15,200.

The amount of married couple's allowance is always based on the husband's total income:

- even if he qualifies for the extra allowance because of his wife's age, i.e. she is 64 (or 74) before the start of the tax year but he isn't
- even if part or all of the married couple's allowance has been transferred to his wife (see p. 83) and her total income exceeds £15,200.

When a married man starts to lose the extra allowances, it is his personal allowance which is reduced first. When it has been reduced to the level of the basic personal allowance, he may then start to lose the extra married couple's allowance.

Your allowances will never be reduced to below the basic personal or married couple's allowances.
ICTA 1988 s257A(5)

Total income

Your 'total income' is basically your gross income less some outgoings. It doesn't include any tax-free income, but *does* include the gross amount of any building society or bank interest – see pp. 37 and 246. Add up your gross (before-tax) income for the tax year, then deduct your tax-allowable outgoings (but *not* your allowances).

Adding up your income Don't forget to include the gross amount of any interest from which tax has been deducted before you get it, e.g. building society or bank interest, share dividends and unit trust distributions (add on the tax credit to get the gross amount) and the whole of any taxable gain on a life insurance policy. Ignore any tax-free income, e.g. from National Savings Certificates.

Deducting your outgoings Some payments you make benefit from tax relief and also reduce the amount of your 'total income', including:

- pension contributions you pay and payments you make to a personal pension
- the gross amount of covenant payments to charity
- charitable donations under the payroll-giving scheme or Gift Aid
- the gross amount of maintenance payments on which you can get tax relief
- interest on certain loans on which you can get tax relief.

Note that from the 1994–5 tax year you have not been able to deduct interest you pay on a mortgage or on a home income plan (see p. 114) from your income. Premiums on private medical insurance are also no longer deductible.

'Total income' over £15,200 – beware!

If your 'total income' for the tax year looks as though it will be above £15,200 but below the point at which you lose the benefit of age-related allowances altogether, you should select your investments carefully. If you have investments which produce income which is included in your 'total income', you would almost certainly benefit by exchanging them for investments which are tax-free (like National Savings Certificates). This applies equally to interest from building societies and banks (which is 'tax-paid', *not* tax-free) and to gains on certain life insurance policies. Since the married couple's age allowance is worked out on the husband's total income, married couples could consider transferring assets which produce a taxable income to the wife's name.

The sliding scale

If your total income is more than £15,200, your extra allowances are reduced by half the excess. For example, if you're aged 73, your personal allowance could be £4,910. But if your total income is £15,500, this is £300 more than £15,200, and your allowance would be reduced by half of £300 = £150. Your personal allowance would be £4,910 – £150 = £4,760.

The table on page 106 shows what your age-related allowances would be for different example levels of 'total income'.

Total income £	Personal allowance 65–74 £	Married couple's allowance 65–74 £	Personal allowance 75+ £	Married couple's allowance 75+ £
15,200	4,910	3,115	5,090	3,155
15,400	4,810	3,115	4,990	3,155
15,600	4,710	3,115	4,890	3,155
15,800	4,610	3,115	4,790	3,155
16,000	4,510	3,115	4,690	3,155
16,200	4,410	3,115	4,590	3,155
16,400	4,310	3,115	4,490	3,155
16,600	4,210	3,115	4,390	3,155
16,800	4,110	3,115	4,290	3,155
17,000	4,010	3,115	4,190	3,155
17,200	3,910	3,115	4,090	3,155
17,400	3,810	3,115	3,990	3,155
17,490	3,765	3,115	3,945	3,155
17,600	3,765	3,060	3,890	3,155
17,800	3,765	2,960	3,790	3,155
17,850	3,765	2,935	3,765	3,155
18,000	3,765	2,860	3,765	3,080
18,200	3,765	2,760	3,765	2,980
18,400	3,765	2,660	3,765	2,880
18,600	3,765	2,560	3,765	2,780
18,800	3,765	2,460	3,765	2,680
19,000	3,765	2,360	3,765	2,580
19,200	3,765	2,260	3,765	2,480
19,400	3,765	2,160	3,765	2,380
19,600	3,765	2,060	3,765	2,280
19,800	3,765	1,960	3,765	2,180
20,000	3,765	1,860	3,765	2,080
20,140	3,765	1,790	3,765	2,010
20,200	3,765	1,790	3,765	1,980
20,400	3,765	1,790	3,765	1,880
20,580	3,765	1,790	3,765	1,790

Using the table: Find your 'total income' and then read off your personal allowance. If you are married, you each have a personal allowance and together you can get the married couple's allowance (based on the husband's total income). Read across to find the amount you are entitled to. The table gives a range of examples for total income. Your allowances will depend on the exact level of your total income.

How pensions are taxed

Some pensions are tax-free. But others are taxable. The following pensions are taxable:

- state retirement pension including any graduated pension, additional pension (i.e. SERPS) or invalidity addition you receive

- non-contributory retirement pension for people of 80 or over who are getting less than the normal state retirement pension
- pension from a former employer paid to a former employee or his/her widow/widower and/or dependants
- personal pension
- retirement annuity.

Married woman's state retirement pension

A married woman's state retirement pension counts as her income whether based on her own National Insurance contributions or, since 6 April 1990, based on her husband's contributions. But any *adult dependency addition* paid, for example, to a husband whose wife has not reached state pension age is counted for income tax purposes as his income.

Tax on state retirement pensions

Although the state retirement pension is taxable, tax isn't deducted from it before it is paid. If the basic state pension is your only income, you won't have to pay any tax because the pension comes to less than your personal allowance. But there may be some tax to pay if your state pension, added to any other taxable income you get (e.g. a pension from your former employer or investment income), comes to more than your total outgoings and allowances.

The amount of pension which will be included in your income is the total of the weekly amounts payable over the tax year. This applies even if your pension is paid monthly or quarterly.

Annuities from pension schemes and plans

An annuity you've bought voluntarily is taxed differently from an annuity which comes from an employer's or a personal pension scheme – see p. 111.

If the annuity was provided by a pension scheme you've belonged to, the full amount of what you get is taxable. Insurance companies will deduct tax from each payment under Pay-As-You-Earn (PAYE), so the correct amount of tax should be deducted. Annuities bought with personal pension plans, as well as pensions or annuities paid by employers' pension schemes, are also paid under PAYE so

again the correct amount of tax, if any, should be deducted.
ICTA 1988 s656, s597 (pensions)

Pensions from abroad

You are normally liable for tax on nine-tenths of any pension from abroad, whether or not it is brought into the UK. With certain pensions, only half the amount is taxable, and certain war widows' pensions are tax-free. Pensions from abroad have generally been taxed on a *preceding year* basis, so your 1995–6 tax bill will have been based on nine-tenths of any pension you got from abroad during 1994–5. However, in 1996–7 transitional rules will apply and from 1997–8 these pensions will be taxed on a *current year basis*. New pensions paid from 6 April 1994 are taxed on a current year basis. Note that pensions paid to the victims of Nazi persecution by the governments of Germany and Austria are tax-free.
ICTA 1988 s196, s330

How tax is collected on pensions

If you get a pension from your former employer, the tax due on the whole of your income will, as far as possible, have been collected under PAYE from your employer's pension. The amount of state pensions and any untaxed investment income the Inland Revenue expects you to receive over the tax year will be subtracted from your allowances on the PAYE Coding Notice so that you get a lower PAYE code and appear to pay tax at a higher rate than before you retired. If the amount to be subtracted from your allowances is greater than your total allowances, your PAYE code will contain a 'K' which will instruct your employer to add an amount to your earnings or pension on which tax is to be paid. At the end of the year you should have paid the correct amount of tax. See Chapter 8 for more information about PAYE.

If you don't get a pension from a former employer, and your state pension plus any other income comes to more than your total outgoings and allowances, you will be sent a statement of the tax you owe, unless the tax on the excess comes to £75 or less, in which case the tax is not normally collected.

If you've paid too much tax on your investments

With most types of investments, including most bank and building society investments, shares, unit trusts and certain British government stocks, income is paid after tax has been deducted at 20 per cent in the 1996–7 tax year. If you don't pay tax – or if your tax bill comes to less than the total of tax deducted plus tax credits received – you will have paid too much tax. So you should claim a rebate.

If you are in a situation like this you may well be sent a special tax claim form R40(SP) instead of the normal kind of tax return. You should fill it in and send it back to your tax office with your tax vouchers (originals, not photocopies, which give details of tax deducted and tax credits). You don't need to wait until the end of the tax year to do this and you can claim in instalments throughout the year. The Revenue will work out how much tax you are owed (if any) and send you a rebate. However, it will pay claims part way through the tax year only if they are for more than £50. If you reclaim less than £50, you won't be paid until the end of the tax year.

If you have to claim tax back regularly but aren't sent form R40(SP), ask your tax office for it. If you claim only occasionally, write to your tax office, giving details of why you are claiming and how much you are claiming (if you know).

Receiving interest without deduction of tax

If the interest you receive from any bank, building society or local authority investment you have, plus any other taxable income you may have (e.g. a pension), totals less than your tax allowances, you can arrange to have that interest paid without any tax being deducted. Banks, building societies, tax offices or tax enquiry centres should all have copies of form R85, which you need to complete to register for gross interest. You will also find a copy of the form with Inland Revenue leaflet IR110 – *A guide for people with savings*.

Private medical insurance

Since 6 April 1990, tax relief has been available on certain private medical insurance policies if you are 60 or over or if you pay premiums on behalf of somebody aged 60 or more. Broadly speaking, policies which qualify are the typical policies which pay for conventional medical treatment, but with one exception: they should not pay a cash benefit of more than £5 a night while you are having treatment as a private patient. There should be no need to work out whether your policy qualifies – your insurer will be able to tell you (and will be able to advise on switching to a policy which does qualify, if necessary).

Since 1994–5 the tax relief has been limited to the basic rate of tax – 24 per cent in the 1996–7 tax year. Relief is given at source: the insurer will charge you the net premium, so even non-taxpayers will benefit. The relief is available on joint policies which a husband and wife have, even if only one is 60 or over.
FA 1989 s54–s57; FA 1994 s79, Sch10

Annuities

Buying an annuity with your own funds (a 'purchased life' annuity) gives you an income for life, and favourable tax treatment. But it's an offer you should refuse if you're under 75 (if a woman) or under 70 (if a man).

What is an annuity?

With an annuity, you hand over your money to an insurance company in return for a guaranteed income for the rest of your life. The older you are at the time you buy the annuity, the higher the income you can get; and a man gets a higher income than a woman of the same age (on average, men don't live as long). To give an example: in return for handing over £10,000, a 75-year-old woman who paid tax at the basic rate could (in January 1996) have got an income before tax of about £1,130 a year for life, however long she lived. But what you get depends on interest rates at the time you buy the annuity. In 1992, for example, the income of the woman in the example would have been around £1,500 a year. Note, however, that once you have handed over your money, you cannot ask for it back.

Type of annuity
This section deals with *immediate annuities*. With these, the company starts paying you the income 'immediately' – in

fact, perhaps one month after you buy the annuity. There are also *deferred annuities*, where you pay a lump sum now and arrange for the income to start much further in the future. The most common type of immediate annuity is a *level annuity* where the income is the same each year. For a given outlay, this type gives you the largest income to start with – though, of course, inflation is likely to erode its buying-power over the years. Another type is an *increasing annuity*, where your income increases regularly by an amount you decide on when you buy.

A *single life* annuity stops when the person buying it dies. A *joint life and survivor* annuity carries on until both the person buying the annuity and someone else, usually a wife or husband, have died.

Should you buy?
Whether or not an annuity proves to be a good buy in the long run depends on three imponderables:

- how long you will live; obviously an annuity will be a better buy if you live for years and years after buying it
- what happens to interest rates (and therefore annuity rates) after you have bought your annuity. If they go up, you'll be left with a return which may be poor in relative terms – if they go down, you have a bargain
- the longer-term effect of inflation on the buying-power of your income.

So weighing up these uncertainties with the one certainty that you lose control of your capital, we conclude that annuities are not a good buy for women under 75 or men under 70. Only for people over these ages may the extra income offered by an annuity – as compared with conventional investments – become significant. And even then, think carefully before buying; be quite sure that you are willing to part with the capital you use, and shop around for the best company.

Tax treatment
If you have bought the annuity with your own money, part of the income from it is treated for tax purposes as your initial outlay being returned to you, and is tax-free. The remainder of the annuity income counts as interest (i.e. as investment income) and is taxable.

The insurance company normally deducts tax from the taxable part of your income before paying you. From

1996–7, tax will be deducted at the 20 per cent rate applying to most savings income. If you are a basic-rate taxpayer, there will be no more tax to pay. If your taxable income from all sources – including income from the *taxable* part of the annuity – is equal to or less than your age-related allowances (see p. 103), you can apply to have your annuity income paid without deduction of tax by completing form R89.

The amount of the tax-free part of the income – called the capital element – is worked out according to Revenue rules. It is a proportion of the income from the annuity. For each type of annuity the tax-free amount is based on your age when you buy the annuity, the amount you pay for it, how often the income is paid and whether payments are guaranteed for a period after you die.

A man gets a larger tax-free amount than a woman (corresponding to his shorter life expectancy).

With increasing annuities, the tax-free amount increases at the same rate as the income from the annuity increases. For example, for a 75-year-old woman buying an annuity that increases by 5 per cent a year, the tax-free amount in the first year would be £50.30 for each £1,000 spent on the annuity (much less than the £77.10 for a level annuity) but increasing by 5 per cent each year.

Pension annuities

There is no tax-free element with an annuity bought with the proceeds of an employer's pension scheme or personal pension plan. All the income from the annuity is taxable.
ICTA 1988 s18(2)–(4) (taxed as interest); s656, s657, s658 (tax-free element)

Postponing buying an annuity

Since the 1995–6 tax year you have been able to draw an income from a personal pension plan when you reach your pension date without buying an annuity. You can put off buying an annuity until the age of 75. You have the option to take your tax-free lump sum when you start drawing an income but once you have taken the benefits from your policy (e.g. the tax-free lump sum), income withdrawals become compulsory until the annuity is bought.

The possible benefit of deferring the annuity purchase is that annuity rates may be low when you reach your pension date but could rise before you reach the age of 75 (though they could go even lower).

Tax warning: annuities and age-related allowances
By and large, if you buy an annuity out of your savings or investments which had been giving you a taxable income, you don't have to worry about the possible effect on age-related allowances (see p. 105). The chances are, in a case like this, that the *taxable* part of your annuity income will be less – or in any event not much higher – than the taxable income you were getting from your savings (a large part of the income from an annuity, remember, is tax-free).

But if you buy the annuity with savings or investments that were *not* earning you a taxable income, and if you are at present getting the benefit of age-related allowances, you might find that your allowance is reduced. The same could apply if, for example, the annuity is bought for you by your pension scheme (in which case the whole of the annuity income is taxable).

EXAMPLE

Shirley Alpine, 75, lives alone on a state retirement pension of £3,179 for the full 1996–7 tax year. She also receives alimony from her former husband totalling £13,735 gross, before deduction of tax; of this £11,945 is taxable (see p. 94). She has no outgoings. Her 'total income' (see p. 104) works out as follows:

state retirement pension	£3,179
taxable part of alimony	£11,945
'total income'	£15,124

Since her 'total income' is under £15,200, she qualifies for an age-related allowance of £5,090. The amount of income on which she will pay tax is £15,124 – £5,090 = £10,034.

To boost her income, she decides to cash in her National Savings Certificates and Premium Bonds (which she's had no luck with) and is thinking of spending the full £25,000 proceeds on an annuity, which will bring in £2,872 a year before tax. The tax-free capital element of the annuity is £1,928, so the remaining £944 would be taxable. Her new 'total income' would be:

state retirement pension	£3,179
taxable part of alimony	£11,945
taxable part of annuity	£944
'total income'	£16,068

Shirley's 'total income' is £868 over the £15,200 limit. Her age-related allowance would therefore be reduced by £1 for every £2 of taxable income over £15,200 – i.e. by £434. Shirley would pay basic-rate tax of 24 per cent on an extra £434, pushing up her tax bill by £104.16. Shirley decides to buy a smaller annuity to keep her total income within £15,200 and she holds on to some of her savings.

Home income schemes

If you're elderly and own your home, you may be able to boost your income with a home income scheme. Some of these schemes have tax advantages. A 75-year-old woman, for example, with a home worth £45,000, could increase her income after basic-rate tax by about £1,245 a year. A man of 75 would get about £580 more.

The basics

An insurance company arranges a loan for you based on the security of your home. Provided you are 65 or over and at least 90 per cent of the loan is used to buy an annuity for you, you'll qualify for basic-rate tax relief on up to £30,000 of the loan. While you live, you get the income from the annuity – after deduction of loan interest and tax. When you die, the loan is repaid out of your estate (possibly, but not necessarily, from the sale of your home).

Basic-rate tax relief on the loan is given to you under the mortgage interest relief at source (MIRAS) scheme – which means that the insurance company will allow for tax relief at 24 per cent (in the 1996–7 tax year) on the loan interest when working out how much income to hand over to you. You get the benefit of this 'tax relief' in full, even if you pay little or no tax. Tax relief for home income scheme loans has not been reduced to the 15 per cent rate which is available when you are buying a home.

The schemes are available for freehold houses, and for

leasehold property with a substantial part of the lease still to run (75 years, say). The most you can borrow is a percentage (e.g. 70 per cent) of the market value of your home. There's usually a minimum loan (£15,001, say) and a maximum loan. You may be able to take part of the loan in cash in return for a rather lower income.

Inflation will reduce the buying power of your fixed income from these schemes, but it correspondingly reduces the value of your debt – so rising prices don't work wholly against you. And provided that the value of your home goes up, you may be able to use the increase in value to get a further loan which could be used to buy another annuity. *ICTA 1988 s365*

How a home income scheme works

Step 1 You mortgage your home to the tune of, for example, £25,000 and get in return an annuity of, say, £2,857.

Step 2 Before you receive the annuity income, 20 per cent tax is deducted from the taxable part of the annuity, say – £216.

Step 3 The mortgage interest you owe is also deducted (after first deducting basic-rate tax relief), say, £1,568.

Step 4 So the extra income you are left with is £2,857 – £216 – £1,568, which equals £1,073.

Should you buy?

It makes very good sense for an elderly person to be able to continue to live in his or her own home, while spending some of the accumulated value of that home. But the financial arguments may be less favourable. It would be realistic to assume that the elderly person concerned may not always be able to cope alone and may sell up and move in with relatives. In this situation, someone who has taken out a home income scheme could lose out (particularly if left with a rather poor-value annuity).

The sale of home income schemes linked to investment bonds rather than annuities – which caused serious problems for investors in the 1980s – has in effect been barred.

All in all, a home income scheme is a useful last resort – try other ways of increasing your income first.

Age-related allowances

The taxable part of your annuity counts towards your total income. It will reduce any age-related allowances you get if your total income exceeds the £15,200 limit (see p. 104). Note that, since 6 April 1994, interest you pay on a loan to buy an annuity no longer counts as an outgoing. It cannot be used to reduce your total income.

If you don't pay tax

You still get the benefit of the basic-rate 'tax relief' on the mortgage. And you should claim back from the Revenue the 20 per cent tax deducted at source from the taxable element of the annuity. You may be able to arrange for this tax not to be deducted in the first place.

7 *SOCIAL SECURITY*

- Some state benefits are taxable while others are tax-free. All are made without tax deducted. Check the overall tax you pay in a tax year carefully, because you could end up having paid too little tax – or you might be due a rebate.

If you're getting social security benefits, you may think you don't have to worry about tax at all. For many people this will be true, as the majority of benefits are not taxable. But pensioners, widows, expectant mothers and sick and unemployed people could all find themselves in the tax net. This chapter explains the rules.

Tax and benefits

	Tax-free	Taxable
unemployed or on strike	part (or all) of income support	unemployment benefit; sometimes part (or all) of income support from October 1996; jobseeker's allowance
families with children	maternity allowance; maternity payments from social fund; child benefit; one-parent benefit; child's special allowance; guardian's allowance; family credit	statutory maternity pay
elderly people	income support	retirement pensions (except additions for children); old person's or over-80s pension

widows	widow's payment; additions paid for children; war widow's pension (including allowances for children and rent)	widowed mother's allowance; widow's pension
disabled or sick	short-term incapacity benefit paid at the lower rate; severe disablement allowance; attendance allowance; disability working allowance; disability living allowance; disablement benefits paid because of injury at work or an industrial disease; disablement pensions paid as a result of service in the forces or the merchant navy or to civilians for war injuries; extra pension paid to police and fire staff injured on duty beyond what they'd have got if retired through ill-health	statutory sick pay; short-term incapacity benefit paid at the higher rate and long-term incapacity benefit (except additions paid for children); invalid care allowance (except additions paid for children); invalidity allowance paid with retirement pension
other benefits	income support (if not unemployed, on short-time work or on strike); £10 Christmas bonus; cold weather payments; social fund community care grant; social fund funeral payment; housing benefit (i.e. rent rebate); council tax benefit; some annuities and pension additions for gallantry awards such as the George Cross; benefits paid by foreign governments similar to tax-free UK benefits; youth training allowance and training for work allowance paid to trainees; special pensions paid by the governments of Germany and Austria to UK victims of Nazi persecution	business start up; youth training allowance paid to employees

ICTA 1988 s617

How are benefits taxed?

Most taxable benefits are paid gross – i.e. before any tax is deducted – and are taxed as the earned income of the person claiming benefit. If you're claiming extra benefit for your spouse (or someone living with you as your spouse), it is taxed as your income. For state retirement pensions this includes the adult dependency addition paid where, for example, the pensioner's spouse has not reached the state pension age. Note, however, that a married woman's pension is paid direct to her and is treated as her own for income tax, even if it is paid as a result of her husband's contributions. Tax-free benefits shouldn't be entered on your tax return, but you do need to give very basic details of any taxable benefit you've received during the tax year.

You will have to pay income tax if your total taxable income, including taxable state benefits, comes to more than your allowances and outgoings. Special rules apply if you're off sick (see p. 122) or claiming unemployment benefit or income support because you're unemployed – see below. For other benefits, if you are working (or getting an employer's pension), any tax due will be collected through Pay-As-You-Earn (PAYE). It will look as if you are paying much more tax than others earning the same amount. But this is because *all* the tax due on your benefits is being collected at the same time as tax on your pay.

If you are not taxed under PAYE, you will be sent a statement telling you how much tax you owe on your benefits.

Special codes

If your taxable state benefits are greater than your tax-free allowances and you're taxed under PAYE, your earnings (or employer's pension) will have to be taxed at a higher-than-normal rate, e.g. at 30 per cent rather than 24 per cent, to collect the tax on your state benefits. Your tax code will then include the letter K.

Tax if you're unemployed

From October 1996, there is a change to the benefits available if you are unemployed. Up to then, you might get unemployment benefit, income support or a mixture of both. Some or all of this benefit will be taxable. Benefit you're claiming because you've been laid off or are on short-time work will also be taxable. To find out how much of what you get is taxable, have a look at the table below. If you're in any doubt, check with your local social security office.

Note that if you are on strike or involved in a strike you

won't get unemployment benefit for yourself. But you may be able to claim income support for your partner (whether you're married or not) and for any dependent children. The taxable part is the smaller of the weekly amount paid to you, or half the income support personal allowance for a couple in your age group, i.e. half of £75.20 (half of £57.20 if you're both under 18).

How much of your benefit is taxable?

Standard weekly rates of benefits 1996–7

Unemployment benefit	**Under state pension age**	**Over state pension age**
Basic benefit	£48.25	£61.15
Addition for dependent adult	£29.75	£36.60
Addition for eldest or only dependent child	–	£9.90
Addition for each additional dependent child	–	£11.15

The taxable part of your benefit is anything you receive in unemployment benefit and/or income support, up to the standard weekly rates above. The addition for dependent children, however, is tax-free, as is anything over the standard weekly rates.

From October 1996, unemployment benefit and income support for the unemployed are replaced by a new benefit called jobseeker's allowance (JSA). If you are already claiming the old benefits, you will carry on receiving them until either October 1997 or until you come off benefit, whichever is the sooner. From October 1996, new claimants get JSA. This is made up of a personal allowance and various premiums (e.g. if you have a family or you are disabled), which are the same as the allowances and premiums for income support. Both these elements of JSA are taxable. There is also an increase if you have a dependent child or children, but this is not taxable.

How much tax?

If you are unemployed and living on benefits for a full year with no other taxable income, your total taxable benefit will be below your allowances – see p. 35. So there'll be no tax to pay.

Because of the way the PAYE system works, if you become unemployed at some point in the tax year, you may have paid more tax on your earnings than you need to have done (see example below). But if you're claiming benefits, you won't get your tax rebate at once. Instead, you'll get it when you start work again or (unless you're on strike or involved in a strike) at the end of the tax year, whichever comes first. In most cases, the rebate will be paid to you by your unemployment benefit office if you are claiming unemployment benefit and/or income support, or by your local Job Centre if you are getting JSA, and you'll also get a statement showing how much taxable benefit you have been paid.

If you think the figure is wrong ask the benefit office or Job Centre to explain it. If you're still unhappy, you should write to the benefit office or Job Centre within 60 days of the date on which the statement was issued. Your tax office will then send you a notice of assessment after the end of the tax year, which you can appeal against in the normal way (see p. 62), but *only* if you've made a written objection to your statement.

EXAMPLE

Joe Doyle becomes unemployed on 5 October 1996 at which point he has earned £7,500 in the 1996–7 tax year and paid £1,135.95 tax under the PAYE system. He claims jobseeker's allowance for himself and his wife, of which £75.20 a week is taxable. He is still unemployed at the end of the tax year and is owed a tax rebate. His tax position is shown below.

earnings	£7,500
taxable benefit	£1,955.20
	£9,455.20
less personal allowance	£3,765
taxable income	£5,690.20
tax at 20 per cent on £3,900	£780
tax at 24 per cent on £1,790.20	£429.60
total tax	£1,209.60
less 15% of married couple's allowance	£268.50
	£941.10
tax paid under PAYE	£1,135.95
rebate due	£194.85

If you are unemployed and not claiming any taxable benefit, you can claim a tax rebate after being unemployed for four weeks. You'll have to claim on form P50 – get this from your tax office.
ICTA 1988 s152

Tax owed after being on strike or unemployed

If you start work again before the end of the tax year after you have been unemployed, your benefit office or Job Centre will give you a new form P45 showing how much taxable income you've had and how much tax you've already paid. Your new employer will then deduct the right amount of tax, including that due on your benefit, from your earnings for the rest of that tax year or, normally, from a later tax year. You will also be sent a statement of how much taxable benefit you've had.

When you return to work after a strike or if you are still unemployed at the end of the tax year, your benefit office or Job Centre will send you a form P60U which includes details of how much taxable benefit you've had in that tax year.

Although you won't get a tax demand from the Inland Revenue straight away, once you're working, your PAYE code will be adjusted so that the tax you owe on benefits will be collected from your earnings.
ICTA 1988 s152, s204

Tax if you're off sick

Employers usually have to pay their employees statutory sick pay (SSP) for their first 28 weeks of a spell of illness. SSP is treated just like your regular earnings, so tax is deducted from it under PAYE. If the amount of sick pay you get is lower than the amount you can earn each week (or month) before paying tax, your employer will give you a refund of some of the tax you've already paid in each pay packet.

If you cannot get SSP, you can claim short-term incapacity benefit paid at the lower rate, provided that you have paid enough National Insurance to qualify. This is not taxable.

After you have been sick for 28 weeks and are in receipt of either SSP or short-term incapacity benefit, you can claim short-term incapacity benefit at the higher rate (again, depending on your National Insurance record). This is taxable.

If you receive both incapacity benefit and a pension from a former employer (or pay from your employer) any tax due will be collected through an adjustment to your PAYE code – i.e. tax will be deducted from your pension or pay.

Tax if you're having a baby

Since October 1994 statutory maternity pay has been paid by employers to all women for up to 18 weeks regardless of how long they have been working for their employer. SMP is taxed in the same way as regular earnings – so tax is deducted under PAYE. If the amount of maternity pay you get is lower than the amount you can earn each week (or month) before paying tax, in each pay packet you will get a refund of some of the tax you have already paid.

If you don't meet all the SMP conditions, you might be able to get maternity allowance for up to 18 weeks. You need to have paid enough in National Insurance to get the allowance, but it's not taxable. You might be able to get incapacity benefit if you can't get either SMP or maternity allowance – it's not taxable, but it does depend on how much you've paid in National Insurance.

8 *Working for an Employer and Spare-Time Income*

- Anecdotal evidence suggests that many people have the wrong tax code and so pay the wrong amount of tax. Check that your code is accurate – see p. 138.
- You don't have to be self-employed to claim expenses, and claiming expenses means cutting your tax bill – see p. 130.
- When you start a new job you could end up paying too much tax unless you get the paperwork right – see p. 145.
- Received a lump sum following redundancy? Don't pay too much tax on it – see p. 149.

For people who work for an employer, tax on wages or salaries is collected under the Pay-As-You-Earn (PAYE) system. Your earnings are taxed in the way described in this chapter if you are employed under a *contract of service* and are paid a wage or salary on a regular basis. If you are employed under a *contract* (or contracts) *for services*, and are paid when you send in a bill or invoice, you are likely to count as self-employed. Details of how self-employed people are taxed are given in Chapter 11.

Earnings from employment are taxed under the rules of Schedule E, earnings from self-employment under Schedule D (see pp. 40–41). See Chapter 9 for detailed rules about fringe benefits, and Chapter 10 if your job involves working abroad for some or all of the time.

One basic tax rule to start off with: if you work for an employer, your earnings from your job are taxed on what's known as a *current year basis* – i.e. in the 1996–7 tax year you pay tax on the pay you receive in that tax year.

It is worth knowing that the PAYE system collects tax on earnings, sometimes on regular freelance earnings and also on pensions. PAYE is often used to collect tax on investment income. If this happens to you, you may be paying tax on the investment income sooner than you need to. You can ask for a separate, and later, bill instead.
ICTA 1988 s19, s617; IR56

Sub-contractors in the building industry

Even though you may regard yourself as self-employed, basic-rate tax will be deducted from all your earnings unless you hold a sub-contractor's tax certificate. Holding a certificate is not necessarily proof that you are self-employed. See Inland Revenue leaflets *IR40* and *IR48* for more details.

Understanding your payslip

When you look at your payslip, you'll see that there's a large gap between your earnings before any deductions – *gross pay* – and your take-home pay – *net pay*. To help you understand your payslip, we've given an example below. Your payslip may well be laid out rather differently, but the same type of information should appear on it.

Not all the deductions on your payslip are to do with income tax. For example, National Insurance (NI) contrib-

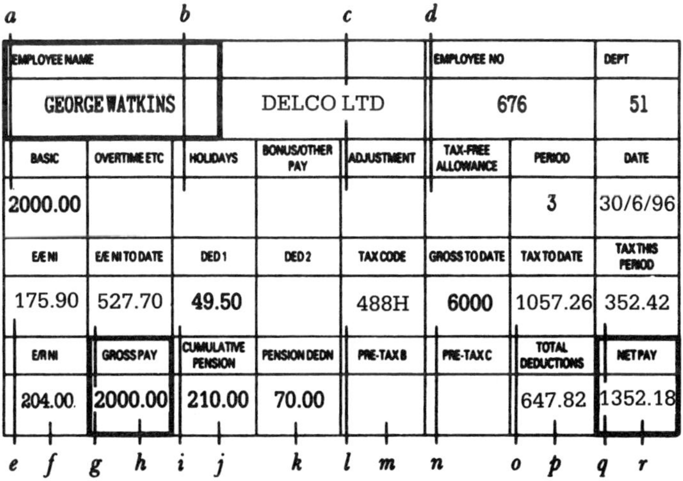

EMPLOYEE NAME					EMPLOYEE NO		DEPT
GEORGE WATKINS		DELCO LTD			676		51
BASIC	OVERTIME ETC	HOLIDAYS	BONUS/OTHER PAY	ADJUSTMENT	TAX-FREE ALLOWANCE	PERIOD	DATE
2000.00						3	30/6/96
E/E NI	E/E NI TO DATE	DED 1	DED 2	TAX CODE	GROSS TO DATE	TAX TO DATE	TAX THIS PERIOD
175.90	527.70	49.50		488H	6000	1057.26	352.42
E/R NI	GROSS PAY	CUMULATIVE PENSION	PENSION DEDN	PRE-TAX B	PRE-TAX C	TOTAL DEDUCTIONS	NET PAY
204.00	2000.00	210.00	70.00			647.82	1352.18

utions you pay should also be shown – more details on p. 147. Other deductions could be for pension contributions, season ticket loans, trade union subscriptions or gifts to charity under a payroll-giving scheme.

How the figures match up
On the payslip above, there's a large difference between £2,000.00 (the figure for gross pay) and £1,352.18 (the figure for net pay). Here's how you get from one to the other.

1. Gross pay	£2,000.00
Deductions	
2. Pension contributions [1]	£70.00
3. Tax	£352.42
4. National Insurance [1]	£175.90
5. Other deductions (in this case, for season ticket loan)	£49.50
6. Total deductions	£647.82
1 *minus* 6	= £1,352.18

[1] What you pay (not your employer's contributions).

A quick check on tax
If you're a basic-rate taxpayer, you can use this to check that the tax deduction on your payslip is broadly correct for 1996–7.

Gross pay	A
Pension contributions, plus payroll-giving, plus tax-free profit-related pay [2]	B
Free-of-tax pay	C

(Take your current PAYE code, add the figure 9 to the end. For example, if your PAYE code is 329 (ignoring any letters), make this 3299; if it's 510, make it 5109. Then divide by 12 if paid monthly or 52 if paid weekly.)

Add B to C and subtract the total from A	D

Multiply D by 0.24 E

Then, to take account of the 20 per cent band, deduct £13 if you are paid monthly, £3 if you are paid weekly.

F

F should be roughly equivalent to the tax deducted for the month or week, and will be the correct deduction *if* you have the right PAYE code.

[2] Don't include if your employer's scheme is not an 'approved' or 'statutory' one.

Key to payslip entries

a **Basic** Pay before additions for things like overtime or bonus.

b **Holidays** Depends on company policy. May include your pay while you're on holiday, or only exceptional payments (e.g. pay in lieu of holiday).

c **Adjustment** On this payslip, statutory sick pay and pay from company's own sick pay scheme (less any amount attributable to contributions you've made to the scheme) or statutory maternity pay are entered here.

d **Tax-free allowance** Depends on company policy. Non-taxable payments (e.g. evening meal or travelling allowance) paid with salary may be entered here.

e **E/E NI** Employee's National Insurance contributions for the month.

f **E/R NI** Employer's National Insurance contributions for the employee.

g **E/E NI to date** Employee's National Insurance contributions since the beginning of the tax year.

h **Gross pay** This is the month's salary before deductions. Would include overtime and bonus if these were paid.

i **Ded.1/Ded.2** Deductions – such as repayment of company loan, an advance on salary, your contributions to your employer's medical bills insurance scheme, a payment under a payroll-giving scheme – would be entered in these boxes. In this example, Ded.1 is the monthly repayment of a season ticket loan.

j **Cumulative pension** Employee's contributions to company pension scheme since the beginning of the tax year.

k **Pension dedn** Employee's contributions to the company pension scheme for the period covered by the payslip. If it is a 'statutory' or 'approved' scheme you get tax relief on contributions you pay (within certain limits – see p. 319) so they will be deducted before tax is worked out on the rest of your pay. 'Statutory' schemes are for civil servants, employees of nationalised industries, etc.; other schemes have to be approved by the Revenue.

l **Tax code** PAYE code number. For how this is worked out see p. 136.

m **Pre-tax B/Pre-tax C** Depends on company policy. Boxes like these could be used to show things like additional voluntary contributions to the company pension scheme or profit-related pay (which are non-taxable and deducted from your pay before calculating tax due) and certain expenses or benefits (e.g. lunch allowance paid in cash) which have to be included in pay for the period and taxed under PAYE. On this payslip, amounts in these boxes will be included in pay to be taxed if marked by a plus sign.

n **Gross to date** Total pay (before deductions) since the beginning of the tax year.

o **Tax to date** Total tax deducted since the beginning of the tax year.

p **Total deductions** Total of all deductions from gross pay for the period covered by the payslip.

q **Tax this period** Tax deducted for the period covered by the payslip (a month in this case).

r **Net pay** Take-home pay – i.e. what's left of gross pay after the figure for total deductions has been subtracted.

Form P60

At the end of each tax year, your employer will give you form P60 (or an equivalent form). This is a record of your total pay (including overtime, etc.) for the tax year – and of how much tax you've paid through PAYE. Note that some P60 forms don't include the contributions to an 'approved' or 'statutory' pension scheme under the figure for pay (i.e. what's shown is pay *less* pension contributions).

What counts as earnings

The basic rule is that any money you get from your employer is taxable, unless: it's a genuine personal gift; or it's spent on an *allowable expense* (see p. 130); or it is genuinely not in any way a payment for the job you do (except for any 'profit-related' pay – see p. 130). So all the following count as pay:

- normal wages or salary; commission; tips; bonuses; holiday pay; overtime; cost-of-living allowance; London weighting; arrears and advances of pay
- fees and other expenses you get for being a company director
- any expense allowance from your employer (though you won't be taxed on anything spent on *allowable expenses* – see p. 130)
- money your employer pays to cover expenses in your job. If you've paid the expenses out of your pocket and your employer pays you back, you're taxed only on any profit you make from the difference. If the expenses are *allowable* – see p. 130 – you're not taxed on what your employer pays
- the taxable value of certain fringe benefits your employer gives you – see Chapter 9
- sick pay from your employer (including *statutory sick pay*); sickness benefits payable from an insurance scheme your employer arranges – see p. 148
- maternity pay (including *statutory maternity pay*)
- pay in lieu of notice and redundancy or leaving payments in excess of £30,000 (though see p. 149)
- most lump-sum payments on taking up a job, including payments made by your new employer before you leave your old job
- taxable unemployment benefit if it is paid to you by your

employer under arrangements with the Department of Employment
- earnings (including all the things above) from any additional jobs.

Other things that count as earnings are pensions from former employers, state retirement pension, and other taxable social security benefits.
ICTA 1988 s131

Profit-related pay

If part of your pay is linked to the profits made by the company you work for, you can get tax relief on your profit-related pay if the scheme meets certain Revenue conditions. It must:

- be set up by a profit-making private-sector employer
- run for at least one year and be open to at least 80 per cent of the workforce or a section of the workforce (a PRP scheme may be set up for a department, say). Employees who have been with the firm for less than three years can be excluded but part-timers – except for part-time directors – can no longer be excluded
- be registered with the Revenue before it starts.

If these conditions are met, you can get tax relief on any profit-related pay you get up to the point where your PRP is £4,000 or 20 per cent of your total pay (whichever is less) – a maximum saving of £480 for a basic-rate taxpayer. You get the tax relief through the PAYE system. National Insurance contributions have to be paid on profit-related pay.
ICTA 1988 s171

Expenses in your job

Two questions you might ask are:

- if I pay expenses out of my own pocket, can I get tax relief on what I pay?
- if my employer pays expenses for me, will I escape being taxed on what my employer pays?

The answer to both questions depends on whether the expenses are *allowable expenses* for tax purposes. The table on pp. 132–5 shows the main items which are, and aren't, aren't, allowable. If an expense is allowable, the answer to both questions is yes. If it's not allowable:

- you get no tax relief on what you pay yourself
- you're taxed on what your employer pays, *less* anything you pay towards the cost.

For an expense to be allowable, the money must be spent '*wholly, exclusively and necessarily in the performance of the duties of your employment*'. So if you get a fixed expense allowance and don't spend all of it on allowable expenses, you are taxed on the difference. Note that '*necessarily*' means necessary within the context of your job, and not simply necessary to you. So if working late means that you'll have to stay in a hotel overnight because your home is a long distance away, the hotel bill won't be allowable if the job could be done by someone else living closer to your workplace. However, small differences in individual circumstances (or in a tax inspector's assessment of them) may mean that an expense disallowed for one person is allowable for someone else. Allowable expenses can be set off only against earnings from your job and not, for example, against investment income.

Expenses paid out of your own pocket

In trades where it's customary to provide your own tools or clothing (e.g. plumbing) many trade unions have agreed a *fixed deduction* for upkeep and replacement of these things. For example, there may be a fixed amount of £70. You can claim the whole fixed deduction as an allowable expense even if you don't spend it all. And if you spend more, you can claim more.

Expenses your employer pays for

If an expense *isn't* allowable, it counts as part of your pay and you're taxed on it – either under PAYE or by getting a separate tax bill. If an expense *is* allowable, how it's dealt with varies:

- has your employer got a *dispensation* for the expense? In broad terms, a dispensation means that your employer doesn't have to give the Revenue details of expenses paid to you and you don't have to declare them in your tax return. A dispensation won't be given unless the

Revenue is satisfied that it's for allowable expenses (and nothing else), and that your employer keeps proper control over expenses

- if there isn't a dispensation, and you count as earning at a rate of £8,500 a year or more (see p. 156), your employer has to tell the Revenue at the end of the tax year about all expenses paid to you (or for you) for which there isn't a dispensation. This is done at the end of the tax year on form P11D. You'll have to enter all these expenses in your tax return, and be taxed on any which aren't allowable. Allowable expenses have to be entered twice – as income and as outgoings. Entering them as outgoings means that you don't pay tax on them
- if you don't count as earning at a rate of £8,500 or more a year, expenses for which there's a dispensation are ignored, as are other allowable expenses, including 'scale payments' (e.g. a mileage allowance) which have been agreed between your employer and the Revenue. Other expenses, if they're not allowable, haven't been taxed as part of your pay and total more than £25 a year, are declared by your employer on form P9D, and any tax due is normally collected under PAYE in a later tax year.

TA 1988 s198, s201, s577

Expenses in your job

	Expenses normally allowed	Not allowed
to get a job	cost of re-training provided by employer to acquire new work skills, if you have left or are about to leave your job. This includes fees, books, travelling and extra living costs for the course	agency fees. Expenses of interview
training	cost of fees and essential books you buy for a full-time external training course lasting for four weeks or more. Your employer must either require you or at least encourage you to attend the course, and must go on paying your wages while you are on it. Possibly, extra cost of living away from home and extra travelling expenses, if away for under a year	fees and book purchases for other courses or evening classes – even if required to take course by employer. Examination fees. Re-sit courses or examinations

	Expenses normally allowed	Not allowed
fees and subscriptions to professional bodies	subscriptions to professional bodies provided membership is relevant to your job. Fee for keeping your name on a professional register approved by the Revenue – but only if this is a condition of your employment	
clothes	cost of replacing, cleaning and repairing protective clothing (e.g. overalls, boots) and functional clothing (e.g. uniform) necessary for your job and which you are required to provide. Cost of cleaning protective clothing or functional clothing provided by your employer, if cleaning facilities are not provided	ordinary clothes you wear for work (e.g. a pinstripe suit) which you could wear outside work – even if you'd never choose to
tools, instruments	cost of maintaining and repairing factory or workshop tools and musical instruments you are required to provide. Cost of replacing instruments and tools, less any amount from sale of old, provided new ones not inherently better than old. Often, fixed amounts agreed with trade unions (see p. 131)	initial cost of tools and instruments, but may be able to claim *capital allowances* (see p. 196)
books and stationery	cost of reference books necessary for your job which you have to provide (e.g. actuarial tables, government regulations). If the book's useful life is more than two years you may have to claim *capital allowances* instead (see p. 196). Cost of stationery used strictly for your job (e.g. business notepaper if you are a sales rep). Possibly, cost of books essential for a full-time training course	cost of other books. Subscriptions to journals to keep up with developments. General stationery (e.g. pens, notepaper, etc.)

	Expenses normally allowed	Not allowed
use of home for work	proportion of heating and lighting costs, and, possibly, proportion of telephone, cleaning and insurance costs. If part of home is used *exclusively* for business, you may be able to claim a proportion of rent. But these expenses are allowed only if it is necessary that you carry out some of your duties at or from home (i.e. if it is an express or implied condition of your employment).	
interest	interest on loans to buy equipment (e.g. car, typewriter) necessary for your job	interest on overdraft or credit card
travelling	expenses incurred strictly in the course of carrying out job. *Running costs of own car*: whole of cost if used wholly and necessarily in carrying out your job, proportion of cost if used privately as well. Work out what proportion your business mileage bears to your total mileage, and claim corresponding proportion of cost. If your employer requires you to use your car for business purposes, and you're paid less for doing so than it costs you, work out the full cost to you and claim the extra. Alternatively, use the fixed-profit car scheme – see p. 135. *Company car*: if you pay for running costs (e.g. petrol, repairs, maintenance), claim proportion of cost of business mileage. Occasional late-night journeys home or extra travel costs if public transport disrupted by industrial action	travel to and from work (but if you travel to or from a job abroad, see p. 177). Cost of buying a car and depreciation – may be able to claim a *capital allowance* (see p. 196) but only if the car is necessary for you to carry on your job and it is necessary for you to provide one
spouses travelling together	allowed only if cost paid by (or for) employer, and if wife or husband has, and uses, practical qualifications directly associated with trip, or if their presence is necessary for essential business entertaining of overseas trade customers, or if your health is so poor that it is unreasonable to travel alone. Often only a proportion of cost is allowed	

	Expenses normally allowed	Not allowed
entertaining	expenses of entertaining customers (but only if you can claim these expenses back from your employer, or pay them out of an expense allowance given specifically for entertaining). Employees of non-trading organisations like schools, local authorities and trade unions can claim all entertaining expenses, but only if spent *wholly, exclusively and necessarily in the performance of your job* (see p. 131 for what this means)	any other entertaining expenses
hotel and meal expenses	if you keep a permanent home, reasonable hotel and meal expenses when travelling in the course of your job. But if, say, you're a single person living in a hostel, and give up your room when travelling, you can claim only extra cost of reasonable hotel and meal expenses over your normal board and lodging	meals, unless you wouldn't normally have had one at that time

ICTA 1988 s198 (travel), s201 (professional fees), s359, s588 and ESC A63 and A64 (training)

Fixed-profit car scheme

If you use your own car for business, it is common for your employer to pay you a mileage allowance. This allowance could come to more or less than the actual costs you incur doing business mileage. If your employer pays you an allowance based on the fixed-profit car scheme, the Revenue ignores any profit you make and the whole allowance is tax-free. If the allowance is less than your actual costs, you can claim the excess as an allowable expense.

From 1996–7 onwards, you can use the fixed-profit car scheme to work out what, if any, tax or tax relief is due, even if your employer does not use the scheme. For example, if you do 3,500 business miles a year in a 1,300cc car, your tax-free allowable motoring costs are 3,500 × 34p = £1,190 a year. If your employer pays you less than this in mileage allowance, you can claim the difference as an allowable expense; if your employer pays no allowance, you claim the whole tax-free amount; if your employer pays you more, you must pay tax on the excess. The advantage of using the scheme is that you do not have to keep detailed records of all your motoring costs. You simply need to note your annual business mileage.

Tax-free rates per mile under the fixed-profit car scheme in 1996–7

Size of car engine	Rate on first 4,000 business miles	Rate on each mile over 4,000 business miles a year
up to 1,000cc	27p	16p
1,001cc to 1,500cc	34p	19p
1,501cc to 2,000cc	43p	23p
over 2,000cc	61p	33p

Pay-As-You-Earn (PAYE)

Principles

PAYE is a way of collecting tax bit by bit over the tax year. The Revenue gives you a PAYE code which indicates an estimate of the amount of free-of-tax pay you're entitled to over the tax year. Any excess over this free-of-tax amount will be taxed. For how the free-of-tax amount is worked out, see the illustrated PAYE Coding Notice on pp. 142–3. Each pay-day, you'll be allowed one fifty-second or one-twelfth (depending on whether you're paid weekly or monthly) of the free-of-tax amount.

Mechanics

The PAYE Coding Notice will show you how your PAYE code is calculated; your employer is just told what your code is. Your employer then uses your code, and *tax tables* supplied by the Revenue, to deduct the right amount of tax from your pay.

The *free-pay tables* allow your employer to work out how much of each month's or week's pay is free of tax. For example, if your code is 376L, this gives you up to £3,769 free-of-tax pay for the tax year. On monthly pay, you'll get one-twelfth of £3,769 (= £314.09) of your pay free of tax each month. If you're paid weekly, you'll get one fifty-second of £3,769 (= £72.49) of your pay free of tax each week. Any excess, after deducting pension contributions to 'statutory' or 'approved' schemes, payments to charity under a payroll-giving scheme and the tax-free part of profit-related pay under an approved scheme (see p. 130), is taxable. The *taxable-pay tables* tell your employer how much tax to deduct.

As the tax tables work on a cumulative basis, this makes dealing with a change to your PAYE code part-way through a tax year comparatively simple – see below.

PAYE code changes during the tax year

If your code goes up (i.e. you get a higher number) you get more free-of-tax pay and so pay less tax. Because the PAYE system works cumulatively, you will have been given too little free-of-tax pay since the start of the tax year so that the first time your new code is used you'll pay less tax than usual to make up for the time you were paying too much; you may even pay no tax and get a rebate. For the rest of the tax year you'll pay less tax each pay-day.

EXAMPLE

Boris's code for the 1996–7 tax year was 376L. This meant that he could earn £314.09 a month free of tax.

On 16 April, Boris got married and became entitled to the married couple's allowance. In August, Boris got around to telling the Revenue he'd got married, and was sent a revised notice showing his new code, 488H. This meant that he was entitled to £407.42 free-of-tax pay for every month of the tax year, i.e. £93.33 a month more than before.

The tax tables (which calculate tax on whole pounds only) give a reduction in his tax bill of £22.32 in some months, £22.56 in others (at the basic rate of 24 per cent).

In addition to this regular monthly saving of £22, Boris got an extra £111.84 in his pay when his employer first used the new code in September. This was a rebate of tax for the first five months of the tax year when he paid too much tax. So Boris's total extra pay in his September pay packet was £134.16.

If your code goes down (i.e. you get a lower number) you will have been given too much free-of-tax pay since the start of the tax year and so paid too little tax. If the amount of underpaid tax is large and would mean a sharp drop in your take-home pay the first time the code is used, the Revenue will tell your employer to apply your new code on a *week 1* or *month 1* basis. For the rest of the tax year you'll get one fifty-second or one-twelfth of your new tax-free pay (depending on whether you're paid weekly or monthly) each pay-day. So on each pay-day, you pay the amount of tax you would have paid if your tax code had been correct at the beginning of the tax year. But you will still owe the underpaid tax from the pay-days before your code was changed. This will be shown as a deduction on next year's notice of your income tax code so that the unpaid tax will be collected over the whole of the following year. If, however, you receive an assessment for the year showing a substantial amount of underpaid tax, you'll be sent a bill for the tax due.

PAYE Coding Notice

Not everyone gets a coding notice each tax year. You're likely to get one if, for example, you're a higher-rate taxpayer, you receive the married couple's allowance, or if certain of your outgoings this year look like being more (or less) than last year. Most notices are sent out in January or February each year and apply for the tax year starting on the following 6 April. These will take account of Budget changes. For other changes, you may get a new notice part-way through the tax year.

You get a separate PAYE code for each job in which your earnings are taxed under PAYE – and, normally, a separate notice giving your code for each job. If possible, all your outgoings and allowances are included in the code for your main job.

Whenever you get a notice, you should check that it's correct. If you think there's a mistake, tell the Revenue at once. The same applies if your circumstances change during the tax year (e.g. if you become entitled to a new allowance or incur a new outgoing). If your PAYE code is not correct at the end of the tax year you'll have paid the wrong amount of tax under PAYE, and either have to claim a rebate, or be faced with more tax to pay in a later year. To get your code changed, write and tell the Revenue why

your code is wrong and send the most recent PAYE Coding Notice if you've still got it. If not, quote the tax reference number which is on all forms and letters the Revenue sends you.
ICTA 1988 s203 Regulations 6(2), 7(b)(d), 9, SI 1993/744

Not sent back your tax return?
If you've received a tax return but haven't returned it, you may get a PAYE Coding Notice showing a special deduction which reduces your PAYE code, possibly to zero, and, as a result, the amount of free-of-tax pay you can have. This is because the Revenue thinks you have income you haven't declared and has decided to estimate the amount of tax you might owe. To get this sorted out – and, if necessary, your code changed – you'll have to send back your completed tax return.

How to read a PAYE Coding Notice
On pp. 142–3 we show you what a PAYE Coding Notice might look like and explain the main headings which might appear, though your notice will include only things which apply to you.

Allowances
Here you'll find details of the personal allowances you are entitled to and the Revenue's estimate of your outgoings on which tax relief isn't given at source.

Note that fixed-rate allowances have to be adjusted for the right amount of tax to be collected. Under the **Allowances** column of the notice, you will see the full amount of the married couple's allowance, widow's bereavement allowance or additional personal allowance of £1,790. If you are a basic-rate or higher-rate taxpayer, you will also see an entry called **Allce restriction** in the other column. This is an adjustment to ensure that the relief you get is restricted to 15 per cent. With the basic married couple's allowance, the restriction will be £447 for 20 per cent taxpayers, £670 for 24 per cent taxpayers and £1,118 for 40 per cent taxpayers.

The figures will be different if you receive an age-related married couple's allowance. You can multiply your allowance by 15 per cent to get a figure for the tax the allowance saves you. To check that the allowance restriction produces the correct tax saving, deduct the allowance restriction from the allowance you are entitled to and multiply by your highest rate of tax. This should give the correct tax saving. If it doesn't, talk to your tax office.

EXAMPLE 2

Bert Fry is a 66-year-old married man. He is entitled to an age-related married couple's allowance of £3,115. Relief is restricted to 15 per cent so is worth £467.25. The allowance restriction on his coding notice is £1,168. Bert deducts £1,168 from the full allowance of £3,115 to get £1,947. He then multiplies £1,947 by 24 per cent (his top rate of tax) to get £467.28, the same figure (apart from rounding adjustments) as the fixed-rate relief of 15 per cent. So the allowance restriction is correct.

Outgoings

Expenses An estimate of any allowable expenses in your job which qualifies for tax relief (see p. 130). If you're counted as earning at a rate of £8,500 a year or more (see p. 156), for example, it will include expenses for which your employer does not have a *dispensation*.

Professional subs Subscriptions to professional bodies which qualify for tax relief.

Ret annuity relief Payments into personal pension plans taken out before 1 July 1988.

Personal pension Payments to a personal pension scheme taken out since 1 July 1988 or into a free-standing additional voluntary contribution (AVC) scheme (see p. 320) if made by a higher-rate taxpayer. If you pay tax at basic rate only, there'll be no entry here as you get the tax relief by making net payments to the pension provider.

Bldg socy int/loan etc int For loans or mortgages where you don't get tax relief under mortgage interest relief at source (MIRAS) there will be an estimate of the interest you'll pay in the 1996–7 tax year adjusted to take account of the fact that tax relief on mortgage interest is restricted to 15 per cent.

Maintenance payments The amount of maintenance you pay which qualifies for tax relief (see p. 91) will be shown here.

Taxed payment Extra tax relief for higher-rate taxpayers on covenant payments to charity will be shown here.

Personal
Details of the allowances you're entitled to will be included here. If you are entitled to one of the higher levels of allowance because of your age, this may be reduced if your income is above a certain amount (see p. 105). An estimate of your total income for the tax year will be shown under the heading **Age est income**.

Deductions
In this section you'll find details of income you get which is taxable but is paid without any tax being deducted, e.g. taxable perks from your job, etc. The tax owed on this income will be collected through the PAYE scheme by deducting the total from your total allowance.

State pens'n/benefit/pension Includes state pensions and benefits, or employers' pensions not taxed before you get them.

Benefits in kind/(Car)/Car fuel Perks from your job which count as taxable income (see Chapter 9).

Taxable expenses pyt Payments from your employer to cover expenses in your job (see p. 131).

Part-time earnings/tips/commission/other earned income Extra income from your main job and freelance or part-time earnings on which you don't pay tax under PAYE.

Adjust unemp benefit Includes taxable benefits you have claimed because of unemployment (see Chapter 7).

Untaxed interest/income from property Interest received without tax being deducted (e.g. from taxable National Savings) and income from property.

Court order Includes maintenance you received from a court order made before 15 March 1988. If you're an ex-spouse, the amount shown will be the payments less the free-of-tax amount you're allowed (see p. 94).

Inland Revenue

PAYE Coding Notice

Your employer or pension payer will use your tax code to ensure you pay the right amount of tax under Pay As You Earn (PAYE)

From: H M Inspector of Taxes

ANYCITY 4
PARK COURT
ANYTOWN ROAD
ANYCITY AC4 6QL
Tel: 01559 666111

MR A TAXPAYER
23 THE STREET
ANYTOWN
AT2 3TH

You should quote both numbers below if you contact us.

297 / 198 / T

ZR | 40 | 57 | 45 | G

Date
14.01.96

The net allowances figure below shows how much of your pay or occupational pension will not have tax deducted from it. This figure is made up of your total allowances less the total reductions shown below. This notice of tax code replaces any previous notice for the year.

If you think the code is wrong, or if your personal circumstances change, you should tell your Tax Office immediately. The 'See note' column refers to notes in *PAYE: Understanding Your Tax Code* (leaflet P3(T)).

See note	Allowances	£	See note	Less amounts taken away to cover items shown below	£
17	PERSONAL ALLOWANCE	3765	25	BENEFITS (CAR)	2800
17	MARRIED ALLOWANCE	1790	25	MEDICAL/HEALTH INS	440
			29	UNPAID TAX £54	216
			33	ALLCE RESTRICTION	670

Less total reductions 4126

Total allowances 5555

Net allowances - the amount of your pay or occupational pension from which tax will not be deducted 1429

Your tax code is worked out from your net allowances. Your code for the year to 5 April 1997 is 142H See note **A** overleaf

P2(T)

Adjustments
Finally, the notice of your income tax code may include other information about adjustments which need to be made.

Unpaid tax If you owe tax for an earlier year (or years) the amount owed will be included here. A deduction from your allowances will be made to collect this tax. If you pay basic-rate tax a deduction of four times the tax you owe will be made; for higher-rate taxpayers the deduction will be two and a half times the amount of tax owed.

Taxed payments If you make covenanted payments and your tax bill is likely to be less than the amount of tax you have deducted, the difference will be included here.

Higher rate adj If you pay tax at the higher rate and have investment income already taxed at the 20 per cent rate, there may be an adjustment here to collect the extra tax owed.

Allce restriction If you claim one of the fixed-relief allowances, there will be an adjustment here to restrict the relief you get from the allowance to 15 per cent (see p. 139).

Less total reductions
This is the total figure for all deductions and adjustments.

Net allowances
This figure is reached by subtracting your total reductions from your total allowances and determines your PAYE code.

The number in your code
This is arrived at by knocking the last figure off the figure in **Allowances set against pay etc**. So if this figure is 950 your code number is 95. Because of the way rounding works, this code entitles you to tax-free pay of £959 instead – an extra £9 of tax-free pay. If it's zero, you have no free-of-tax amount to be deducted.

The letter in your code
L if you get the personal allowance.
H if you get the personal allowance plus the married couple's allowance or additional personal allowance and

are likely to pay basic-rate tax.
P if you get the full personal allowance for someone aged 65 to 74.
V if you get the full personal allowance for someone aged 65 to 74 plus the married couple's allowance for someone aged 65 to 74 and are likely to pay basic-rate tax.
T under certain circumstances – e.g. if you get a personal allowance for someone aged 75 or more, or if you get a reduced amount of age-related personal allowance because your income is above a certain level. Your code will also include T if you have a company car or if you don't want your employer to know about your age or marital status.
K if the total deductions shown on your notice come to more than your total allowances; the Revenue will have to collect tax under PAYE at a higher-than-normal rate.
NT if no tax is due on your pay.
BR if all your allowances have been given elsewhere and all your earnings will be taxed at the basic rate. You're most likely to get this if it is a code for a second job.
D if all your allowances have been given elsewhere and all your earnings will be taxed at the higher rate. Again you're most likely to get this if it is a code for a second job.

PAYE enquiries
If you pay tax under PAYE, it's possible that your tax office is a long distance away. This may make resolving any tax problems you have more difficult. In this situation, check to see if there's a local tax office or tax enquiry centre – look in the telephone book under *Inland Revenue*. If necessary, details of your tax affairs can be sent to the local office so that the people there can discuss your problems with you, give you advice and chase up matters (e.g. a long overdue tax rebate) for you.

Starting work

Your first job

If you've started work for the first time after full-time education (and haven't claimed unemployment benefit or income support) your employer will ask you to complete form P46. If your earnings are below the PAYE threshold (about £72 a week or £314 a month in the 1996–7 tax year) you won't pay any tax. If you are paid more than this you will be given an emergency code – 376L for the 1996–7 tax year – which assumes that you're entitled only to the basic personal allowance. This code gives you £314.09 of tax-free pay each month (£72.41 each week) – i.e. roughly 1/12 (or 1/52) of £3,765.

Tax won't be deducted until the free-of-tax pay since the beginning of the tax year has been used up. So, for example, if your first monthly pay-day is in the fourth month of the tax year, you are entitled to four months of free-of-tax pay on code 376L, i.e. £314.09 x 4 = £1,256.36. So on your first pay-day tax will be deducted only on any excess over £1,256.36. If your total pay for the month is less than this amount, the balance of the free-of-tax pay owing to you will be given to you on subesquent pay-days until it runs out. Note that if you don't complete form P46, the emergency code will be operated on a *week 1* (or *month 1*) basis. See *Returning to work* below for what this means.

As well as form P46, you should ask for a Coding Claim form P15 to complete in case you're entitled to other outgoings or allowances. When you return it to the Revenue your proper code will be worked out. You will be sent a PAYE Coding Notice and your employer will be told your new code. This new code may allow you a higher amount of free-of-tax pay than the emergency one. If so, any tax over-deducted will be refunded to you.

Working in the vacation

A student who gets a vacation job won't be taxed on weekly (or monthly) earnings even if these are more than £72 a week (£314 a month), if his or her earnings and other taxable income for the whole year won't exceed the personal allowance of £3,765. Both the student and the employer have to complete form P38(S) to get this exemption.

Returning to work

If you haven't worked for some years (e.g. because you've stayed at home to look after the children), the procedure is broadly the same as that described in *Your first job* on p. 145.

However, if your earnings for the 1996–7 tax year are more than £72 a week (£314 a month) your employer will operate the emergency code (376L for the 1996–7 tax year) on a *week 1* or *month 1* basis. This means that no account will be taken of any free-of-tax pay due from the beginning of the tax year to the time you started working, and tax will be deducted straight away. When the Revenue has received your Coding Claim (form P15), and allocated your proper code to you, any tax you've overpaid will be refunded to you.

Changing jobs

When you change jobs, your old employer should give you a form P45. This shows your PAYE code and details of the tax deducted from your total pay for the year to date. Give this to your new employer on your first day so that the correct amount of tax can be deducted from your pay.

If you don't do this, your employer will follow the procedure described above in *Returning to work* and you may pay too much tax for a while.

National Insurance contributions

If, in the 1996–7 tax year, you earn £61 or more a week (£265 or more a month), you'll have to pay Class 1 National Insurance contributions. These will be deducted from the whole of your pay on up to a maximum limit of £455 weekly earnings (or £1,972 monthly). These limits apply to each job, if you have more than one job.
Social Security Act 1975 s1–s4

Temporary work through an agency

If you work through an agency, e.g. as a temp, you will be treated as an employee (normally of the agency) and taxed under PAYE. But there are exceptions to this rule: you may be able to work through an agency and be treated as *self-employed* if you're an entertainer, model, sub-contractor in the building industry, or if all your work is done at or from your own home.
ICTA 1988 s134

Other temporary or casual jobs

Tax won't be deducted unless your earnings are more than £72 a week (£314 a month). If you are paid more than this amount, the basis on which you are taxed depends on whether or not you can give your employer form P45. With a P45, the procedure is as described under *Changing jobs* above. Without a P45, the emergency code (376L for the 1996–7 tax year) will be used on a *week 1* (or *month 1*) basis. Special rules apply to the building industry – see p. 125.

Interrupting work

Off sick

Statutory sick pay (SSP) paid by your employer and sick pay you get from your employer's own sick pay scheme are taxable under PAYE. But if the amount you get is lower than the amount of free-of-tax pay you are entitled to, your employer will refund some of the tax you've already paid, in each pay packet. You get statutory sick pay only for a limited period; then you may get state incapacity benefit which is taxable (see Chapter 7).

Some employers have *sick pay insurance schemes* which pay out income when you're off sick. Tax will normally be deducted from payments you receive from these schemes. But if you contribute towards the insurance premiums, you'll be taxed only on the part of the payment attributable to your employer's contributions. If you've taken out your own sick pay insurance policy, income from it is not taxable, from 6 April 1996 onwards. Before that date, it was tax-free for the first 12 months of payment only.
ICTA 1988 s149

Maternity

Statutory maternity pay (SMP) and any extra maternity pay paid by your employer is taxable under PAYE. If either SMP or maternity pay is paid when (or before) you stop working, the tax deducted will depend on your PAYE code. If it's paid *after* you've stopped working, i.e. after you have received a P45, tax is deducted at the basic rate. This could mean too much tax is deducted. If so, claim a rebate.

State maternity allowance isn't taxable.
ICTA 1988 s150

Laid off, on short-time, on strike

If you have been laid off, put on short-time or gone on strike, too much tax may have been deducted from your pay since the beginning of the tax year. If you've been laid off or put on short-time, any tax refunds due will be given on your normal pay-days by your employer. But strikers (or those involved in strikes) will have to wait until they return to work (or the end of the tax year if sooner) for their tax refunds.

Stopping work

Redundancy

If you're made redundant, earnings your employer owes you and paid when you leave your job, are taxed in the normal way under PAYE, e.g. normal wages, pay in lieu of holiday, pay for working your notice period, commission. But the following payments are tax-free:

- any lump sum for any injury or disability which meant you couldn't carry on your job
- compensation for loss of a job done entirely or substantially outside the UK
- gratuities from the armed forces (but if for early retirement, balance over £30,000 may be taxable)
- certain lump sum benefits from employers' pension schemes
- money your employer pays into a retirement benefit scheme or uses to buy you an annuity (if certain conditions are met)
- outplacement counselling services paid for by your employer for employees who are or become redundant, to help them find new work.

Other payments are also tax-free if, added together, they total less than £30,000. These are:

- redundancy payments made under the government's redundancy payments scheme or a scheme 'approved' by the Revenue
- pay in lieu of notice, in most circumstances, provided your conditions of service don't say you're entitled to it
- other payments made to you, as long as they are not payments for work done, not part of your conditions of service, and, technically at least, unexpected. This would normally cover redundancy payments over and above the government minimum.

Anything more than £30,000 is added to the rest of your income and taxed in the normal way.

Your employer has to deduct tax under PAYE on the excess over £30,000 before paying it to you. Unless a special, reduced tax payment is negotiated with your tax office, too much tax will be deducted because the tax tables don't allow for these special rules, and you'll have to claim a rebate.
ICTA 1988 s148, s188, s191, s589, Sch 11 (tax-free payments)

Employer going bust

Pay in lieu of notice is normally tax-free. But if you lose your job because your employer goes bust, and get pay in lieu of notice from the liquidator (or trustee in bankruptcy), basic-rate tax will be deducted from the whole amount. You can't claim a full rebate, but if this tax is more than the tax that would have been deducted if you'd received it as normal pay, you can get a refund of the difference. You get the refund from your local Redundancy Payments Office.

Dismissal

Earnings your employer owes you will be taxed under PAYE. In most circumstances pay in lieu of notice together with any other payments (provided they are not payments for work done, not part of your conditions of service and, technically, unexpected) totalling less than £30,000 are tax-free. Anything over £30,000 is taxed in the normal way.

If you are awarded compensation for unfair dismissal by an industrial tribunal, the amount you get for loss of wages will be paid after deduction of basic-rate tax, though any compensation for loss of your job would not be taxed. As with pay in lieu of notice paid by a liquidator (see above), the only tax rebate you can get is the difference between the amount actually deducted and any (smaller) amount that would have been deducted if you'd received the money as normal pay.

Refunded pension contributions

If you leave an employer's pension scheme within two years, you may be offered a refund of your contributions, but 20 per cent tax will have been deducted. This can't be re-claimed.

Spare-time income

Many people who have jobs in their spare time don't realise that they almost certainly need to tell the Revenue about the income they get. The most common examples of how you might get spare-time income are:

- you have a second job in the evenings, or at weekends (e.g. working behind the bar at your local pub), completely different from your main job
- you're someone with a skill (e.g. electrician, plumber, carpenter, motor mechanic), and you normally work full-time for an employer, but you get spare-time income doing work for other people, often for cash
- you're a professional person (e.g. schoolteacher, architect). Again, you use your professional skills and knowledge to get spare-time income (e.g. if you're a teacher, you may give private tuition)
- you have some extra income (e.g. commissions from running mail-order catalogues)
- you own a second home or a caravan which you let out, or you let rooms in your house.

How the Revenue finds out about your activities

- If you are employed, your employer should tell the Revenue that you have started work, and ask for a PAYE code for you to be able to work out how much tax to deduct from your pay.
- If your activities consist of a trade or business, or the letting of property, and you advertise in local or national papers, the Revenue has a department which monitors these ads and checks to see that the income has been declared.
- The Revenue has wide powers to compel employers to send details of payments they make to freelance staff, consultants, caterers, etc. – in short, any people who do work for them.
- The Revenue also gets a number of letters from informants – some of them anonymous, and a few of them paid by the Revenue. What they say may or may not be taken seriously, but it may tie in with suspicions the Revenue already has, or it may alert it to taking an interest in your affairs.

Since the Revenue can get to know of your income

without your telling them, it makes it more important for you to report your income yourself. If the Revenue starts an inquiry into your affairs as a result of information received you're more likely to be charged penalties in addition to the tax due than if you disclose your income voluntarily.
TMA 1970 Part III, Part X

Telling the Revenue

If you get a tax return
If you get a tax return, you must list all your income on the return. Where exactly on the form you need to show your spare-time income depends on what sort of income it is (e.g. from a second employer, or from renting out your house). If you're not sure where to show the income, don't worry too much: the important thing is for it to appear somewhere. The Revenue can, if need be, transfer it to the right heading. Broadly speaking, the income will probably fall under one of these headings:

- **income from employment** If you get a wage from your spare-time work (e.g. £40 a week for working in a chip shop in the evenings), enter the name and address of your employer and the amount of your earnings, including any tips, in the section of the tax return dealing with income from employments. Enter any *allowable expenses* (see p. 130) separately.
- **income from trades, professions or other business activities** If your spare-time income comes from a trade or business (e.g. you put small ads in the newsagent's window saying that you decorate houses), use the section of the form dealing with trades, professions or vocations. Say what your trade or business is (e.g. painter and decorator), give the address from which you work (e.g. your home), and declare the amount of your profit for the tax year.
- **income from lettings** If you let a property or rooms, you should show in the section dealing with income from property the gross rental income due for the tax year and all your expenses (see p. 230).
- **income from other activities** If none of the headings above applies, there's a special section of the return which asks for details of any other income or profits. Enter full details of your income and expenses.

See pages 132 and 193 for details of the types of expenses which you can claim against your income.

If you don't get a tax return
If you *don't* get a tax return, you must still tell the Revenue about your income within six months of the end of the tax year in which the income arose – e.g. income earned in August 1996 must be reported to the Revenue by 5 October 1997 at the latest – so that the Revenue can send out a tax return. If you fail to do this you can be charged a penalty when you eventually tell the Revenue about the income, or the Revenue finds out about it from other sources. You will also be charged interest from the date on which the tax ought to have been paid to the date on which it was actually paid.
TMA 1970 s7, s88, s93

How will your income be taxed?

Income from spare-time activities can be taxed in a number of ways:

- under Schedule E if your income is from an employment
- under Schedule D Case I or II if it amounts to a trade or business
- under Schedule A if your income is from the letting of property
- under Schedule D Case VI if the income doesn't fit in anywhere else, or arises from activities which do not amount to a trade or business and are not an employment, e.g. a casual commission. Income under this Case will almost always be taxed as investment income.

For more about Schedules, see p. 38.

Why bother about the Schedules?
The most important reason is the type and level of expenses which you can claim and the treatment of any losses. These differ from Schedule to Schedule. The rules for allowable expenses under Schedule E are more stringent than the rules under Schedule D Cases I and II. For example, the cost of travelling between your home and your place of work is not allowable under Schedule E. But if you're in business and work from your home, the cost of travelling to see your clients or customers is allowable under Schedule D Cases I and II.

9 *FRINGE BENEFITS*

- Some fringe benefits provide a valuable tax-free addition to your pay.
- Loans can be tax-free if they do not exceed £5,000 – see p. 166.
- Company cars are taxable, but there are several ways to keep the tax bill down – see p. 163.

If your employer lets you use a company car, gives you Luncheon Vouchers, or pays for private medical bills insurance, fringe benefits are a part of your life.

Are fringe benefits worthwhile?

Yes, because the tax system treats most fringe benefits favourably compared with a rise in salary. Getting a fringe benefit can often be worth more to you than a salary rise costing your employer the same to provide.

But there are disadvantages to getting fringe benefits:

- no choice – you may find that your fringe benefits aren't the things you'd choose to spend your money on
- lower pension, life insurance and redundancy money – all these are often linked to your pay in cash, *excluding* the value of the fringe benefits you get.

A fringe benefit – or an expense?

Some payments which you might get from your employer are on the borderline between a fringe benefit, which is generally taxable, and an allowable expense, which isn't. These include mileage allowance, removal expenses and overnight allowances, and are normally regarded as expenses because your employer is reimbursing you for money you have to spend in the course of your job. They are all tax-free as long as they count as *allowable expenses* – see p. 130.

Your employer may have what's called a *dispensation* for certain expenses and fringe benefits you get, such as a mileage or subsistence allowance. You don't have to pay tax on these expenses and benefits. Your employer can tell you which, if any, benefits have a dispensation. If you get expenses and benefits for which there is no dispensation, your employer will give details to your tax inspector on form P11D if you earn more than a certain amount – see below.

ICTA 1988 s166, s198

How are fringe benefits taxed?

Fringe benefits are taxed in one of three ways:

- some are tax-free
- some are taxed only if you count as earning £8,500 or more a year
- the rest are taxed whatever you earn.

See p. 157 for how individual benefits are taxed.

Swapping pay – a warning

No matter how much (or little) you earn, if you can swap some of your pay for a fringe benefit (or *vice versa*) the Inland Revenue may tax you on the amount of pay you give up if this is more than the taxable value of the fringe benefit under the normal tax rules. However, if you have a choice of having a company car or being paid more cash, you will be taxed on the taxable value of the car if you choose the car, or the cash if you choose the cash. And measures announced in the 1995 Budget aim to stop job-related accommodation being valued at an artificially low cash alternative.

Heaton v. Bell 46 TC211; Tennant v. Smith 3 TC 158

Tax-free fringe benefits

There are many fringe benefits which you can get without having to pay any tax, provided certain conditions are met. Some of the more common ones include pension contributions from your employer, free life insurance and sick-pay insurance, cheap or free drinks and meals.

Taxable fringe benefits

With these benefits, you pay tax on the *taxable value* of the benefit. This is also the amount you have to enter in your tax return. The taxable value will be the amount your fringe benefits cost your employer to provide, less anything you pay towards the cost (but see p. 163 for exceptions) *if you count as earning £8,500 a year*. If you don't, the taxable value will be the *second-hand value* of your fringe benefits. The taxable value of fringe benefits which don't have a second-hand value (e.g. free hairdressing at work) is nil.
ICTA 1988 s156

Do you count as earning £8,500 or more?

For the 1996–7 tax year you will count as earning £8,500 or more a year if you're paid *at a rate of* £8,500 or more a year. At a rate of means you'd be caught if, say, you were paid £4,300 for six months' work. If you are paid at a lower rate than £8,500 a year, you will still count if the total of the following comes to more than £8,500: your earnings from your job; your fringe benefits *valued as though you did earn £8,500 or more*; any expenses reimbursed to you by your employer for which there is no dispensation (see p. 155), even if these count as allowable expenses.
ICTA 1988 s167

If you have more than one job with the same (or an associated) company and your total earnings and expenses from these jobs come to £8,500 or more, you'll also be caught. This also applies to directors – see below.

Directors

A director is normally treated as earning £8,500 or more whatever he or she earns. But a director earning at a rate of less than £8,500 a year doesn't count if he or she:

- owns or controls 5 per cent or less of the shares in the company (together with close family and certain other associates), *and*
- is a full-time working director of the company, *or* works for a charity or non-profit making company, *and*
- is not a director of an associated company.
  ICTA 1988 s167, s168 (8–12)

EXAMPLE 1

Joseph Jones is paid a salary of £7,800. His employer lets him use a car in which he drives over 18,000 miles on business. The list price of the car when registered was £12,000. To find out if he counts as earning £8,500 or more, Joseph needs to add the taxable value of the car, assuming he does fall into this category, to his salary. This is £1,400 for the 1996–7 tax year, which takes him over the limit of £8,500. So Joseph does count as earning £8,500 or more.

How each fringe benefit is taxed

Benefit	How it is taxed if you count as earning £8,500 or more	How it is taxed if you don't count as earning £8,500 or more
board and lodging, i.e. job-related accommodation (see also *living accommodation*) *ICTA 1988 s145, s163*	accommodation provided for you, tax-free; for other benefits, pay tax on what employer pays out *less* anything you pay towards employer's costs up to a limit – see p. 167	see left
clothes specially needed for work, e.g. overalls *Ward v. Dunn 52 TC 517*	tax-free	tax-free
company car, including use of the car for private purposes; employer pays costs, e.g. repairs, insurance *ICTA 1988 s156, s157, s158, s159, s168, Sch 6*	pay tax on the taxable value of car – see p. 163	tax-free
company van which your employer makes available to you for your private use	you pay tax on a standard amount of £500 if the van is less than four years old or £350 if the van is more than four years old. A *pro rata* amount will be calculated if you share the van with other employees or if you had use of the van for only part of the year. Vans over 3.5 tonnes are tax-free	see left

Benefit	How it is taxed if you count as earning £8,500 or more	How it is taxed if you don't count as earning £8,500 or more
crèche or day-nursery provided by employer *FA 1990 s20, s21; ICTA 1988 s155*	tax-free – but see p. 168 for cash payments or vouchers	see left
credit cards, charge cards *ICTA 1988 s142, s144*	taxed on what employer pays out, *less* anything you pay towards employer's costs and *less* allowable expenses	see left
discounts on goods and services, if employers sell their own products cheap to employees	tax-free, as long as employer doesn't end up out of pocket	see left
employees' outings, including Christmas party *ESC A70*	normally tax-free (up to £75 per head per year)	see left
fees and subscriptions to professional bodies and learned societies *ICTA 1988 s201*	tax-free if organisation approved by the Revenue and relevant to employment; if not, taxed on cost to employer	see left
food and drink – includes free or cheap meals, tea, coffee, etc. *ICTA 1988 s155 (5); ESC A74*	tax-free, if provided for all employees – even if separate facilities are provided on the employer's premises for different groups of employees	see left
gifts, if they are genuinely personal, such as wedding or retirement gifts (but not a gift of money on retirement) *Herbert v. McQuade 4TC 489; Moorhouse v. Dooland 36TC 1*	tax-free	tax-free
gifts of things (not cash) from someone other than your employer *ESC A70*	tax-free, provided they cost £150 or less	see left

Benefit	How it is taxed if you count as earning £8,500 or more	How it is taxed if you don't count as earning £8,500 or more
gifts of something previously lent, e.g. furniture, TV *ICTA 1988 s156 (3), (4)*	pay tax on taxable value – see p. 169	pay tax on second-hand value
hairdressing at work *ICTA 1988 s156 (1), (2)*	pay tax on cost to your employer	tax-free
liability insurance e.g. professional indemnity insurance provided by or paid for by your employer	tax-free	tax-free
life insurance – cost of providing this under a scheme approved by the Revenue *ICTA 1988 s155 (4)*	tax-free	tax-free
living accommodation, e.g. rent-free or low-rent home *ICTA 1988 s145, s146, s163*	sometimes tax-free – see p. 167	see left
loans of money *ICTA 1988 s160, s161, Sch7; SI 1989/1297*	if loan qualifies for tax relief – see p. 166; pay tax on taxable value of other loans if the total of the cheap loans is more than £5,000 – see p. 167	tax-free
loans of things, e.g. furniture *ICTA 1988 s156*	pay tax on taxable value – see p. 169	tax-free
long-service awards, e.g. gifts of things or shares (but not a gift of money) *ESC A22; Weston v. Hearn 25 TC 425*	tax-free, if given for service of 20 years or more with the same employer. The cost must not be more than £20 for each year of service and you must not have had such an award within the past 10 years	see left
luncheon vouchers *ESC A2*	15p each working day is tax-free	see left

Benefit	How it is taxed if you count as earning £8,500 or more	How it is taxed if you don't count as earning £8,500 or more
medical bills insurance *ICTA 1988 s155(6)*	pay tax on cost to your employer (tax-free if insurance is to cover working abroad)	tax-free
mobile phones – including fixed car phones *ICTA 1988 s159A*	pay tax on fixed taxable value of £200	tax-free
mortgage – low-interest or interest-free *ICTA 1988 s160, s161, Sch 7*	pay tax on the taxable values less tax relief if the loan qualifies – see p. 166	see left
pension contributions your employer pays into an 'approved' or 'statutory' pension scheme for you *ICTA 1988 s590, s592*	tax-free	tax-free
petrol or diesel – if you get any for private use in company car *ICTA 1988 s158, s157(3), s167(2)*	pay tax on taxable value – see p. 166	pay tax on cost of petrol or diesel unless directly provided by employer – see p. 165
relocation allowances towards extra expenses in higher-cost housing areas *ESC A67*	tax-free (within limits)	see left
removal expenses (if reasonable) including solicitor's, surveyor's and estate agent's fees, stamp duty, removal costs, an allowance for carpets and curtains, temporary subsistence allowance, rent while you're looking for a new home and, in certain circumstances, the interest on a bridging loan even if the loan takes you over the £30,000 limit *ICTA 1988 s191, Sch 11; ESC A5*	normally tax-free up to a limit of £8,000, if you have to move to take a new job or are transferred by your employer	see left

Benefit	How it is taxed if you count as earning £8,500 or more	How it is taxed if you don't count as earning £8,500 or more
scholarship and apprenticeship schemes awarded to you by your employer *ICTA 1988 s331; SP 4/86*	tax-free if you are enrolled for at least one academic year and attend full-time for an average of at least 20 weeks a year. Rate of payment (including lodging, subsistence and travelling allowances but excluding tuition fees) must not be above £7,000 or the amount of a grant from a public body such as a research council, if higher – otherwise taxable in full. Payments for time at work taxable in normal way	see left
scholarships awarded by your employer to your children *ICTA 1988, s154, s165*	normally pay tax on amount of scholarship. Amount is tax-free if scholarship awarded before 15 March 1983 as long as first payment was made before 6 April 1984 *and*, for payments made after 5 April 1989, your child is still at the same full-time school or college. Special rules apply if scholarship comes from a trust fund	tax-free
season ticket loans *ICTA 1988 s160, s161, Sch 7*	tax-free if the total of the cheap loans from your employer is £5,000 or less – see p. 167	tax-free
shares bought cheap (or free) in your employer's company through an approved employee share scheme *ICTA 1988 s185, s186, s187, Sch 9, Sch 10*	usually tax-free – but see p. 170	see left

Benefit	**How it is taxed if you count as earning £8,500 or more**	**How it is taxed if you don't count as earning £8,500 or more**
sick pay insurance – cost of insurance paid for you by employer *ICTA 1988 s149, s154 (2)*	cost of insurance met by employer is tax-free if the scheme meets the Revenue's conditions. Income from scheme normally taxed as part of your earnings. If you pay some of the premiums, only the income provided by the employer's contributions is tax-free	see left
social and sports facilities *ICTA 1988 s197*	tax-free if provided for staff use generally. Facilities for limited groups of staff may be taxable	tax-free
staff suggestion schemes – awards from schemes *ESC A57*	tax-free up to an overall maximum of £5,000	see left
training, e.g. attending a course or studying on normal pay; tuition fees *Humbles v. Brooks 40 TC 500; ESC A63; ESC A64 ICTA 1988 s588, s589*	pay is taxed in the normal way. Books and tuition fees paid for by your employer for some UK external training courses are tax-free. If you're away less than 12 months, extra travel expenses and living costs met by your employer may not be. Similar expenses if you are leaving or have left your job for retraining in new work skills are also tax-free	see left
transport between home and work for severely disabled employees who can't use public transport *ESC A59*	tax-free	tax-free
travel costs, e.g. for taxi, hire car for late-night journeys from work *ESC A66*	tax-free, provided you have to work to 9pm or later, it doesn't happen regularly or frequently and public transport would be difficult	see left

Benefit	How it is taxed if you count as earning £8,500 or more	How it is taxed if you don't count as earning £8,500 or more
travelling and subsistence allowance when public transport is disrupted by industrial action *ESC A58*	tax-free	tax-free
vouchers – such as travel voucher (e.g. British Rail season ticket) or any other voucher exchangeable for goods or services (e.g. a letter to a tailor ordering you a new suit) or for cash (e.g. a cheque) *ICTA 1988 s141, s143 s144*	pay tax on amount your employer pays out *less* anything you pay towards the cost. If you work for a transport organisation, any transport voucher under a scheme in operation on 25 March 1982 is tax-free	see left

Some fringe benefits in more detail

We give here details of the special rules for:

- use of cars and fuel
- cheap loans
- living accommodation
- workplace nurseries
- loans of things and their subsequent gifts to you
- employee share schemes.

Company cars

The basic taxable value of a company car which you have for both private and business use is 35 per cent of the car's list price (including extras) at the time it was first registered (if you count as earning £8,500 or more a year – if you don't, there's no tax on your company car). However, depending on the age of your car, the business miles you do and whether or not you pay anything for the private use of your car, you may be able to reduce the basic taxable value of your car. The amounts by which the basic taxable value is reduced are shown in the table overleaf:

Reason for reduction	Amount of reduction
car over four years old at the end of the tax year	one-third of the taxable value (but see below)
you travel between 2,500 and 17,999 business miles in the tax year	one-third of the taxable value (but see below)
you travel 18,000 business miles or more in the tax year	two-thirds of the taxable value – this replaces the one-third reduction for business miles up to 17,999 (but see below)
you pay your employer for private use of your company car	the taxable value will be reduced by the amount you pay your employer
you have use of the car for only part of the year	the taxable value will be reduced in line with the amount of time the car was available to you
you are disabled and your car has been converted to suit your special requirements	the costs of supplying and fitting accessories designed specifically for disabled people

If you qualify for a double reduction because of the age of the car *and* the business mileage you drive, you take one-third off the basic taxable value. Then using the figure you get after doing that sum, you take a further one-third or two-thirds off (as appropriate). It does not matter in which order you make the reductions – the answer will be the same.

EXAMPLE 2

The list price (including extras) of Jonathan Jones's company car was £12,000 when it was first registered. So its basic taxable value is £4,200 – 35 per cent of £12,000.

But Jonathan qualifies for a double reduction. He travels more than 18,000 business miles and the car is over four years old. First he takes two-thirds off £4,200 to give £1,400, then one-third off £1,400, to get a figure of £933. (He could have taken one-third off £4,200 to get £2,800, then two-thirds off £2,800 to reach £933.)

The taxable value of Jonathan's car in 1996–7 is £933. He is a higher-rate taxpayer, so will pay tax of 40 per cent of £933, which comes to £373.20.

Special rules for old and valuable cars

The Revenue will use the open market value to work out the basic taxable value of cars for which there is no list price. The open market value will also be used if the car is over 15 years old and its open market value is over £15,000, even if the car's list price is lower than the open market value.

Second cars

The basic taxable value of a second company car (provided for you or a member of your family) will be 35 per cent of its list price when registered. You can reduce the basic taxable value by one-third only if you use the second car to do more than 18,000 business miles. There is no reduction if you do a lower number of business miles. If the second car is four or more years old at the end of the tax year, the taxable value can be reduced by one-third.
ICTA 1988 s157, Sch 6, s168

Motoring costs for a company car paid by your employer

If your employer pays certain costs, such as repairs, business petrol, insurance, direct (e.g. settling a company account), it doesn't affect your tax position. But if *you* pay them, claim the business part of what you pay as *allowable expenses* in your tax return, i.e. the proportion attributable to your business mileage. And if your employer reimburses you in full or in part (e.g. by a mileage allowance), also enter what you get under *expense allowances*, unless your employer has a dispensation (see p. 155).

If your company car has a telephone, you have to pay extra tax. And if your employer provides you with a telephone for your own private car, there'll be tax to pay on private use unless you reimburse your employer.

A free car-parking space provided at or near your place of work isn't taxable. And there will be no tax to pay if your employer pays for a parking space (or reimburses the cost).
ICTA 1988 s155(1A) s157, s158, s159A, Sch 6; ESC A71

Pool cars

A pool car doesn't count as a fringe benefit and there is no tax to pay by the people who use it. To qualify as a pool car, the car must be made available to (and used by) more than one employee, and it mustn't normally be kept overnight at, or near, an employee's home. Any private use of the car must be incidental to business use – e.g. occasional travel between home and office as part of genuine business trips. *ICTA 1988 s159*

Car fuel
Fuel you get from your employer for private use is taxable. If you count as earning £8,500 or more a year, fixed taxable values (based on engine size and shown in the table below) apply if you get *any* petrol for private use from your employer which you don't pay for in full – no matter how much or how little. If you don't count as earning £8,500 or more, you pay tax on the cost of the petrol unless it is provided directly by your employer.

Size of engine	Charge for petrol	Charge for diesel
1400 cc or less	£710	£640
1401 to 2000 cc	£890	£640
over 2000 cc	£1,320	£820

Cheap loans

If your employer lets you have a loan on which you pay little or no interest, there may be tax to pay. How much depends on whether or not the loan qualifies for tax relief.

Loans which qualify for tax relief If the loan (or part of it) that you get from your employer qualifies for tax relief, the taxable value of the cheap loan (i.e. what you pay tax on) is:

- the amount of interest you would have had to pay if you didn't get the cheap loan (worked out using the official rate of interest which was 7.75 per cent in December 1995)
- *less* the interest you pay your employer (this deduction will be zero if it's an interest-free loan).

This amount is added to your taxable income and tax is charged at your top rate. However, you can then deduct tax relief to reduce your tax bill. This is done by subtracting tax relief at 15 per cent of the interest (at the official rate rather than the actual rate you pay) on the first £30,000 of the loan.

So if you get a cheap mortgage of £50,000 on which you pay interest at 2 per cent, the taxable value of the loan will be £2,875 – i.e. 7.75 per cent of £50,000 less 2 per cent of

£50,000. If your top rate of tax is 24 per cent, your cheap mortgage will add an extra £690 (i.e. 24 per cent of the taxable value of £2,875) to your tax bill. But you can reduce your tax bill by deducting the tax relief. This is 15 per cent of £2,325 (i.e. interest at the official rate of 7.75 per cent on £30,000 of the loan), which reduces your tax bill by £348.75.

Other loans Cheap loans you get from your employer which don't qualify for tax relief – e.g. season ticket loans – are tax-free *unless* you count as earning £8,500 or more *and* the total of all cheap or interest-free loans from your employer (which don't qualify for tax relief) comes to more than £5,000. If the total of your loans is over the £5,000 limit, you'll pay tax on the difference between the interest you actually pay and the interest you would have paid if you had been charged the official rate of interest *on the total of all your loans* – i.e. *not* your total loans less £5,000. So to avoid paying tax on your cheap or interest-free loans, don't borrow more than £5,000 from your employer.

Living accommodation

A rent-free or low-rent home can be a tax-free fringe benefit if one of the following applies:

- it is necessary to live in the home to do your job properly (e.g. you are a caretaker)
- living in the home enables you to do your job better, and it is customary for people doing your sort of job to live in such a home (e.g. you are a publican)
- there is a special threat to your security, and you live in the home as part of special security arrangements.

A home provided for a company director for either of the first two reasons above qualifies as a tax-free fringe benefit only if he or she owns 5 per cent or less of the shares in the company, *and* is a full-time working director *or* the company is non-profit making or a charitable body.

There are special rules for free or cheap accommodation abroad – see p. 178.

Even if the home does count as a tax-free benefit, if you count as earning £8,500 or more you will have to pay some tax on what your employer pays for heating, lighting, cleaning, decorating or furnishing (but the value put on these by your tax inspector cannot be more than 10 per cent of your earnings not including these benefits).

If a rent-free or low-rent home doesn't count as a tax-free fringe benefit, the Revenue values the benefit at either the *gross value* of the home (the figure the rateable value used to be based on, but with an adjustment in Scotland) or the rent your employer pays if greater, less any rent you pay. For properties which don't have a gross value (such as property built since the abolition of rates) your employer will estimate what the gross value would have been and agree a figure with the Revenue. This method of valuing the benefit applies whether or not you count as earning £8,500 or more. If you share the right to use a property with other employees, the strict letter of the law means that you could each be charged tax on the full value of the benefit as described above. However, by a concession backdated to 1995–6 onwards, the total tax bill for all the users cannot come to more than the amount which one person with sole use of the property would pay. The Revenue will decide how much each user pays according to the relevant facts.

If the home costs your employer more than £75,000 to provide, there could be an extra tax bill. The extra tax bill is worked out by finding how much the accommodation cost to buy and set up and deducting £75,000. You then multiply this figure by the *official rate of interest* on cheap loans – 7.75 per cent in December 1995. You must use the official rate at the start of the tax year, i.e. 6 April 1996 for the 1996–7 tax year. But you can deduct any rent paid in excess of the *gross value*. From 1995–6 onwards, if the taxable value of the home is based on the full market rent, the extra tax bill will not apply.

Agricultural workers whose employers give them free board and lodging may be able to take higher wages and arrange their own accommodation instead. That would normally make the value of their board and lodging taxable. But by a concession, agricultural workers who don't count as earning £8,500 or more will generally avoid the tax.
ICTA 1988 s145, s146, s163; ESC A56, A60; ESC 28 November 1995

Workplace nurseries

The cost of workplace nurseries provided by employers has not been taxable since 6 April 1990. The exemption applies to nurseries run by the employer at the workplace or elsewhere and to nurseries set up jointly with other employers, voluntary bodies or local authorities (provided the employer participates in the cost and management of the scheme). Facilities provided for older children after school or during school holidays are also tax-free.

Any cash payments or vouchers provided by an employer to cover child care (e.g. childminders or private nurseries) are still taxable for all employees. Any child-care places bought by an employer in other companies' schemes where the employer is not involved in the management are also taxable.

ICTA 1988 s155

Loans of items and their subsequent gift to you

If you count as earning £8,500 or more and your employer lends you something like furniture or a TV, your tax inspector will value it at 20 per cent of the market value at the time your employer first loaned the thing out, *less* anything you pay for the use of it. For items first loaned out before 6 April 1980, the 20 per cent figure becomes 10 per cent. Anything your employer pays for servicing (or any other costs) is added to the taxable value.

If your employer gives you something previously lent to you, your tax inspector will value it at the market value at the time your employer first loaned it out, *less* anything you've paid towards it, and *less* any amount you've already paid tax on (e.g. under the 20 per cent rule). But if this value is lower than the market value when the item is given to you, you'll be taxed on the higher (market) value, *less* anything you've paid towards it. And if the item was first loaned out before 6 April 1980, its value is taken as the market value when the item was given to you (*less* anything you've paid towards it).

If you count as earning £8,500 or more and you use something for which your employer pays rent (e.g. a flat, a TV) your tax inspector can value the benefit at the amount your employer pays in rent, running costs, etc., *less* anything you pay, if this comes to more than the value using the normal method.

If you don't count as earning £8,500 or more, there's no tax on a loan and you're taxed on the *second-hand value* of a gift.

ICTA 1988 s156

Employee share schemes

An employee share scheme is organised by an employer and is a way in which an employee can get a stake in the company he or she works for. The following sorts of schemes have considerable tax advantages if they are *approved* by the Revenue:

- profit-sharing schemes
- share option schemes you joined before 17 July 1995
- Save-As-You-Earn (SAYE) share option schemes
- company share option plans

Profit-sharing schemes
Under an *approved* scheme you can get shares in your employer's firm free of tax. The yearly limit is £3,000 worth of shares, or 10 per cent of your earnings, whichever is higher, with an overall limit of £8,000-worth of shares a year. To get approval, the scheme must meet various conditions. For example, the shares must be held in trust for you. They can't normally be handed over to you from the trust for at least two years (unless you reach retirement age, are made redundant, or stop work through injury or disablement). And if you withdraw your shares from the trust within three years of getting them, there will normally be some income tax to pay (unless the shares are withdrawn because you die).

If you sell the shares for more than their value at the time you were given them, the gain you make counts as a chargeable capital gain, and there may be capital gains tax to pay (see Chapter 15). And any dividends you get count as part of your income for the tax year in which you get them.
ICTA 1988 s186, s187, Sch 9, Sch 10

Share option schemes
A share option scheme gives you the right (or *option*) to buy shares in your employer's company at some future date, but at today's market price. There is no income tax to pay on any gain you make when you exercise your option, if the scheme is an *approved* one and you were given rights under the scheme before 17 July 1995. Instead, any gain you make when you sell (or give away) the shares will count as a chargeable capital gain.

Any tax will be based on the difference between the price you paid to buy the shares, and the price when you sell (or give away) the shares – see p. 295. To get approval, the scheme must meet certain conditions. For example, you must be able to exercise your option at the market price at the time the option was made. The option must be used at some time between three and ten years.

If you are in a share option scheme which is *not approved*, or your rights were granted on or after 17 July 1995, you will pay income tax on the difference between the market value when you exercise your option and the cost to you of the shares, including any amount paid for the option. You might have to pay capital gains tax when you sell (or give away) your shares, based on the difference between their market value when you exercise your option and their value when you dispose of them.
ICTA 1988 s135, s185, s187, Sch 9

Savings-related share option schemes
Your company can run a savings scheme giving you the option to buy its shares some years in the future at a price fixed now. Provided the scheme is an *approved* one and you buy the shares with the proceeds of an SAYE scheme – which normally runs for three, five or seven years – there will usually be no income tax to pay when the option is given to you, nor on the difference between the value of the shares when you buy them and the price you pay for them (which must not be less than 80 per cent of their market value at the time the option is given). But if you sell (or give away) the shares, there could be capital gains tax to pay based on the difference between the price you buy at and the market value when you sell or give them away. The maximum saving is £250 a month and the minimum can't be more than £5.
ICTA 1988 s185, s187, Sch 9

Company share option plans
With the removal of tax relief from 17 July 1995, share option schemes (see above) are no longer so attractive. However, in the 1995 Budget, the government proposed a scheme called the company share option plan. This is identical to the old share option scheme except that the maximum value of options per employee is £20,000 (compared with £100,000 or four times earnings under the old share option schemes) and the exercise price of the options must not be at a discount to the market price of the shares (which was allowed with share option schemes).
Budget Press Release, 28 November 1995

Company takeovers and share option schemes

It is possible for employees in a company which is taken over to exchange their existing share options under an approved share option (including savings-related schemes) for options to buy shares in the company which takes over. The replacement options can only be granted if certain conditions are met to ensure that the employees concerned will be no better or worse off than if the takeover had not happened.

ICTA 1988 Sch 9(15)

Single-company PEPS

Shares acquired under an all-employee profit-sharing and savings-related share option scheme can now be transferred, tax-free, into a single-company personal equity plan (PEP, see p. 252). Shares with a value of up to £3,000 can be invested in a single-company PEP. The transfer into a PEP must be made within 90 days of the employee acquiring the shares.

ICTA 1988 s333

10 *WORKING ABROAD*

- You can work abroad and still visit the UK without incurring a tax bill – but it is vital that you arrange your visits in a 'tax-efficient' way.

If you want to keep the Inland Revenue's hands off your hard-earned guilders, dinars or even pounds, you'll have to earn them abroad. But just earning them abroad isn't enough. You'll have to be absent from the UK for at least a year to get your earnings free of UK tax.

Where you live – according to the Revenue

In general, the UK tax system aims to tax all earnings made in the UK, and all earnings paid to people who are *resident* and *ordinarily resident* in the UK, even if the money is earned outside the country. But if you're paid money abroad and aren't allowed to take it out of the country (because of a ban on doing so, or a war, say) you can ask the Revenue to let you off paying tax on it until it is possible for the money to be sent to the UK. You'll then have to pay tax on the income whether or not it is sent to the UK.

The terms 'resident' and 'ordinarily resident' have not been defined by Act of Parliament, so their interpretation is up to the courts. Whether you are resident and/or ordinarily resident is decided separately for each tax year. But you will always be treated as resident if you're in the UK for at least six months (183 days) of the tax year. The 183 days may be made up of one visit or a succession of visits. Under current Revenue practice, the day of your arrival and the day of your departure do not normally count towards the 183 days. You're also likely to be treated as resident if, over a four-year period, you come to the UK for an average of three months or more each year.

For tax years before 1993–4 you could also be treated

as resident if you had accommodation in the UK available for your use and you visited the UK, no matter how short the visit.

The term 'ordinarily resident' is less clear-cut and is to do with your intentions and way of life. If you are treated as being resident in the UK year after year, you are likely to count as ordinarily resident too.

A person can be resident (or ordinarily resident) in two or more countries at the same time – or even none at all.

If you are married, your residence status depends on your own circumstances and need not be the same as that of your spouse.

ICTA 1988 s334–s336, s19(1) (2), s192; IR20

Domicile

You'll generally be considered to be *domiciled* in the UK if this is where you have your permanent home and where you're likely to end your days. If you're considered to be domiciled in the UK, it will largely affect your liability to capital gains tax and inheritance tax, even if you're currently living abroad.

How you're taxed

If you're resident and ordinarily resident in the UK, you'll be taxed on all you earn abroad unless you qualify for a *foreign earnings deduction* of 100 per cent of your earnings for that period. If you do qualify, all your earnings from abroad will be treated as free of UK tax.

The foreign earnings deduction

If you're abroad for a 'qualifying period' of 365 days or more (not necessarily coinciding with a tax year), all your earnings will be tax-free. Where possible (e.g. you work for a UK company which has sent you abroad), the deduction is given in your Pay-As-You-Earn (PAYE) code, and if the Revenue is satisfied you'll qualify for the 100 per cent deduction, you'll get a 'no tax' code (see p. 144) for those earnings.

Even if you come back to the UK during your 365 days, you may still qualify for the 100 per cent deduction. The Revenue adds together:

- the continuous days abroad immediately *before* your UK visit
- the number of days in your UK visit
- the number of days abroad immediately *after* your UK visit.

If the number of days in your UK visit comes to more than one-sixth of this total *or* to more than 62 days, the continuity of your 365 days is broken at the end of your first period abroad. And a new period of 365 days starts at the beginning of your second period abroad. But if your UK visit is one-sixth of the total above (or less) and not more than 62 days, the whole time, including the days in the UK, counts towards your 365 days. If you come back to the UK for another visit, the whole period which counted towards your 365 days is included when working out the continuous days immediately before your second UK visit, and the total number of days that you've spent in the UK in previous visits is added to the number of days in your latest visit – see the example below. The 62-day limit doesn't apply to the cumulative total for UK visits. The process is repeated for each UK visit.

Note that the 100 per cent deduction applies only to work done entirely abroad, unless your work in the UK is regarded as *incidental* to the overseas employment. Things like getting further instructions, or reporting to head office, would be treated as incidental; beyond this the Revenue deals with each case on its merits.
ICTA 1988 s132(4), s193(1)

Qualifying days

A day of absence is a day at the end of which you are absent from the UK. The day you leave the UK to travel to your job counts, but the day of your return doesn't. For the purposes of the foreign earnings deduction, aircrews and seafarers count as working abroad during trips that take them to or from (or between) places abroad.
ICTA 1988 s132(4), s193(1), Sch12(4)

EXAMPLE

Angela Tavistock and Brian Duckworth work for the same company. They both have to go abroad three times in the next 16 months or so, for a total of 400 days away. They know when they have to be away and when they will come back for UK visits, so they work out if they are entitled to the 100 per cent deduction.

Neither of Angela's UK trips exceeds the limits, so her earnings will be free of UK tax.

Brian's first visit to the UK breaks the one-sixth rule, and his second and third trips abroad (including the 20 days of his visit to the UK) don't add up to 365 days. So he can't claim the 100 per cent deduction. If Brian could arrange another working trip abroad which linked to his third trip abroad without breaking the one-sixth rule, and he then met the 365-day requirement, he could claim the 100 per cent deduction for his second and third trips abroad and the final one that took him over the 365-day requirement.

If Angela's work (other than work incidental to overseas employment) was done partly in the UK during visits home, she would not get the 100 per cent deduction from all her earnings. It would be given against earnings shown to be *reasonable* given the nature of the duties, the time devoted to them in the UK and abroad, and all other relevant circumstances.

Angela	Days	1/6 limit exceeded?	**Brian**	Days	1/6 limit exceeded?
1st trip abroad	100		1st trip abroad	100	
1st UK visit	20		1st UK visit	60	
2nd trip abroad	150	no (20/270)	2nd trip abroad	150	yes (60/310)
2nd UK visit	60		2nd UK visit	20	
3rd trip abroad	150	no (80/480)	3rd trip abroad	150	no (20/320)*

*Note, however, Brian hasn't met the 365-day requirement since the beginning of his second trip abroad.

When the normal rules don't apply

It can happen that your visit to the UK is either caused, or extended, for reasons beyond your control. For example, you may have been working in one of the Gulf states at the outbreak of the Gulf crisis in 1990 and had to return to the UK for safety reasons. Maybe you were already on a visit to the UK and could not return abroad because of the outbreak of a crisis or because you were ill. Days spent in the UK because of exceptional circumstances won't be taken into account in working out how long you have stayed in the UK, so long as you intend to resume full-time employment abroad. However, these days will be taken into account when it comes to the 183-day rule (see p. 173)
SP 2/91

Crown employees

Crown employees (e.g. UK diplomats and members of the armed forces) working abroad are, for most income tax purposes, taxed as if they worked in the UK. But any extra allowance paid for working abroad isn't taxable.
ICTA 1988 s132, s319

Personal allowances while you're away

If you're resident in the UK, you'll get your full personal allowance for the tax year. So if, say, you get the 100 per cent deduction, you'll be able to use all your personal allowances against other income you get in the UK – e.g. National Savings interest, dividends, UK earnings.

Travelling expenses

You don't have to pay tax on what your employer pays towards the cost of travel to a job abroad (and back again when you've finished), or between countries where you're working. If your employer doesn't pay and the duties of the employment are carried out wholly abroad, you can get tax relief against your taxable earnings from your job abroad for the costs you incur. If you get the foreign earnings deduction no other relief is due.

You can now make any number of visits to the UK, paid for or reimbursed by your employer, without being taxed on the travel expenses, providing your job can be performed *only* outside the UK and you go abroad purely for work purposes. And, providing you're working abroad continuously for at least 60 days and there are no more than two return trips for family members per tax year, what your employer pays towards some other journeys is tax-free too:

- visits by your wife (or husband) or children under 18
- return trips that you make to visit them.

But if *you* pay for these trips, the costs cannot count as *allowable expenses*. There's no tax to pay on costs, met by your employer, of travel in the UK at the beginning or end of your journey, e.g. from a UK home to the airport.
ICTA 1988 s193, s194, s195

Board and lodging abroad

If your job is done wholly abroad, and your employer pays (or reimburses) the cost of board and lodging which enables you to carry out your duties, there'll be no tax to pay on this fringe benefit. But you *will* be taxed on the cost to your employer of board and lodging for your husband or wife and children, and of any board and lodging for a holiday abroad. If your employer doesn't pay, you can't claim any board and lodging as an *allowable expense*.

If your job is done partly in the UK and partly abroad, there'll normally be no tax to pay on what your employer pays towards *your* board and lodging, and if your employer doesn't pay, you may be able to claim the cost as an allowable expense. See p. 130 for details.
ICTA 1988 s193

Golden handshakes

If you're a UK resident, redundancy payments you get after working abroad may be wholly tax-free, even if they're over £30,000 (see p. 149). Payments you get are tax-free if any of the following apply:

- you worked abroad for at least three-quarters of the time you did the job
- you worked abroad for all of the last 10 years
- you did the job for over 20 years, and at least 10 of the last 20 years *and* at least half the total time was spent working abroad.

Where the payment isn't wholly tax-free, part may be. An amount will be deducted from the payment equal to:

$$\frac{\text{number of years you worked abroad} \times \text{the amount which would otherwise have been taxable}}{\text{total number of years' service}}$$

You count as working abroad if you weren't both resident and ordinarily resident or if you got the foreign earnings deduction (see p. 174).
ICTA 1988 s188, sch 11

Double taxation relief

If you pay local income tax on what you earn abroad, you may be eligible for *double taxation relief*. The UK has a large number of double taxation agreements with other countries, which prevent you paying tax both abroad and in the UK on the same income. This is done either by giving exemption from UK tax on certain types of income (e.g. earnings, dividends, business profits) or by reducing the UK tax bill by the smaller of the overseas tax liability and the UK tax liability.

If there is no double taxation agreement, you may be able to claim *unilateral relief* if you're a UK resident earning income which has been taxed abroad. You'll be allowed to offset the tax you paid abroad against your UK tax bill.
ICTA 1988 s788–s790

Tax if you're non-resident

As a non-resident, you pay UK income tax on only your UK earnings – at the appropriate rate depending on how high your income is. You'll also have to pay tax on your UK investment income but other than income from property in the UK and income from trading in the UK through a broker or investment manager, the tax charge is limited to the tax (if any) which is deducted at source. You may get relief under a double taxation agreement – see above. (Note: You won't normally have to pay UK tax on bank and building society interest and some British government stocks have a tax-free return for anyone who is not ordinarily resident.)

Becoming non-resident

If you leave the UK to work abroad full-time under a contract of employment, you may count as non-resident and not ordinarily resident if the period spent abroad includes a complete tax year. Your visits back to the UK must total less than 183 days in any tax year and average less than 91 days a tax year, measured over a maximum of four years. You'll count as non-resident from the day after you leave to the day before you come back. As a concession, an accompanying spouse whose visits to the UK meet the same limits may also count as non-resident and not ordinarily resident even if he or she is not in full-time employment.

If you're not employed full-time abroad, in addition to meeting the requirements above you'll have to produce some evidence to support your claim to non-residence – e.g. selling your home in the UK and setting up a permanent home abroad. If you can do this, your claim may be accepted provisionally. It will normally be confirmed when you've been away for a complete tax year, providing your visits back to the UK have averaged fewer than 91 days in the tax year. If you're unable to provide sufficient evidence, the decision is delayed for three years, and your tax liability will be worked out provisionally as though you were still resident (except for any tax year in which you don't set foot in the UK at all). After the three years are up, you'll be able to claim back any overpaid tax if it's confirmed that you're non-resident.
IR20

Personal allowances

British citizens, other Commonwealth citizens, citizens of the Irish Republic and, from 1996–7, citizens of all states within the European Economic Area can claim personal allowances as if resident in the UK. A non-resident husband can give unused married couple's allowance to his wife in most cases.
ICTA 1988 s278

11 *WORKING FOR YOURSELF*

- The self-employed will notice a significant difference under self-assessment and should master the new rules as soon as possible.
- Transitional rules for tax bills in 1996–7 could mean you pay less tax – see p. 186.
- The self-employed can claim more allowable expenses than employees – see p. 192.
- There are various ways to treat business losses and the route you choose can have a big impact on the tax you pay – see p. 202.
- It's all change for partnerships – see p. 209.

Being self-employed includes all sorts of occupations – owning a shop, being a wholesaler, working as a doctor, barrister or writer, and so on. Most of this chapter is for people in business on their own ('sole traders', in the jargon), but we also tell you something about partnerships on p. 209. Casual earnings are dealt with in Chapter 8 on p. 151.

Self-employed people can generally claim more than employees in expenses to reduce their tax bills. Tax is not deducted from the earnings of the self-employed before they are paid, as it is for employees. This is because they are taxed under the rules for Schedule D Case I or Case II, rather than as employees under Schedule E (see pp. 40–1).

Do you count as self-employed?

To be treated as self-employed, you must convince the Inland Revenue that you are genuinely in business on your own account. If you own a shop or offer a mobile car mechanic service, say, provide all your own equipment and find all your own customers, there is little doubt that you are self-employed. But there can be circumstances in which, though you may regard yourself as self-employed, the Revenue says you are not.

In general, you are on dangerous ground if all (or nearly all) your work comes from just one source – from one company you have a contract with, say – and you are paid on a regular basis without having to send in an invoice. The Revenue may decide you are an employee with a *contract of service* rather than a self-employed person with a *contract for services*. If the Revenue says you have a contract of service, you may be taxed under Schedule E as an employee and the company will have to deduct income tax and National Insurance from your pay under the Pay-As-You-Earn (PAYE) system. This is particularly likely to happen if all the work you do is carried out on the company's premises.

Each Revenue and Department of Social Security (DSS) local office has someone responsible for saying whether or not you will be treated as self-employed, and who will confirm decisions in writing if you wish. Also, see Inland Revenue leaflet *IR56*.

If you are a director of a limited company, no matter how small, you are an employed person, not self-employed.

What is trading?

You may be taxed as if you're a business, even if you don't think you are, if your tax inspector says you are *trading*. You might be said to be trading if, among other points:

- you frequently buy and sell similar items
- you sell items which you haven't owned for very long
- you alter the items so that you can sell them for more
- your motive in buying and selling is to make a profit.
  ICTA 1988 s18, s832

When profits are taxed

Unlike employees, who pay tax on their pay as they earn it, the self-employed have a delay between earning their profits and paying tax on them. How long this delay is depends on which tax rules apply to you and when your accounting year ends.

From April 1997, everyone who receives a tax return will have to pay tax under the new system of self-assessment.

This means that, instead of simply declaring all your income and gains to your tax office, you will also be given the option to calculate how much tax is due on them.

To simplify the calculations, self-employed people and partnerships are to be taxed under new rules. The new rules apply immediately for businesses which started up on or after 6 April 1994. For businesses that started before 6 April 1994, they will apply from 1997–8 onwards, but there are transitional rules before then which may affect your business from its 1995–6 accounting year onwards.

Rules for businesses starting on or after 6 April 1994

Your profits are normally taxed on a *current-year basis*, e.g. tax in the 1996–7 tax year will be based on profits for the accounting period which ends in the 1996–7 year.

If you choose your accounting year to coincide with the tax year – called *fiscal accounting* – working out your tax is very straightforward, because you are taxed simply on what you have earned during each tax year. To operate fiscal accounting, your year-end does not have to be exactly 5 April – it can be a day or two earlier or later – and the Revenue will accept a year-end of 31 March as fiscal accounting, if you ask.

If you choose some other year-end, your tax affairs will be more complicated, especially in the opening years. To find out which profits are taxed in the first two or three years of business, you need to work through the following steps:

- find the first tax year that includes the end of an accounting period falling at least 12 months after the date you started in business. Tax for that year is based on profits for the 12 months up to the end of that accounting period
- tax for the next and subsequent tax years is based on profits for the accounting year ending in that tax year – i.e. normal current-year basis applies
- there will be one or two opening tax years falling before the one you identified in the first step. For the first of these you are taxed on your actual profits for the tax year – i.e. from the date you start in business until the following 5 April
- if there is a second opening year and the end of an

accounting period falls during that year, you are taxed on your profits for the first 12 months of business. If no accounting period ends during the year, you are taxed on your actual profits for the tax year – see Example 1 below.
FA 1994 s200–201

Splitting your profits between tax years
Sometimes, you are taxed on your actual profits for the tax year, or your profits for 12 months rather than profits for an accounting period. This can happen in the opening and closing years of a business. To find the relevant amounts, you may need to take a proportion of the profits for one or more accounting years. Where just one accounting period needs to be apportioned, you can do this as follows:

$$\text{Profits for tax year} = \text{Profits for accounting period} \times \text{number of months of accounting period falling into the tax year} \div \text{total months in accounting period}$$

If two periods straddle the tax year, you will need to add to the sum above a proportion of the second accounting period's profits worked out in the same way.

Your tax office will usually accept apportioning done on a monthly basis, but strictly speaking it can insist that you do the sums on a daily basis. You should, in any case, choose the daily basis if it would produce a lower tax bill.

EXAMPLE 1

Peter Piper started in business on 1 October 1994. He wants his year-end to be 31 December and opts to end his first accounting period on 31 December 1995. His profits for the first two accounting periods are as follows:

1 October 1994 – 31 December 1995 (15 months) £15,000
1 January 1996 – 31 December 1996 (12 months) £16,000

Peter finds the first tax year in which an accounting period ends more than 12 months after the start of business. This is 1995–6. Tax for that year is based on profits for the 12 months to 31 December 1995 – i.e. £15,000 × $^{12}/_{15}$ = £12,000. Thereafter, current-year basis applies, so tax for 1996–7 is based on profits for the accounting year ending in that tax year – i.e. £16,000.

For the first year of business, 1994–5, Peter's actual profits are taxed. This means his profits for the period from 1 October 1994 to 5 April 1995 – a period of roughly six months. Therefore, he takes £15,000 × 6⁄15 = £6,000. To summarise, the profits to be taxed in the first three years of business are:

1994–5 tax year (6⁄15 × £15,000)	£6,000
1995–6 tax year (12⁄15 × £15,000)	£12,000
1996–7 tax year	£16,000

Overlap profit

Part of your profits may be taxed twice, because of the opening-year rules. For example, Peter Piper (see Example 1) was taxed twice on part of the profits for his accounting period: (6⁄15 × £15,000) + (12⁄15 × £15,000) = £18,000. That's £3,000 more than his profits for that period. The £3,000 is called his *overlap profit*.

You eventually get tax relief on your overlap profit, but usually not until your business ceases, by which time inflation may have seriously eroded the value of the relief. You may get the relief earlier if you change your accounting date.

FA 1994 s205

Choosing your accounting year-end

The date you choose for drawing up your accounts is an important decision for tax planning:

- if you expect your profits to rise steadily, consider a year-end early in the tax year. This will maximise the delay between earning your profits and paying tax on them, which is good for your cash-flow
- a year-end early in the tax year also gives you plenty of time to sort out your tax accounts before sending them to your tax office – this will be especially important once the new self-assessment system starts in April 1997
- but a year-end early in the tax year means carrying forward higher overlap profits
- if you want your tax affairs to be as simple as possible, opt for fiscal accounting (see p. 183).

Rules for businesses which started up before 6 April 1994

Apart from the opening years, your profits are taxed on a *preceding year basis* – i.e. your tax bill for 1995–6 is based on profits for the accounting year which ended in the 1994–5 tax year.

If you started your business in 1993–4, special opening-year rules may still apply to you:

- for 1994–5, you had a choice of being taxed on either profits for the first 12 months of business or actual profits made during the tax year
- for 1995–6, the preceding-year basis applies, if you chose to be taxed on the first 12 months' profits last year. If in 1994–5 you chose to be taxed on actual profits, you will also be taxed on actual profits this tax year
- for 1996–7, if the preceding-year basis applied last year, the transitional rules (see below) will apply for this year. If you were taxed on actual profits in 1995–6, you will once again be taxed on actual profits in 1996–7.

Transitional rules for 1996–7

The 1995–6 tax year is the last one in which you were taxed on a preceding year basis. From 1997–8 onwards, the current year basis will apply. Meanwhile 1996–7 is a transitional year during which profits for two accounting periods (the year ending in 1995–6 and the year ending in 1996–7) need to be taxed. To avoid huge tax bills for 1996–7, you will be taxed on *half* the sum of the profits for these two accounting years.

Since half your profits for the accounting years ending in 1995–6 and 1996–7 will escape tax, it is worth having as high earnings as possible during these two years. But there are new anti-avoidance rules, including hefty fines, to stop your artificially boosting your profits. Basically, the rules will catch you if the main benefit of any change you make is a tax advantage. Changes for purely commercial reasons should be accepted as genuine.

FA Sch20, Inland Revenue Press Release 29 November 1994

EXAMPLE 2

Beth James runs a design consultancy as a sole trader. She has been in business since 1992 and makes up her accounts each year to 30 September. This is how her trading profits are taxed so she is ready for a current year basis of assessment in 1997–8.

Tax year	Trading period used to calculate tax	Basis of assessment
1994–5	12 months to 30.9.93	preceding year
1995–6	12 months to 30.9.94	preceding year
1996–7	12 months to 30.9.95	transitional year
	12 months to 30.9.96	
1997–8	12 months to 30.9.97	current year

As can be seen, for the tax year 1996–7 two trading years' profits will have to be assessed so that Beth's accounts are up-to-date in time for assessment on a current-year basis in 1997–8. However, she won't have to pay two years' tax at one time. Profits from the two trading years making up the transitional period will be added together and an *appropriate percentage* of the profits will be determined for the calculation of tax. Broadly, this will work out at 50 per cent of the total profits over the two-year period – see Example 3, below.

EXAMPLE 3

Beth James's transitional period covers the two trading years 1.10.94 to 30.9.95 and 1.10.95 to 30.9.96 (24 months). The *appropriate percentage* of the profits to be taxed is found using the formula 365 ÷ *n*, where *n* is the total number of days in the transitional period. However, the Revenue will accept any other reasonable time-based calculation, e.g. weeks, months or even fractions of months. For our example we will use months, in which case the formula is 12 ÷ 24 (24 being the number of months in the transitional period).

Profits for trading year 1.10.94 to 30.9.95	£10,000
Profits for trading year 1.10.95 to 30.9.96	£12,000
Total profits for transitional period	£22,000
The appropriate percentage (12 ÷ 24)	0.5
£22,000 divided by 0.5	£11,000

So £11,000 is the figure that will be assessed for tax during Beth's transitional period; i.e. only half of the profits she made during that time will be taxed.

Closing a business

If your business started on or after 6 April 1994, for the year in which your business closes down you are taxed on profits for the period running from the end of the last accounting year to the date of closure. From these profits, you deduct any overlap relief (see p. 185) due to you, before tax is worked out.

More complicated rules apply if you started your business before 6 April 1994. In the last tax year in which you are in business, you are taxed on your actual profits for the year. In your last-but-two and last-but-one tax years, your tax inspector can choose to revise your tax bills and base them both (not just for one year) on actual profits for each of those tax years. The inspector will do this if it will result in a higher tax bill than under the normal preceding-year rules.

FA 1994 s204, ICTA 1988 s63

Income and expenses after you close down

If you get any income from your business after you have closed, it will be taxed under Schedule D Case VI (see p. 41) as earned income in the tax year in which you get it. However, if you receive it within six years of closing down, you can choose within two years to have it treated as income you got on the last day of your business.

Usually, if bills come in after you have closed down, you can claim tax relief on them only if you also have some late income from the business against which you can set the expenses. But from 29 November 1994 you can set certain expenses against any other income or gains which you have in the year the bill turns up. The expenses which qualify for this relief are:

- the costs of putting right a defective product or service which you supplied, the cost of insuring for such claims against you and legal costs connected with such claims
- debts which you had taken into account in drawing up the profits of your business but which now turn out to be bad debts; and the costs of collecting debts that had been included in your profits.

ICTA 1988 s103–110, Budget Press Release 29 November 1994

When tax is paid

For 1996–7, tax is due in two equal instalments on 31 January 1997 and 31 July 1997. Some people, mainly sole traders and partners, will have to make payments on account for the tax year before the return for that year is due. These payments will be made on 31 January of the tax year and 31 July following the end of the tax year. So for the 1996–7 tax year, the first payment on account will be due by 31 January 1997 with the second payment due by 31 July 1997.

If these two payments amount to more or less than the tax actually due for the year, then a balancing payment (if you have paid too little tax) or repayment (if you have paid too much) will be made on the following 31 January. If you need to make a payment on account in January 1997, the Revenue will notify you in good time (by October 1996).

When you submit your tax return, you don't always need to send a balance sheet and you don't need to have your accounts audited. If your total turnover is less than £15,000 a year, you can submit only *three-line accounts* giving your total turnover, total business purchases and expenses, and your net profit. It is a good idea to make sure the records you have provide you with all the information you will need to cope with self-assessment. You can do this by asking your tax office to send you a copy of the new tax return so that you can check on the questions you will need to answer. You can also get a copy of the Inland Revenue's booklet *A guide to keeping records for the self-employed* (SA/BK3). Alternatively, check with your accountant if you use one. Basically, however, make sure you keep records of:

- all receipts and expenses
- all goods purchased and sold
- all supporting documents relating to the transactions of the businesses such as accounts, books, deeds, contracts, vouchers, receipts and computer records.

There are stiff penalties for failure to keep records – see p. 78.
TMA 1970 (as amended by FA 1994 and 1995) s12B (1)(b), (2), (3), (6)

Avoiding problems

There are some simple rules to cut down the chances of being investigated by the Revenue (see p. 76):

- find out the profit margin for people in similar businesses and, if yours is lower, send a note saying why

- if the income you take out of the business is very low, e.g. because you are living on savings, tell your tax inspector why this is so
- try to send your accounts in on time
- don't miss out simple things, such as National Savings Investment account interest, from your tax return
- if possible, send a balance sheet and list of fixed assets as well as a profit and loss account
- if you've made a loss, explain it.

ICTA 1988 s60–s63; TMA 1970 s31, s55, s86, FA 1994 Sch 19 s29

Checklist: starting a business

- decide whether to register for value added tax (VAT) – see p. 207
- inform the DSS
- inform your local tax inspector
- make a list of fixed assets, e.g. office equipment, car
- get cash books to show cash paid into (and taken out of) the bank, and a book for petty cash
- set up an accounting system (e.g. in a book or on a computer) to show details of sales and purchases. Sort the purchases into different types, e.g. stationery, travel, heating and lighting
- if you need stocks of raw materials and other goods, keep records of what you've bought, what you've sold, and what has gone from stock
- get written receipts and file them in date order
- get a notebook to record items for which there's no receipt
- plan how you are going to pay your tax bill – e.g. by putting money aside each month
- if a car is used partly for your business, keep a record of business mileage, petrol, and all running costs
- if you are going to use in your business items you already own, e.g. a car, typewriter, computer, include them in your accounts. You will be able to claim capital allowances on them (and you may be able to recover the VAT)
- choose your accounting year-end – see p. 185
- consider employing your spouse or making your spouse a partner – see p. 206
- ask for any expenditure before you start business to count as pre-trading expenses – see p. 192
- if you make a loss in the first year, remember you can set it off against other income – see p. 203
- make sure you have adequate life insurance and pension cover. Think about *permanent health insurance* in case you're ever too ill to work.

Working out taxable profits

You pay tax on the taxable profits of your business. If you were working out your taxable profits from scratch, it would be your takings during your accounting year, i.e. cash received during the year for the sales you make, plus:

- money owed *to you* at the end of the accounting year
- money owed *by you* at the beginning of the year
- the increase in value of your stocks during the year (see p. 196)

less the following deductions:

- allowable business expenses – see p. 192
- money owed *to you* at the beginning of the year
- money owed *by you* at the end of the year
- capital allowances – see p. 196
- losses – see p. 202.

In practice, you may start off by working out your profit under normal accounting rules. You then turn this into your taxable profits by adding back things which aren't allowable business expenses (e.g. depreciation and your wages) and deducting things on which you can get tax relief (capital allowances).

In a very few cases (e.g. a barrister) your sales figure may be taken as the cash you receive during your accounting year for work done – regardless of when you actually did the work. So you can ignore money owed at the start or end of the accounting year.

If you take items out of stock for your own use you normally have to include these in sales at the normal selling price.
CIR v. Gardner Mountain & D'Ambrumenil 29 TC 69; Sharkey v. Wernher 36 TC 275

Other income

If you have any other income which is not part of your trading income, it is not part of the taxable profits of your business. How any non-trading income is taxed depends on where it comes from. For example, bank interest is taxed as investment income.

Allowable business expenses

An expense is allowable only if incurred *'wholly and exclusively'* for the business. Table 1 opposite lists expenses you will probably be allowed and those you will not. But business needs vary widely and an expense allowable for one business may not be for another. If in doubt, claim.

Note that the *'wholly and exclusively'* rule does not mean that you can't claim anything if, for example, you sometimes use your car for business, sometimes for private purposes. If the car is used wholly for business purposes on some occasions, then you can normally claim the proportion of car expenses which is attributable to business use; you'll have to agree the proportion with your tax inspector. You can usually claim the same proportion of your car expenses as your business mileage bears to your total mileage. However, if you use the car for a trip which is part pleasure, part business, you may not be able to claim any of the costs of the trip as an allowable expense. This is known as the *dual-purpose rule*. For example, you can't normally claim the expenses of a business trip which is combined with a holiday. However, if you attend a conference during the trip, the conference fee will be allowable.

You can normally claim part of your home expenses, e.g. heating, lighting, insurance, if you use part of your home for business. Home expenses are usually shared out on the basis of the number and size of rooms. If you claim costs of using your home for business, beware of a possible capital gains tax bill if you sell your home – see p. 225.

Capital expenditure, e.g. what you spend on buying cars, machinery, improving property, is not an allowable expense, nor is depreciation, such as that on cars. But you may get capital allowances – see p. 196.
ICTA 1988 s74

Pre-trading expenses

If you spend money, e.g. rent and rates on your business premises, expenses incurred up to seven years before your business actually starts will probably count as pre-trading expenditure. It will be treated as a loss in your first year of trading, and you can get loss relief – see p. 202.
ICTA 1988 s401

Table 1: Business expenses

	Normally allowed	Not allowed
basic costs and general running expenses	cost of goods bought for resale and raw materials used in business (see p. 196 for how much to claim); discounts allowed on sales; advertising; delivery charges; initial cost of computer software with a limited useful lifetime (see p. 200); heating; lighting; cleaning; business rates; proportion of the council tax on a second home if let out or used for business; telephone; rent of business premises; replacement of small tools and special clothing; postage; stationery; relevant books and magazines; accountants' fees (mostly); bank charges on business accounts; VAT if you're not registered (see p. 209)	initial cost of buildings, machinery, vehicles, equipment, permanent advertising signs – but see *Capital allowances*, on p. 196; any money paid as a result of extortion (on or after 30 November 1993)
use of home for work	proportion of telephone, lighting, heating, cleaning, insurance; proportion of rent and domestic rates for periods prior to their abolition (they have not been abolished in Northern Ireland) if you use part of home *exclusively* for business – but watch out for capital gains tax (see p. 225)	council tax paid on your main home
wages and salaries	wages, salaries, redundancy and some leaving payments paid to employees; payments on counselling for employees made redundant; pensions for ex-employees and dependants	your own wages or salary, or that of any business partner
workplace nurseries	cost of some types of child-care provision for employees' children	cost of premises and equipment – but see *Capital allowances*, on p. 196
tax and National Insurance	employer's National Insurance contributions for employees; VAT on allowable expenses if you're not a registered trader for VAT (and, sometimes, even if you are – see p. 209)	income tax; capital gains tax; inheritance tax; your own National Insurance
entertaining	entertainment of own staff, e.g. Christmas party	any business entertainment

	Normally allowed	Not allowed
gifts	gifts costing up to £15 a year to any single person so long as the gift advertises your business and is not food, drink, tobacco or vouchers for goods	most other goods
travelling	cost of travel and accommodation on business trips; travel between different places of work; *running costs of own car*: whole of cost, excluding depreciation, if used wholly for business, proportion if used privately too; provided trips are exclusively for business purposes, the cost of travel to and from the UK to carry on business performed wholly outside the UK	travel between home and business; meals, except the reasonable cost of evening meals and breakfast on overnight trips; cost of buying a car or van – but see *Capital allowances*, on p. 196
interest payments	interest on, and costs of arranging, overdrafts and loans for business purposes – see p. 30	interest on capital paid or credited to partners; interest on overdue tax
hire purchase and leasing	hire charge part of payments (i.e. the amount you pay *less* the cash price); rent paid for leasing car or machinery, for example, though it may be restricted for expensive cars	cash price of what you're buying on hire purchase (you may get *capital allowances* on cash price – but see p. 199)
hiring	reasonable charge for hire of capital goods, including cars	
insurance	business insurance, e.g. employer's liability, fire and theft, motor; life insurance, personal accident insurance, permanent health insurance and private medical insurance for employees	your own life, accident, permanent health and private medical insurance
trade marks, designs and patents	fees paid to register trade mark or design; or to obtain a patent	cost of buying a patent from someone else – you may get *capital allowances*, see p. 201

	Normally allowed	Not allowed
legal costs	costs of: recovering debts, defending business rights, preparing service agreements, appealing against rates on business premises, renewing a lease with the landlord's consent for a period not exceeding 50 years (but not if a premium is paid)	expenses (including stamp duty) for acquiring land, buildings or leases; fines and other penalties for breaking the law; costs of fighting a tax case
repairs	normal repairs and maintenance to premises or equipment	cost of additions, alterations, improvements
debts	specific bad debts and, in part, doubtful debts	general reserve for bad or doubtful debts
subscriptions and contributions	payments which secure benefits for your business or staff; genuine contributions to approved local enterprise agency; payments to professional bodies which have arrangements with the Revenue (in some cases only a proportion); contributions to Training and Enterprise Councils	payments to political parties, churches, charities (but small gifts to *local* churches and charities may be allowable)
training	subject to certain conditions, cost of training employees to acquire and improve skills needed for their current jobs; cost of training employees who are leaving or who have left in new work skills	
secondments	cost of seconding employees on a temporary basis to certain educational bodies, including local education authorities and institutions maintained by them, and to charitable institutions	

ICTA 1988 s74; Coltness Iron Co v. Black 1 TC 287 (machinery); ICTA 1988 s577; FA 1988 s72 (entertaining); ICTA 1988 s577 (gifts); Newsom v. Robertson 33 TC 452, Caillebotte v. Quinn 1975, 50 TC 222 (subsistence when travelling); TMA 1970 s90 (interest on overdue tax); Darngavil Coal Co v. Francis 77 TC1 (hire purchase); ICTA 1988 s83, s520 (trade marks, patents, etc.); Smith's Potato Estates Ltd v. Bolland 30 TC 267 (legal costs); ICTA 1988 s79, s577; ICTA 1988 s86, s588 (training and secondments); ICTA 1988 s155 (workplace nurseries)

Stock

You can claim as an allowable expense the cost of raw materials you use in your business, and the cost of things you buy for resale. But you can claim only the cost of business materials which you actually sell during your accounting year – i.e. the value of your stocks of these things at the start of the year *plus* anything you spend on buying more during the year, *minus* the value of your stocks at the end of the year.

If you have stocks which can be sold only for less than you paid for them, you will normally be allowed to value them at what they would fetch if sold now. This means for tax purposes that you can value stock *at the lower of cost or market value*. No other method of valuing stock is allowed by your tax inspector, regardless of what is allowed under accounting rules.

When you value your stocks at the start and end of the accounting year, you need to add in the value of *work-in-progress*. This is the value of work which has begun, but which isn't completed, e.g. products half-way through the manufacturing process, or part-completed work if you're a builder, solicitor, engineer, etc. Work-in-progress can be valued in one of the following ways:

- cost of raw materials used
- cost plus overheads
- cost plus overheads plus profit contribution.

Once you've chosen a way of valuing work-in-progress, this is how it must be valued each accounting year.

If you are closing a business, your stock will be valued either at the price it's sold at, if sold to someone else in business, or at the price it would fetch if sold in the open market.

ICTA 1988 s100–103, SP 3/90

Capital allowances

When you work out your taxable profits, you can't deduct anything you spend on capital assets or equipment, e.g. machinery or cars. Money spent in this way is not an allowable business expense. But you can still get tax relief on these sorts of things by claiming capital allowances on:

- plant and machinery (e.g. vans, machines, typewriters, computers)
- motor cars
- buildings (e.g. industrial, agricultural, hotels, in enterprise zones)
- patents, know-how and scientific research.

To get a capital allowance, expenditure must be '*wholly and exclusively*' for the business. But again, on anything used partly for business, partly privately, you will get a proportion of the capital allowance, depending on the proportion of business use.

If you buy equipment for private use and then use it in your business, you can claim a capital allowance on its market value at the time you start using it for business.

How you pay for the equipment doesn't make any difference to the capital allowance. If you pay by a loan or by bank overdraft, the interest is an allowable business expense, not part of the cost of the asset. In the same way, hire-purchase charges are a business expense.
CAA 1990, FA 1994, s211

VAT
For how to deal with VAT on items on which you claim a capital allowance, see p. 209.

Plant and machinery
You can get a capital allowance of up to 25 per cent of the cost of plant and machinery for the accounting year in which you buy it. The rest of the cost is written off over the following years at up to 25 per cent of the remaining value each year. This is how it works. The cost of plant or machinery you buy goes into a *pool of expenditure*. At the end of the year, you can claim up to 25 per cent of the value of the pool as a *writing-down allowance* – this can be deducted from your profits for that year. You have to claim your allowance within two years.

The pool is reduced by what you claim: what's left is known as the *written-down value*, and becomes your pool for the start of the next accounting year. Any purchases in the next year are added to the pool, and at the end of the year you can claim 25 per cent of whatever the pool is now worth. Note that you can claim less than the full 25 per cent writing-down allowance (see Example 5, below) – you deduct only what you claim from your pool.

If you sell something on which you have claimed capital allowances, the proceeds (up to the original cost of the item or sometimes the market value) must be deducted from your pool of expenditure before working out your writing-down allowance for the year in which you sell. If the proceeds come to more than the value of your pool, the excess (the *balancing charge*) is added to your profit.

You can claim capital allowances in full only on expenditure which is 'wholly and exclusively' for the business. Things bought partly for business, partly for private use, should be kept separate from other business assets in their own pools. You can claim a proportion of the maximum capital allowances, in line with business use.
CAA 1990 s24, s25, s140, s141

EXAMPLE 4

Herbert Hughes works out what he can claim in capital allowances for his accounting year ending on 30 April 1996. His pool of expenditure at the start of the year was £6,782. During the year, Herbert had bought a new van, costing £8,880, trading in his old van for £2,650. He also bought some shelving for his stock room for £960.

Herbert first adds the new purchases to his pool of expenditure: £6,782 + £8,880 + £960 = £16,622. He then subtracts the trade-in value of his old van: £16,622 – £2,650 = £13,972; this is the value of his pool of expenditure on 30 April 1996. He can claim a maximum writing-down allowance of 25 per cent of his pool of expenditure, i.e. 25 per cent of £13,972 = £3,493.

The value of his pool of expenditure at the start of his next accounting year is £13,972 – £3,493 = £10,479.

EXAMPLE 5

Mary Worsley bought some machinery costing £10,000 in her accounting year to 30 June 1995. She could claim a writing-down allowance of 25 per cent of this, i.e. 25 per cent of £10,000 = £2,500. However, her taxable profit for the year is just £6,000, while her outgoings and allowances come to £4,000. Assuming that she has no other taxable income, she will pay tax on £6,000 – £4,000 = £2,000 of taxable income. If she claims the full £2,500 capital allowance, she will have wasted £500 of allowances. So she decides to claim just £2,000 of capital allowances, 20 per cent of her pool expenditure.

That leaves £8,000 as the written-down value of Mary's pool of expenditure, to be carried over to next year.

Leasing

If, instead of buying an asset, you choose to lease it, you can claim the lease rental as an allowable expense, as long as you are using the asset in your own business. The person or company from whom you lease can normally claim the capital allowances.

Cars

As with plant and machinery, you can claim a writing-down allowance of up to 25 per cent for each year in which you own the car. Cars must go into a separate pool of expenditure. Lorries and vans do not count as cars – they can go into the main pool with other plant and machinery.

If the car cost more than £12,000, it has its own pool of expenditure (i.e. separate even from other cars). In this case, the maximum writing-down allowance in any year is £3,000.

CAA 1990 s34–s36, s41

Assets with a life of less than five years

With things like computers, which last for only a few years, you could find yourself still claiming capital allowances for the cost after you had got rid of them. Suppose, for example, you bought a personal computer for £1,000, and claimed the full 25 per cent capital allowance on it each year. The following table shows what the written-down value would be year by year:

Year	25 per cent allowance	Written-down value at end of year
1	£250	£750
2	£188	£562
3	£140	£422
4	£106	£316
5	£79	£237

If you scrapped the computer after four years, there would still be a written-down value of £316 in your pool of expenditure, and you'd write this off only over several more years.

With equipment which you expect to scrap or sell within five years, you can opt for special treatment which allows you to write off the value of the equipment when you get rid of it. You must keep each such *short-life asset* in its own pool of expenditure. If you sell it for less than its written-down value, the difference can be subtracted from your profits for the year, as a *balancing allowance* (if you scrap it, you can claim the whole written-down value as a balancing allowance). If you sell it for more than its written-down value, the difference is added to your profits as a balancing charge (see p. 198). If you still have the equipment after five years, its written-down value is added to your main pool of expenditure as if it had never been treated separately.
CAA 1990 s37, s38

Computer software
The yearly writing-down allowance of 25 per cent for plant and machinery is normally available for software whether or not bought at the same time as computer hardware. If the software has a useful life of less than two years, or some other limited period if your tax office agrees, you can instead claim the cost as an allowable business expense – see p. 192.

For software bought before 9 March 1992 you can choose to add it to your pool of expenditure on capital assets or as a business expense in the year of purchase.
CAA s67, Revenue Tax Bulletin, November 1993

Buildings
You can claim writing-down allowances on some buildings at 4 per cent of their original cost excluding land:

- industrial buildings, e.g. factories, warehouses
- homes built for letting on assured tenancies, provided certain conditions are met

- agricultural buildings, including farmhouses, farm buildings, cottages, fences, roads
- hotels or hotel extensions of 10 bedrooms or more which meet certain conditions.

With industrial buildings and hotels in enterprise zones, you can claim 100 per cent of the cost in the first year, including the cost of fixed plant or machinery in the buildings. If you claim less than 100 per cent, you can claim a writing-down allowance of up to 25 per cent of the original cost, starting the following year.
CAA 1990 s1–s21 (industrial buildings and hotels); s84–s97 (homes let on assured tenancies); s122–s130 (agricultural buildings)

Patents, know-how and scientific research
You can claim a 25 per cent writing-down allowance on the cost of buying a patent to use in your business, in the same way as for plant and machinery. Note that you cannot claim an allowance for the cost of creating and registering your own patent (though you may be able to claim expenses for these – see p. 192).

You can get 25 per cent allowances for the cost of know-how – any industrial information or techniques likely to assist in manufacturing, mining, agriculture, forestry or fishing. And you can claim 100 per cent of the cost of capital expenditure for the purposes of scientific research (though not on land or houses), in the year of expenditure only.
ICTA 1988 s520–s533; CAA 1990 s136–s139

New (and closing) businesses
For business set up before 6 April 1994, working out capital allowances when you start up or close down can be complicated. Some of your profits may be taxed twice and others not at all. By contrast, capital allowances are worked out according to a separate system which ensures that allowances are given for all eligible expenditure but are given only once. The rule is that you get the allowances in the first tax year available (and not in the following tax year if the assessment is based on the same taxable profits).

If you've bought something in an accounting period and the profits for that period are *not* assessed for tax purposes, you get the allowance as if you had bought the equipment in the following accounting period. But if the following accounting period is the last year of the business (because you're closing it down), you get the allowance in the preceding year.

A much simpler system applies to businesses set up on or after 6 April 1994 and to all businesses from 1997–8 onwards. Even though some profits may be taxed twice in the early years of your business, the system of relief for overlap profit ensures that over the lifetime of your business, all your profits are taxed just once. So capital allowances can be given as a straightforward deduction in working out your profits.

CAA 1990 s147, s160, FA 1994, s211

Combining capital and other allowances

Claiming your full capital allowances each year could cause other allowances and reliefs to be wasted. When deciding how much to claim, first work out by how much personal and any other allowances and any loss relief (see below) will reduce your profits. Capital allowances are not wasted if you claim less than the full amount. What you do not claim will remain in your capital pool, making larger allowances possible in future years.

Losses

If you make a loss in your business, there are several things you can do with it. The options open to you depend on whether your business is new, ongoing or closing down, and whether your business was set up before or after 6 April 1994.

For businesses that started up before 6 April 1994 a loss within an accounting year that does not coincide with a tax year should, strictly speaking, be apportioned to the correct tax years. In practice, your tax inspector will normally let you treat it as a loss for the tax year in which the accounting year ends. The only time this won't be allowed is during the opening years of a new business.

For businesses starting up on or after 6 April 1994, new rules apply: losses will be calculated in the same way as profits – i.e. a loss for a given tax year will be the loss for the accounting period ending within that tax year. The new rules will also apply to pre-April 1994 businesses from 1997–8 onwards, with transitional rules applying to losses and loss relief for the 1996–7 tax year.

New businesses

As well as the reliefs available to an ongoing business (see below), there is a special option if you make a loss during the first four tax years of your business. You can set it against other income (including earnings from a job) in the three tax years before the year in which the loss was made, and so get a tax rebate. You start by setting the loss against the earliest year first.

To get this relief, you must be able to show that you have been trading on a commercial basis and can be expected to make profits within a reasonable period.

Claim this relief within two years of the end of the tax year in which the loss occurred.

ICTA 1988 s381

Ongoing businesses: relief against other income and gains

For businesses set up before 6 April 1994, you can ask for the loss to be set against:

- any other income being assessed in the tax year in which the accounting year ends – e.g. profits from the previous accounting year, earnings from a job, income from investments, and so on, or
- income of the following tax year, provided the business carries on during that year.

Similarly, for businesses set up on or after 6 April 1994, and for all business from 1997–8, you can ask for the loss to be set against:

- any other income being assessed in the year the loss occurs, or
- income in the previous tax year.

For all businesses, whichever of the two options you choose, the whole of the loss must be used up against that year's income, or as much as possible if the income is too low. This means that other outgoings and allowances which you qualify for could be wasted. You can use the second option to take up any unused part of the loss relief. If the loss exceeds your income, you can set off the unrelieved part against any capital gains.

The time limit for claiming relief against other income or gains is two years from the end of the tax year of the loss.

ICTA 1988 s380

Ongoing businesses: relief against future profits

If you can't use up all the loss against other income and capital gains, you can set the loss against the income of the business in future years. The losses can be carried forward indefinitely until used up. The advantage of doing this is that it is relatively straightforward, but there are disadvantages too:

- the loss can be set off only against income from the same business
- there may be a long delay before the loss can be translated into cash savings – see Example 7 below
- the whole loss has to be set off against the available profits before any outgoings or allowance which may, therefore, be wasted.

To carry forward losses indefinitely until they are used up, submit a claim within six years of the end of the tax year in which the loss occurred.
ICTA 1988 s385

EXAMPLE 6

Suppose you have other income of £10,000, and outgoings and allowances of £4,000. In this case your taxable income will be £6,000. If you have losses of £8,000, and ask for them to be set against other income, the whole of the £8,000 will be set off first against your other income, even though you need only £6,000 in losses to reduce your tax bill to zero. You will not be able to carry forward the remaining losses to the future, so you will have lost the benefit of £2,000 of outgoings and allowances.

EXAMPLE 7

Jessica Jones has a part-time job as a book-keeper from which she earns £10,000 a year. She has outgoings and allowances that (to simplify the Example) remain constant at £4,000 a year.

Jessica has also run a business as a theatrical costumier for many years. She makes up her accounts to 31 December each year and her recent profits are:

Accounting year	
1 January – 31 December 1993	£10,000
1 January – 31 December 1994: loss	(£15,000)
1 January – 31 December 1995	£5,000

1 January – 31 December 1996	£10,000
1 January – 31 December 1997	£15,000

Instead of insisting that Jessica splits the loss made in 1994 between the two tax years it straddles, the tax inspector allows her to treat it as a loss for the 1994–5 tax year. Jessica has to decide the best way to claim relief for the loss. Her options are set out in the following table:

	Tax years: 1994–5	1995–6	1996–7	1997–8
Income without loss relief				
Business	£10,000	nil	£ 7,500 [1]	£15,000
Job	£10,000	£10,000	£10,000	£10,000
TOTAL	£20,000	£10,000	£17,500	£25,000
Setting loss against other income for 1994–5				
Income	£ 5,000	£10,000	£17,500	£25,000
less				
Allowances	£ 4,000	£ 4,000	£ 4,000	£ 4,000
Tax to pay[2]	£ 200	£ 1,340	£ 3,215	£ 5,090
Total tax with this option: £9,845				
Setting loss against income for the following year (1995–6)				
Income	£20,000	nil	£12,500 [3]	£25,000
less				
Allowances	£ 4,000	nil [4]	£ 4,000	£ 4,000
Tax to pay [2]	£ 3,850	nil	£ 1,965	£ 5,090
Total tax with this option: £10,095				
Setting loss against future profits (1996–7 onwards)				
Income	£20,000	£10,000	£10,000	£17,500
less				
Allowances	£ 4,000	£ 4,000	£ 4,000	£ 4,000
Tax to pay [2]	£ 3,850	£ 1,340	£ 1,340	
Total tax to pay with this option: £9,745				

[1] Transitional-year profits – see p. 186.
[2] 1994–5 tax rates for that year. 1995–6 rates for subsequent years.
[3] Part of loss carried forward to this year.
[4] With no income, Jessica's allowances can't be used.

Although carrying the loss forward to set against future profits would result in less tax in total over the years, Jessica chooses to claim immediate relief by setting the loss against her other income for 1994–5. This cuts her tax bill at the time she makes the loss, which helps her cash flow.

You as an employer

When you employ staff on a permanent basis you have several duties as an employer. These include:

- acting as a collector of taxes and deducting income tax and Class 1 National Insurance contributions from your employee's pay (assuming your employee earns more than a certain amount – £61 or more a week in the 1996–7 tax year)
- paying National Insurance as an employer – for rates see box below.

Your spouse
You may be able to save tax by employing your spouse. If he or she has no other income, you can pay your spouse up to £3,765 in the 1996–7 tax year before any tax is due on it. But if weekly earnings exceed a certain amount (£61 a week – equivalent to £3,172 a year – in the 1996–7 tax year) both of you will have to pay National Insurance contributions.

National Insurance rates for employers in 1996–7

There's no National Insurance to pay on earnings below £61 a week. Above £61, rates are on a graduated scale. For earnings:

- from £61 up to £109 a week, 3 per cent on all earnings
- from £110 up to £154 a week, 5 per cent on all earnings
- from £155 up to £209 a week, 7 per cent on all earnings
- from £210 a week, 10.2 per cent on all earnings with no upper limit.

Note that rates are different where an employer runs a *contracted-out* pension scheme.

For employee rates, see p. 313.

Your own National Insurance contributions

You will have to pay Class 2 National Insurance contributions (unless your earnings from self-employment will be less than £3,430 for 1996–7) and you may also have to pay Class 4 contributions depending on your earnings.

Class 2 contributions are payable each month by direct debit. Class 2 is a flat-rate payment of £6.05 a week for the 1996–7 tax year. Paying Class 2 contributions entitles you to most contributory benefits, but not unemployment benefit or the earnings-related portion of the retirement pension.

Class 4 contributions are earnings-related and collected along with your tax payments. Until the 1995–6 tax year, you would have received tax relief on half your Class 4 contributions, but from 6 April 1996 this has been abolished. To compensate, the Class 4 contribution has been reduced to 6 per cent of net profits between £6,860 and £23,660 for the 1996–7 tax year. Paying Class 4 contributions doesn't entitle you to any benefits over and above those you get by paying Class 2.

There are special rules to prevent you paying more than a certain amount in all classes of National Insurance – see DSS leaflet *NP18*.

Value added tax

The current rate of VAT is 17½ per cent (8 per cent on domestic fuel). There are some goods on which the rate is zero, e.g. most food, books, newspapers, children's clothing and transport. And some goods are *exempt*, e.g. land, insurance, postage, education, and so on. But if you buy any goods or services for your business, it's likely that on some of those things you will be paying VAT. If you are registered for VAT, you will be able to claim that tax back once every three months. By doing this, you are lowering your costs. However, you must add VAT on to all the bills you send out or sales you make if, of course, they are items on which VAT is payable at 17½ per cent. By doing this you are increasing your selling prices, but not your income, because you have to hand over the VAT to Customs and Excise.

Handing over VAT on income you haven't yet received can cause cash-flow problems. But businesses with a yearly turnover below £350,000 have the option of handing over VAT only on income actually received. (This is known as *cash accounting* by Customs and Excise.)

Registering for VAT

From April 1996, you have to register for VAT if, at the end of any month, the value of your taxable supplies in the last year exceeds £47,000. You must also register if at any time you think it likely that the value of your taxable supplies over the next 30 days will exceed £47,000. Taxable supplies in this case means any supplies which are not exempt – so it includes zero-rated goods and services.

Below these levels, you can choose whether or not to register. Your choice depends upon:

- how much you can cut your costs by claiming VAT back on goods and services you buy for use in your business (which you can do if you register)
- whether your customers will be able to claim back VAT which you must add to your selling prices, and
- how tedious you find the record-keeping necessary to be registered for VAT.

For more information about VAT, contact your local VAT office (under *Customs and Excise* in the phone book).

Keeping records

If you are registered, you have to:

- give your customer a bill (and keep a copy yourself) which shows, among other things, your VAT registration number, your name and address, the amount payable before VAT and the amount of VAT due. (If you're a shopkeeper and the bill, including VAT, is £100 or less, you needn't show all these)
- keep a VAT account in your books which shows the amount of VAT you are reclaiming and the amount of VAT you are handing over
- fill in a form (VAT return) every three months (normally) and send it to Customs and Excise, showing what you are claiming and what you are handing over. Businesses which have been registered for VAT for at least a year, pay VAT regularly and have a yearly turnover of below £350,000 can opt for a yearly return (but you have to pay an estimated amount of VAT monthly by direct debit).

If you have charged more VAT on your sales than you can claim on your purchases, then you have to send the difference to the VAT Collector. If you can claim more on what you've bought than you can charge on what you have sold, the VAT Collector will pay you the difference.

Business expenses and capital allowances

If you *are not* a registered trader for VAT, include any VAT when claiming the cost of allowable business expenses. Also include VAT in the cost of any 'machinery or plant' on which you can claim a capital allowance.

If you *are* a registered trader for VAT, *don't* include VAT when claiming business expenses or capital allowances. However, you should include in your claim for expenses or capital allowances any VAT which you can't claim back through the normal VAT system, e.g. because it relates to part of your sales exempt from VAT.

But with cars (unless you're a car trader), include VAT in the cost you base your claim on for business expenses and capital allowances. The reason is that VAT on cars you buy can't be reclaimed, even if the expense is related to part of your business liable to VAT. Since 1 August 1992, however, private taxi and self-drive hire firms and driving schools have been permitted to recover the VAT they pay on cars purchased for their businesses.

Partnerships

If you are a business in a partnership with others, much of what has gone before about expenses and capital allowances is relevant. Self-assessment from April 1996 will also affect partnerships (see p. 71). Here is the old system of taxing profits; there are some special rules which apply only to partnerships.

Partnerships set up before 6 April 1994

Partnership profits are worked out in the same way as profits for a trade or business. But when it comes to working out how much tax to pay on those profits, the rules can, in some cases, be strange:

- **Rule one** All partners are *jointly and severally liable* for all tax on the profits from the partnership. This means that if one partner doesn't pay up, the others can be made to pay up instead.
- **Rule two** Rule one doesn't apply to the capital gains of a partnership, or to non-trading income (e.g. interest from a bank deposit account). In these cases, each partner pays the tax on his or her share, and if one doesn't pay, the others don't have to.

- **Rule three** The amount of tax charged on the partnership profits depends on the rates of tax paid by the individual partners. For example, a partnership might have very modest profits – £2,000, say. But if one of the partners is paying tax at the top rate of 40 per cent, part of the profits (in normal cases) will be taxed at 40 per cent.
- **Rule four** When the Revenue works out the bill on the partnership profits, the profits are divided between the partners in the same proportion as the partners themselves are sharing the profits in that tax year. So if the profits are £20,000, and there are two partners sharing the profits equally, the £20,000 will be divided equally between them. If one partner pays tax at 25 per cent, and the other at 40 per cent, the tax bill on the profits will be 25 per cent of £10,000 *plus* 40 per cent of £10,000 = £2,500 plus £4,000 = £6,500.
- **Rule five** Partnership income has been taxed on a preceding year basis – i.e. the partnership pays tax on profits from its accounting period ending in the previous tax year – but see p. 212 for transitional rules.
- **Rule six** The partners can agree to pay the tax in any proportions they like – they don't have to pay the tax on their share of the profits.

The effect of rules four and five

Rule four is based on the division of profits in the current tax year. But the income taxed in that year will – because of rule five – be from an earlier year, and may have been divided quite differently.
ICTA 1988 s277

EXAMPLE 8

Alice, Barbara and Caroline are in partnership. In the 1995–6 tax year, they decided to split the income of the partnership equally between them. But the tax bill for the 1995–6 tax year is based on the profit for their accounting period ending in the *previous* tax year (i.e. the 1994–5 tax year). Those profits *weren't* shared on an equal basis. Alice took half the profits, and Barbara and Caroline took 25 per cent each. The profits amounted to £30,000.

In the 1995–6 tax year, Alice pays tax at a top rate of 25 per cent (the basic rate of tax for 1995–6). The other two both pay tax at a top rate of 40 per cent. Here's how tax is calculated on the £30,000:

Total partnership profits for the 1995–6 year of assessment [1] £30,000

Partner	Received	Share [2]	Equals	Tax rate	Tax
Alice	£15,000	one-third	£10,000	25%	£2,500
Barbara	£7,500	one-third	£10,000	40%	£4,000
Caroline	£7,500	one-third	£10,000	40%	£4,000
	£30,000		£30,000		£10,500

So the partnership has to pay £10,500 in tax.

[1] i.e. the profits from the accounting period ending in 1994–5
[2] Divided on the 1995–6 basis of sharing

It looks as though Alice has done very well – £2,500 in tax on her share of £15,000. But of course the partners can divide up the tax bill in any way they like (see rule six). If they wish, they could agree that Alice pays half the £10,500 (£5,250) and Barbara and Caroline a quarter each (£2,625) – or any other split.

A new partner

Each time a partner joins (or leaves) the partnership, the partnership can come to an end. In fact it *will* come to an end, unless everyone who was a partner before the change *and* everyone who is a partner after the change agrees that it should continue (technically, by making a *continuation election* to the Revenue), *and* at least one of the partners before the change is still a partner after the change. If a partnership continues, the calculation of tax on partnership profits can be even more bizarre.
ICTA 1988 s113(2)

Partnerships set up on or after 6 April 1994

A new system of taxation applies to partnerships set up on or after 6 April 1994. The main changes from the old system are:

- partners are no longer jointly and severally liable for tax on the partnership profits. Instead, each partner is treated as if they run their own individual business based on their share of the partnership profits. Each partner is responsible only for tax on their own share of the profits
- the profits are both allocated between the partners and taxed on a current year basis, so the mismatch caused by

the effect of rules four and five (see p. 210) no longer applies
- under the pre-April 1994 system, partners have been able individually to claim expenses and capital allowances. Under the new system, these have to be deducted from the partnership income when profits are calculated
- for practical reasons each partnership will be asked to nominate one person who will send in a *partnership return* with details of all the partners and the allocation of profits between them. Partnership expenses must be claimed on the partnership return and if there are any queries the individual partner's tax returns will remain open until enquiries into the partnership return is complete. The nominated partner will deal with any enquiries concerning the partnership return and this person can be replaced by a partner nominated by the Revenue if he or she fails to complete it
- continuation elections are no longer relevant when the members of a partnership change. Because each partner is treated as if they run their own business, the normal opening and closing rules (see pages 183 and 188) apply individually to each of the partners affected by the change.

FA 1994 s215

Transitional rules and tax planning

For partnerships set up before 6 April 1994, the new system will apply from 1997–8 onwards. The transitional rules described on p. 186 will apply for calculating profits for the 1996–7 tax year.

However, established partnerships can move on to the new system earlier than 6 April 1997 if there is a change in the members of the partnership and the partners do not make a continuation election. The existing partnership is deemed to cease from the date of the changes and the old-system closing-year rules apply (see p. 188). A new partnership is deemed to start up from the date of change and the new-system opening rules apply (see p. 183). Partnerships which move on to the new system early are not affected by the transitional-year rules.

Whether switching early to the new system results in less tax to pay overall depends on the pattern of profits. Ask your accountant to work out the most advantageous option and timing for your partnership.

Partnership losses

Partnerships have much the same options as individuals for dealing with losses – see p. 202. If a partnership makes a loss, the individual partners 'own' the losses in the same proportion as they would have actually received the profits. Carrying back of losses isn't allowed, except for a new partner. And it isn't allowed if the new partner is married to an existing partner and the partnership continues.

Individual partners can treat losses in different ways – i.e. they don't all have to treat them in the same way. For example, one could set losses against other income and capital gains for the same tax year; another could carry them forward against future profits from the partnership.

Limited partners

The losses a limited partner can set against other income is limited broadly to the amount of capital he or she has contributed.
ICTA 1988 s117

Pension for partners

There are special rules where a pension is paid to a partner, or to the widow or dependant of a partner. In brief:

- take the partner's *actual profits* – i.e. what he or she actually declared in the tax return – for the last seven years in which he or she spent substantially the whole of his or her time in acting as a partner
- separately for each year, multiply the profits by the Retail Prices Index (RPI) for December in the final tax year and divide them by the RPI for December in the year in which the profits were charged to tax
- take the average of the three highest figures and divide by two.

The result is the maximum pension which counts as earned income (though it can be increased by the RPI every December). Payments above that limit are investment income. The payments reduce the partnership's income for tax purposes, but payments *within* the limit can't reduce the partnership's (or anyone else's) investment income.
ICTA 1988 s628

12 *HOMES AND LAND*

- Tax relief on mortgage interest is usually restricted to loans totalling no more than £30,000, but there are six instances where you can breach the £30,000 limit – see p. 215.
- If you are letting out your home, you may be better off not claiming tax relief under MIRAS – see p. 232.
- If you have more than one home, choose the right one to be exempt from capital gains tax – see p. 219.
- If you work from home, make sure you claim your allowable expenses – see p. 225.
- You may not have to pay tax on the rent your lodger pays – see p. 233.

In this chapter, we explain the tax rules that apply to owning a home – whether you live there, work there or let it. We also look at the rules that apply if you employ someone in your home – a housekeeper, say.

Tax relief for buying your home

Buying a home is by far the largest transaction most people enter into, and few can afford to pay for their home outright. Tax relief on loan interest has been eroded. In the 1995–6 tax year it was reduced to 15 per cent of the interest on the first £30,000 of your mortgage – down from 20 per cent in the 1994–5 tax year. It remains at 15 per cent in 1996–7.

In general, you can get tax relief on the interest you pay on up to £30,000 of loans used to buy your home. If you have more than one home, you normally get tax relief only on loans used to buy your *main* home. In most cases, this is the one you in fact live in most of the time.

You can be away from this home for up to a year at a time and still get tax relief, and you can be away for longer if your employer requires you to live elsewhere, or if you live in a home which counts as a tax-free fringe benefit, or if you're self-employed and have to live in accommodation provided under the terms of your business – see *Your home and your work* on p. 225.

If you take out more than one loan on the same day, they are treated as a single loan. If you're taking out two loans which total more than £30,000 (e.g. a building society mortgage and a more expensive top-up loan) try to arrange things so that you take out the more expensive loan at least a day before the cheaper loan. You'll then get tax relief on more of the total interest you pay.

EXAMPLE 1

Richard Powell owes £40,000 on his mortgage. In the 1996–7 tax year he is charged £2,800 interest, and he gets tax relief on £2,100, which is ¾ of the interest (i.e. $\frac{30,000}{40,000} \times 2,800$).

His tax relief will be 15 per cent of £2,100 = £315, so the cost of the interest to him will be £2,800 – £315 = £2,485.

When you can exceed the £30,000 limit

You will be able to get tax relief on the interest you pay on loans in excess of £30,000 in the following cases.

- **Getting married** If you get married, and each partner has a home with a mortgage, see p. 87 for the extra relief for which you may be eligible.
- **Moving home** If you have to take out a loan (e.g. a mortgage or a bridging loan) on the house you are buying before you've sold your old home, you can continue to get tax relief on the old home. The loan on the old home is ignored when working out how much tax relief you're entitled to on the new loan. For 12 months (longer in deserving cases) you can get tax relief on both loans. It doesn't matter which of the two homes you live in during these 12 months. You can continue to get the relief on the old home even if you do not buy a new home, in the same way.
- **Joint purchases before 1 August 1988** Before 1 August 1988, each individual and each married couple could get

tax relief on the interest on their share of a loan(s) of up to £30,000 even when they were buying a property with other people. This meant that, for example, two single people buying a property together could get tax relief on the interest on loans of up to £60,000. Since 1 August 1988 the £30,000 limit has been applied to each individual property for new loans. If you are still getting multiple tax relief, beware of re-mortgaging. You will lose tax relief. Two joint owners who get married will also lose relief.

- **Arrears** If at some time in the past you didn't pay all the interest which was due and it has been added to what you owe the lender, you can get tax relief on interest on up to £1,000 of arrears added to the outstanding capital provided the original loan was £30,000 or less.
- **Buying property to let** You can normally get tax relief on the interest you pay on a loan to buy a home which you let (and which isn't also your main home). The rules on this are quite separate from the rules for tax relief on your main home; the £30,000 limit doesn't apply nor is relief restricted to 15 per cent – see p. 232.
- **If you are over 65** If you are 65 or over, in addition to the normal £30,000 limit, you can get tax relief at a rate of 24 per cent on the interest on further loans of up to £30,000 to buy an annuity. The loan(s) must be secured on your home. A home income plan is an off-the-peg scheme combining loan and annuity – see p. 114.

ESC A35, SP10/1980 (getting married); ESC A27 (living away from home); ICTA 1988 s356 (joint purchases), s357 (arrears), s355 (letting property)

Loans taken out before 6 April 1988

Certain loans were eligible for tax relief until 6 April 1988:

- home improvement loans
- loans to buy a home for a dependent relative
- loans to buy a home for a former spouse.

Such loans taken out before that date will get 15 per cent tax relief, but will count towards the £30,000 limit. Beware of re-mortgaging: you'll lose the tax relief.

ICTA 1988 s353, s355, s357, s367; FA 1991 s26

Which loans qualify for relief?

Interest on a loan qualifies for tax relief only if you spend the money you borrow on:

- buying the home, or
- buying an *interest* in the home (e.g. buying a half share, or buying someone else's stake).

Part of the loan can be spent on the cost of acquiring the property, e.g. solicitor's fees, surveyor's fees, stamp duty, removal costs. The loan doesn't have to be secured on the home you're buying. Nor does it matter if you have other savings or made a profit on your previous home which made it unnecessary for you to borrow – see Example 2. But note: if you own your own home outright (or have a mortgage of less than £30,000) you can't get yourself a cheap loan (i.e. one that attracts tax relief) by arranging an artificial sale of the property to, say, your spouse or some other accomplice and then buying it back.

EXAMPLE 2

Bill and Linda Adams plan to sell their London flat for £70,000 and pay off the £25,000 owing on their mortgage. Their new home in Norfolk will cost them £50,000, and their moving expenses will come to nearly £5,000. They have £70,000 – £25,000 – £5,000 = £40,000 to pay towards their new home, so need a loan of only £10,000. But they decide to get a £30,000 mortgage and keep the extra £20,000. They will get tax relief on the interest on the whole £30,000.

The interval between getting the loan and acquiring the interest in the property must not normally be more than 12 months (it doesn't matter which comes first). If you get the money before acquiring the interest in the home, you mustn't spend it on anything in the meantime, though you can place it on deposit and get interest. If interest becomes payable on the loan in this period, you can claim tax relief on it when the purchase is completed. You can also claim tax relief on interest you've paid to the vendor because you haven't paid the full price, or because you moved in before completion.

If you pay off a qualifying loan (or part of it) and, within six months, replace it with another loan on the same property, you get tax relief on the interest you pay on the new loan. But if the new loan is bigger than the amount you paid off, you don't get any relief on the interest you pay on the excess (unless the new loan is taken out within six months of buying the home). It doesn't matter if the loan you pay off was interest-free.

You can't get tax relief on a loan which has to be repaid within 12 months of being taken out, unless the interest is paid in the UK to a bank, stockbroker or discount house. Nor is there any relief on a bank overdraft or a credit card debt (except as a business expense) though you can get relief if you convert to another type of loan within 12 months.

ICTA 1988 s354(1), s355(5), s367(2); IR11 (1988)

Which homes qualify?

The home must be in the UK or the Republic of Ireland. It can be freehold or leasehold. A caravan or mobile home can qualify, as can a houseboat, if it has been designed or adapted for living in.

ICTA 1988 s354, s367(1); FA 1991 s28

How you get tax relief

Tax relief is given on most loans by the borrower paying a reduced amount to the lender under the system known as mortgage interest relief at source (MIRAS). You get this 'tax relief' even if you pay little or no tax. The government pays the difference between the net amount you've paid and the gross amount direct to the lender.

Most lenders have government approval to operate MIRAS, but a few don't. If your lender is not in the MIRAS scheme you'll have to pay the gross amount to the lender and claim the relief you're entitled to from the Revenue. You'll then get the tax relief in your Pay-As-You-Earn (PAYE) coding or by getting a lower tax bill. You cannot normally get tax relief under MIRAS if you let more than one-third of your home. If your loan is in MIRAS and you start letting more than one-third of your home, you should tell both your lender and your tax office straight away.

With a loan which takes you over the £30,000 limit, lenders calculate your payments so that you pay the correct net amount of interest on the first £30,000 of the loan and the gross amount of interest on the rest.

ICTA 1988 s353, s369, s373, s376

Claiming tax relief

If your loan comes under MIRAS, the forms you fill in when you get the loan will entitle you to get your tax relief by making reduced payments. The lender will tell you the net amount to pay. If the loan doesn't come under MIRAS, get a *Certificate of Interest Paid* from the lender at the end of each tax year and send it to your tax inspector. If you are not in MIRAS and are on a low income, you may not pay enough tax to receive all the tax relief you would otherwise get. You may still be able to get the relief by writing to Financial Intermediaries and Claims Office* in Bootle with details of your mortgage.

Your home and capital gains tax

Any gain you make when you sell your home is normally exempt from capital gains tax (CGT). Exceptions are listed on p. 220. Any gains on other homes or land you own will normally be liable to CGT.

A 'home' means a freehold or leasehold house, flat or maisonette. A caravan or a houseboat won't normally be liable to CGT, whatever the circumstances (though the land on which a caravan stands won't be exempt unless you can show that the caravan was your only or main home for the whole time you owned the land).

For general details of CGT (including how the indexation rules are applied), see Chapter 15.

TCGA 1992 s222, s223(1)

More than one home

If you have two or more homes it's only your 'main' home which is exempt from CGT. (In certain cases, homes bought for relatives before 6 April 1988 can be exempt in addition to your main home. See leaflet CGT4 for the exact rules.)

You can choose which home you want to be regarded as your main one – it doesn't have to be the one you spend the most time in though in most cases you must live in it at some stage. And it needn't be the one with a mortgage you get tax relief on. It's best to nominate the one on which you think you'll make the largest *chargeable gain* (see p. 276 for what this means).

Make your choice by writing to the Revenue within two years of acquiring the second home. You can alter the choice at any time, simply by telling the Revenue, but this cannot affect the period more than two years before you make your new choice. A married couple must both sign the letter, unless all the homes are owned by one of you.

If you don't tell the Revenue within the two-year period which is your 'main' home, it will be decided for you. If the decision doesn't suit you, you can appeal within 30 days but you will have to prove that the home selected is *not* in fact your 'main' home.

If you live mainly in a rented home – or in one which goes with your job (e.g. as a caretaker or clergyman) – but also own a home where you spend some of your time or intend to live eventually, it is vital that you nominate the one you *own* as your main home. If this has applied for more than two years the Revenue may accept a late request.
TCGA 1992 s222 (5), (6), (8)

When your only or main home isn't exempt

You may not get full exemption from CGT on your only or 'main' home in any of the following cases:

- the home wasn't your main one for CGT purposes for all the time you owned it
- you lived away from home
- you let out all or part of the home
- you used part exclusively for work
- you converted it into self-contained flats and then sold them
- you built a second home in your garden and then sold it
- you sold the house on its own, and the land around it afterwards
- the garden (including the house area) was bigger than half a hectare
- the home was one of a series of homes you bought, or spent money on, with the object of making a profit.

The detailed rules are given in the next three pages (except that aspects to do with your work are covered on p. 225 and property you let is covered on p. 235). In many cases, only *part* of the gain you make when you sell your only or 'main' home will be taxable – see below.
CGTA 1979 s101–s103; FA 1991 s81

If you have lived away from your only or 'main' home

The capital gain you are assumed to have made during periods when you were living away from your only or main home will normally not be exempt from CGT. For example, if you have lived away from the home for 7 years out of the 15 you owned it, 7/15 of the gain you made would not be exempt from CGT. But there are six situations in which absence from the property is ignored:

- **Before 6 April 1982** Generally, only gains made after 31 March 1982 are subject to CGT, so any absence before this date becomes irrelevant. For the rules on when you might want to take account of the value of your house before this date, see p. 281.
- **The first year** If you can't move into your new home straight away because you're having a new home built on a plot you've bought, or because you're having the home altered or redecorated, or because you can't sell your old home, you will still get exemption from CGT for up to a year (two years if there's a good reason). You must live in the home within the one- or two-year period.
- **If you live in job-related accommodation** A home which you (or your husband or wife) own and which you intend to live in one day can be exempt from CGT while you are living in a home which goes with your job, or are self-employed and have to live in accommodation provided under the terms of your business – see pp. 227–8.
- **Because of your work** Certain periods when you have to be away from home because of your job are exempt – see p. 225.
- **The last three years** Any absences in the last three years before you dispose of a home which has been your only or main home at some time are always exempt. It doesn't matter why you're away, or if you have another home which you've nominated as your main home during this period. If you're away for more than three years before you sell, the gain for the excess over three years won't be exempt unless one of the other exemptions applies.
- **Any other absences** for any reason totalling up to three years will not affect exemption, as long as you use the home as your main one for a time both before the first such period and after the last one.

Except in the first year or last three years, you can't get the exemptions above if any other home of yours is exempt. None of the exemptions above is lost if you let the home while you're away.
SPD4; ESC D3, D4; TCGA 1992 s222, s223

If you divide the property, or change its use

Exemption from CGT for your only or main home is likely to be partly lost if you divide up the property or use part of it for something other than living in. For example, if you convert part of your home into self-contained flats, part of the gains you make when you sell the flats would not be exempt (see *Working out the chargeable gain*, on p. 223). If you build a second home in your garden, the gain you make when you sell it would not be wholly exempt. If you use part of the property exclusively for a trade or business or some other non-residential use, you may also lose exemption on that part. If you and your tax inspector cannot agree on what is taxable, the amount of the gain which is not exempt is whatever the commissioners (see p. 63) consider to be just and reasonable, but will normally be based on the proportion of the property affected.

For example, if you bought a home for £37,000 (after deducting buying costs) and spent £8,000 having part of it done up to sell, the cost of acquiring the whole home is taken to be £37,000 + £8,000 = £45,000. If you sell part for £40,000 when the whole home is worth £90,000, the cost of acquiring the part you sell is taken to be four-ninths of £45,000 = £20,000. So the gain (before allowing for selling costs or indexation) on the part you sell would be £40,000 − £20,000 = £20,000. Not all this gain is chargeable. The chargeable amount is the gain *less* what the commissioners reckon your gain would have been (on that part) if you hadn't spent money improving the property. So if, without the additional expense, the gain would have been £15,000, the chargeable part is £20,000 *less* £15,000 = £5,000.

If what you get for part of a property is no more than £20,000 and its market value is not more than 20 per cent of the value of the whole property, you can elect for the sale not to be treated as a disposal until you sell the rest of the property.
TCGA 1992 s42, s224(2), (3), s242, s244; SP/D1

Your garden

The garden of your main home is not normally liable to CGT even if you sell off part of it while you still own the home. But if it's over half a hectare, the gain on the excess will not be exempt unless the Revenue considers that a larger garden is appropriate for that house.

If you sell the home and retain some of the land, the gain you make on the land from the time when it stopped being part of your garden may be liable to CGT.
TCGA 1992 s222(1)–(4); Varty v. Lynes, 1976 3 All ER p. 447

The profit motive

If there is evidence that you bought your home wholly or partly with the object of selling it at a profit, you get no exemption from CGT – even though it was your only or main home. Of course, it's not easy to prove what was in your mind when you bought it, but if you moved frequently from house to house – buying them in a derelict state and improving them, say – it would look as though your main aim was profit. The Revenue might even class you as a property-dealer, and tax your gain like income.

If you make major changes to your home (such as converting it into flats, buying the freehold if it's leasehold) in order to increase the price you get for it, the *extra* gain you make may not be exempt.
TCGA 1992 s224(3), (4); ICTA 1988 s18(1)–(4)

Compulsory purchase

If part of your property is compulsorily purchased, special rules apply for working out any CGT bill.
TCGA 1992 s245

Working out the chargeable gain

In many cases, only *part* of the gain you make when you sell your home will be chargeable. For example, normally only gains made after 31 March 1982 are liable for CGT. If you have let your home while you lived away for a few years (unless you lived away for one of the reasons listed on p. 221), or nominated another home as your main one for part of the period you owned this one, you will be liable for tax on the part of the gain you are assumed to have made in that period. In general, the Revenue assumes the value of your home has increased by even monthly steps from the price you paid for it to the price at which you sell.

First, the gain over the whole period is worked out as outlined in Chapter 15. Broadly speaking, this is the amount you sold the home for *less* the amount you paid for it – but certain *allowable expenditure* (see below) may reduce your tax bill, as will the indexation rules (see p. 282). The Revenue then works out the chargeable gain for the period when the home was *not* exempt from CGT by the *time apportionment method*. This gain is:

$$\text{gain over whole period} \div \text{total number of months you owned it} \times \text{number of months it was liable for tax}$$

See Example 3 for how this works in practice.

Allowable expenditure normally includes:

- any costs of acquiring *and* disposing of the asset (e.g. commission, conveyancing costs, stamp duty, valuation)
- capital expenditure which has resulted in an increase in the value of the asset (e.g. improvements, but not ordinary maintenance).

There are special rules for limiting the chargeable gain arising from letting your only or 'main' home – see p. 235.
TCGA 1992 s38, s223(2), s224

EXAMPLE 3

Sarah Keighley bought her home in May 1986 and sold it in May 1996 for £76,000, making a total gain of £20,000 (after deducting buying and selling costs, and after indexation).

Because Sarah lived in another home which she had nominated as her main home for four years, the home she bought in 1986 was not exempt for four years i.e. 48 months. She owned the home for a total of 120 months. Her chargeable gain is £20,000 ÷ 120 × 48 = £8,000.

Your home and your work

If you work for an employer

If you work at home

You may be able to claim a proportion of heating and lighting costs, and, possibly, of telephone, cleaning and insurance costs as an allowable expense to set against your earnings. If you use part of your home *exclusively* for your work, you may be able to claim a proportion of your rent. But it's unlikely you'll be able to claim *any* of these expenses unless it's an express or implied condition of your employment that you carry out some of your duties at or from your home.

Using part of your home exclusively for your employment will mean that any gain on that part is liable to CGT (although you won't lose your exemption for the rest of your home), even if you are allowed tax relief for your expenses.

ICTA 1988 s198, TCGA 1992, s223

Working away from home

If you're getting tax relief on the mortgage on your only or main home, you're allowed to be away from the home for up to a year at a time before you stop getting relief. And if your employer *requires* you to live away from home, you continue to get tax relief if you're likely to return to that home within four years. If you don't move back within four years (or if you sell the home without moving back), you don't lose any of the tax relief you've had. But there's no further tax relief for that home until you move back. If you move back for at least three months, you can have another four years' absence. You get the tax relief even after four years if you live abroad as a Crown servant.

Being away from the home you've nominated as your 'main' home for CGT purposes may not mean you lose exemption. Any periods when you were employed (but not self-employed) and all your duties were carried on outside the UK are exempt from CGT, however long they are; taking leave in the UK or elsewhere doesn't affect this exemption. In addition, you can be away from your home for up to four years without losing exemption if you have to live away because of the location of your job. If you are away for more than four years in total, the excess won't be exempt unless another exemption on p. 221 applies, e.g. it was the last three years you owned the home. To get any of the exemptions on account of your work, you must have lived in the home as your only or main home at some time before the first absence, and, unless you can't return home because your job requires you to work away from home again, you must also live in it after the last absence. A married couple still get these exemptions even if one partner owns the home and the other has the job causing the absence.

ESC A27 (interest relief); CGTA 1979 s102; ESC D3, D4 (capital gains)

EXAMPLE 4

In September 1996 Hamish MacDonald was trying to sell his home in Edinburgh which he bought in December 1973. He didn't always live in his home, and when he was away he let it.

- The first absence: from August 1976 to May 1979 he lived in Wales.
- The second absence: from September 1982 to February 1983 he lived abroad where he was employed.
- The third absence: from March 1984 to February 1990 he was working in London.
- The fourth absence: in September 1996 he bought a new home in London where he now lives. He is trying to sell his empty Edinburgh home.

How do the absences affect his exemption from CGT?

- The first absence is prior to 1 April 1982 and irrelevant to the calculation. Any tax bill would be based only on the rise in value (taking account of indexation) after 31 March 1982, so Hamish would have to find out what the house was worth then. But if there is a tax bill, the time apportionment method (see p. 224) will take account only of the period Hamish has owned his home since then. In fact, Hamish probably won't have to pay any tax.
- The second absence will be exempt because he was employed abroad.
- The third absence: the first four years will be exempt because Hamish had to live nearer his job in London; the last two years will be exempt because he is allowed to be absent for periods totalling three years for any reason, so long as he lived in the home after the absence (which he did, from March 1990 to August 1996).

- The fourth absence will be exempt provided he sells within three years of September 1996 (even though he has now nominated his London home as his main home).

If you live in job-related accommodation
You can get income tax relief indefinitely on a loan used to buy a home which you (or your spouse) own and in which you intend to live. And, if you nominate the home you own as your 'main' one for CGT purposes, any gain you make when you sell the home is exempt from CGT so long as you are living in a home which goes with your job. It doesn't matter if you change your mind and sell the home without ever living in it, as long as you intended to live in it at some stage. To qualify on either count, at least one of the following must apply to your job-related accommodation:

- you need to live there to do your job properly (e.g. you're a social worker living in a children's home)
- living where you do enables you to do the job better *and* it is common for people doing your sort of job to live in such a home (e.g. you're a caretaker)
- you live there because there is a special threat to your security.

A director can qualify for the first two reasons above only if he or she owns or controls 5 per cent or less of the shares in the company, *and* is a full-time working director of the company *or* works for a charity or non-profit-making company.
ICTA 1988 s356 (interest relief); TCGA 1992 s222(8) (capital gains)

If you're self-employed

If you work at home
If you're self-employed (or do some freelance or spare-time work) and do part of your work at home, you can claim as an allowable expense the proportion of the cost of running your home that's attributable to business use – see p. 193.

But if you use part of your home *exclusively* for your business, the part you use will not be exempt from CGT for the period you use it. The exact *proportion* of the gain you make when you sell the house which will be liable to tax will have to be negotiated with your tax inspector (in one of the same ways as would be adopted if you had let part of your home – see p. 235). However, if your business is on a modest scale, and if you've got an understanding tax inspector, you may be able to get the best of both worlds by using a room *almost* exclusively for business – enough to be allowed heating and so on as an expense, but not so exclusively as to risk a CGT bill.

Even if there is a chargeable gain when you sell the home, you won't be liable for any tax at the time if you use the proceeds from selling the part of the home you used for your business to buy another property where you will carry on the same business or a similar one. The new building counts as replacement of a business asset, and the gain is *rolled over* (see p. 291). If you don't use all the proceeds in this way, only the part you use can qualify. If you eventually qualify for *retirement relief* (see p. 292), you may avoid a CGT bill entirely.

ICTA 1988 s74 (expenses); TCGA 1992 s224(1), s152, s163 (capital gains)

Accommodation provided under the terms of your business

If you live in accommodation provided under the terms of your business (e.g. you're a licensee publican) and you're buying a home elsewhere which you intend to live in one day, you can get tax relief on your mortgage and exemption from CGT as if you were an employee in job-related accommodation (see p. 227).

ICTA 1988 s356

Letting property

If you let land or property, there are two main points to consider:

- how rents you receive are taxed, and what expenses and interest you can set against the income
- CGT when you sell the property. If a property is not your only or main home, the gain you make will be liable to CGT. If you let part of your own home, the gain on the let part may be liable to tax, unless you were away from the home on a qualifying absence (see p. 221).

Income from property and land you let

The 1994 Budget heralded a major change to the way in which income from land and property is taxed. Until 5 April 1995 income of this type could be taxed under various different tax Schedules, depending on the source of the income. The result could be confusing, particularly if you had more than once source of income of this kind, because, for example, different Schedules allow different expenses to be deducted and handle losses in varying ways.

The new system, which has applied since 6 April 1995, treats virtually all property income as Schedule A income, which is investment income. The distinction between furnished and unfurnished property letting is gone. But tax is worked out in the same way as income from a business (i.e. Schedule D, Case 1 – see Chapter 11). A welcome improvement arising from this is that all your Schedule A income from property in the UK can be added together and treated as one pool. This includes rents you receive, ground rents, feu duties (in Scotland) and premiums on leases (though there are special rules for premiums on leases – check with your tax office). The new rules also apply to immobile caravans and permanently moored houseboats.

The following are the only types of income to which the new rules do *not* apply:

- income from a hotel or guesthouse continues to be taxed as a business under Schedule D Case 1, as does income you get from taking in lodgers if you provide services such as meals or laundry. (See Chapter 11 for how businesses are taxed.)
- mineral rents and mining royalties are taxed partially under Schedule D Case 1 and partially as capital gains
- rental income from abroad is also now taxed under Schedule A, but cannot be pooled with income from property in this country – see p. 235
- if you had income from property in the 1994–5 tax year, but stopped getting income from that source in 1995–6, any income will be taxed under the old rules.

You may not need to grapple with tax at all if you are letting a room in your home. Under the rent-a-room scheme, explained on p. 233, the first £3,250 of rent can be tax-free altogether.
ICTA 1988 s21–43, s122, FA1995, s33, s35

Letting land and property

In any tax year, you are taxed on the income you are entitled to receive in that year. This applies even if you haven't yet received the income, but not to debts you've tried unsuccessfully to recover. For tax years before 1995–6, you could ask to be taxed on your profits for your accounting year ending in the tax year. If your tax bill was based on accounting years before 6 April 1995 check with your tax inspector how you will be brought into a current-year basis. Very few tax payers are affected by this.

You are allowed to deduct certain expenses and interest (see below) which you have actually paid during the tax year when you work out your profits. If the expenses and interest come to more than your income, you will have made a loss – see p. 233.

The tax on all the property income you are entitled to receive in the 1996–7 tax year is due on 31 January 1997. If you pay tax through PAYE and your taxable rental income is small, your PAYE code may be adjusted to collect the tax you owe.

If you are letting UK property while you live abroad, your tenants have to deduct basic-rate tax from the rent if it is paid directly to you. If, however, it is paid to an agent, the collection of any tax will depend on your residence status in the UK. Check your position with your tax office.
ICTA 1988 s42A, FA 1995 s40, S1 2902

Allowable expenses

You can deduct certain expenses from your income from letting when you work out your profits as long as they are 'wholly and exclusively' incurred for the letting. If you let only part of your home, or let it for only part of each year, you and the Revenue will have to agree on the proportion you can claim. You can't claim anything for your own time. For a list of business expenses which are normally allowable, see p. 193. The following expenses related to letting homes are allowable:

- water rates, ground rent, feu duty (in Scotland)
- normal repairs and decoration, but not repairs necessary when you bought the property, nor improvements, additions or alterations to the property
- management expenses as a landlord (e.g. stationery, telephone bills, accountant's fees, cost of rent collection)

- cost of insurance and any necessary valuation for insurance
- legal fees for renewing a tenancy agreement (for leases of up to 50 years)
- estate agent's fees, accommodation agency fees, cost of advertising for tenants
- rent you pay for a property which you, in turn, sub-let
- cost of lighting common parts of property
- cost of services you provide, including wages of people who provide such services (e.g. cleaners, gardeners). It could be worth paying your husband or wife to provide the services if he or she is not fully using his or her tax-free allowances – see Example 5 below
- cost of maintenance and repairs made necessary by improvements you've made, as long as you haven't changed the use of the property
- cost of maintaining roads, drains, ditches, etc. on an estate you own, if for the benefit of tenants.

The new rules introduce some new allowable expenses: the cost of statutory redundancy payments for staff and the cost of training or counselling staff. In addition, you can now deduct expenses incurred before you actually start letting, so long as they would have been allowable if incurred once the letting had begun.

You can also deduct interest you pay on a loan used to buy or improve property – see below. If you buy any machinery or equipment (e.g. a lawnmower or ladder) for upkeep or repair of property, you can claim *capital allowances* as if you were self-employed (see p. 196).

If you incur expenses while the home isn't actually occupied by a tenant, they should still qualify for tax relief as long as they were 'wholly and exclusively' incurred for the letting.

Note that if you let furnished accommodation to a tenant who pays you separately for any services you provide (e.g. meals, cleaning, laundry), what you get for these services counts as earnings from a business and is taxed under Schedule D Case 1.

ICTA 1988 s25–s28, FA 1995 s33

EXAMPLE 5

Brian Wallis lets out three furnished flats and gets £10,000 a year in rent. His student son provides the tenants with an evening meal, cleans the flats twice a week and collects the rents. Brian pays his son £3,900 a year for this (but has to deduct some tax and National Insurance from what he pays). As his son has no other taxable income, £3,765 (the personal allowance) of this will be tax-free. Brian deducts the £3,900 wages from his letting income of £10,000, and will be taxed on £6,100, less the National Insurance he pays, and less any other allowable expenses.

Interest

Since 6 April 1995, interest you pay on a loan to buy or improve a home you let out has been treated as an allowable expense and deducted from your rental income.

Note that the rules were more complicated *before* April 1995. You got tax relief only if, in any 52-week period, your property was let at a commercial rent for more than half the period. (And for the rest of the period it had to be available for letting, or used as your only or main home, or unused while building or repair work was going on.)

If it is your only or main home you are letting out, you may meet the rules for mortgage interest relief (see *Tax relief for buying your home* p. 214) and you would get relief at 15 per cent on interest on the first £30,000. But under the rules for let property, you will be eligible for tax relief on all the interest, at your top rate of tax – though you can deduct the interest only from your rental income.

If you are eligible for both types of relief, you can choose which you prefer. You can ask to be taken out of the MIRAS. Tell your tax office within 22 months of the end of the year to which it relates, i.e. by 5 February 1999 for the 1996–7 tax year. Full tax relief under the rules for let property will usually be the best option unless your rental income is so low that you have too little income to set against the interest – see Example 6. However, once you have opted out of MIRAS you can't opt back in until you have stopped letting.

EXAMPLE 6

Henry Birchall has a £40,000 mortgage on his home, which he is letting out while he is working abroad. Mortgage interest relief for 1996–7 would be 15 per cent of the interest on the first £30,000 of the loan. If the interest rate averages 7 per cent during the year, the interest qualifying for tax relief would be £2,100 and the tax relief would be worth 15 per cent of £2,100, i.e. £315.

Under the rules for let property, Henry could deduct the interest on the whole £40,000, i.e. £2,800, from his rental income. So, if he pays basic-rate tax on his rental income, the tax relief would be worth 24 per cent of £2,800, i.e. £672.

ICTA 1988 s354(1), s355, s367, FA 1995 s33, s36

Wear and tear

Capital allowances cannot be claimed for equipment let in a residential property. Instead, you can claim an allowance for wear and tear on fixtures, furniture and furnishings – e.g. chairs, cookers, lampshades, beds and sheets. You can claim *either* the actual cost of fixtures, furniture, etc. you replace during the year (called *renewals basis*), *or* a proportion (normally 10 per cent) of the rent *less*, if you pay them, service charges and water rates. Once you've chosen a basis, you must stick to it.

SP/A19

Losses

A loss can be set off against any income from property but see *Letting Property Abroad*, p. 235. If you haven't enough other property income to set it all against, you can carry what's left forward and set it against income from property in future years if you're still letting the property you made the loss on. Losses brought forward from before 6 April 1996 can be set against property income in 1996–7 and carried forward to future years if still unused.

FA 1995 sch 6 (18)

Rent-a-room

Since 6 April 1992, tenants and owner-occupiers have been able to take advantage of the rent-a-room scheme. If you let furnished accommodation in your only or main home you can receive a gross rental income of £3,250 (£62.50 a week). If your rental income exceeds £3,250, you can choose *either* to pay tax on the excess, without any relief for allowable expenses; *or* to pay tax on the whole lot but claim expenses in the normal way. If you choose to claim the £3,250, you must tell your tax inspector within one year of the end of the relevant tax year. Your choice will remain in force until you decide to change to the normal method of assessing rent. There is no need to make this choice if your rental income is £3,250 or less. If two or more people

receive rental income, the tax-free limit is £1,625 for each person. Note that the definition of 'only or main home' is not the same as the one used for CGT (see p. 219). It is the home which is, *in fact*, your main home – for example, the one for which you're entitled to MIRAS.
FA 1992 (no. 2) s59, Sch 10

Furnished holiday lettings

Income from letting property (including caravans) which is let as furnished holiday accommodation for part of the year is treated as earnings from a business, even though, strictly speaking, it is assessed under Schedule A. (Until 5 April 1995 it was taxed under Schedule D Case VI.)

The advantage is, for example, that you can claim roll-over relief (see p. 291) and retirement relief from CGT (see p. 292).

To qualify, both the following must apply:

- the property is available for letting to the general public at a commercial rent for at least 140 days (which need not be consecutive) during each 12-month qualifying period (not necessarily a tax year)
- it is actually let out as holiday accommodation for at least 70 of those days, and during at least seven months of the 12-month period it isn't normally occupied by the same tenant for more than 31 days at a stretch.

If you let more than one unit of accommodation, you can average the days they're actually let to pass the 70-day rule.

If a furnished letting counts as holiday accommodation, all the income you get from it in the tax year counts as earned income. But if only part of the let accommodation counts as furnished holiday lettings only a proportion of the income counts as earned income.
ICTA 1988, s504

EXAMPLE 7

Winston Fry started letting out a furnished bungalow in Skegness for holidays on 1 June 1996. It will count as a furnished holiday letting for the 1996–7 year of assessment, as long as it's available to the public at a commercial rent for 140 days during the 12 months from 1 June 1996 to 31 May 1997, and as long as he lets it out for 70 of those days, mainly for periods of 31 days or less.

Letting property abroad

Since 6 April 1995 income from letting property you own abroad has in effect been taxed in the same way as income from property in this country (though it actually comes under Schedule D Case V). In particular, you can deduct from your rental income interest you pay on a loan to buy the property abroad – something which wasn't possible before. However, you *cannot* pool your income from property abroad with that from property in the UK – for example, to offset losses.

If you are currently receiving income from property abroad which is taxed on a preceding-year basis (see p. 186) this will continue until self-assessment is fully in place in 1996–7.

Capital gains on let property

If a home has been your only home or nominated as your main one for the whole time you've owned it, the whole of your gain will be exempt from CGT even if you've let it out while you were away, as long as all your absences count as qualifying absences (see p. 221). But the gain attributable to any other period you let it while you were away (worked out by the time apportionment method shown on p. 224) won't be exempt.

If you let part of your only or main home, you don't lose any exemption for having lodgers who share your living rooms and eat with you. In other cases it depends on whether you have occupied the part of the home you've let at any time. If you haven't, the gain on the part you let will not be exempt from CGT. The chargeable gain will normally be based on the number of rooms you let or the floor area of the part you let, but could alternatively be based on the rateable value of the part you let, or on its market value. It's up to you and the Revenue to agree which method to use; if you don't agree, you can appeal to the general or special commissioners (see p. 63).

If you have lived in the part of the home you've let out, the gain on the let part is apportioned according to the period you've let it. In addition, this gain (after allowing for indexation – see p. 282) will remain exempt from CGT if it's not more than the (exempt) gain attributable to your occupation of the home (after allowing for indexation), *and* if it's not more than £40,000. If either limit is exceeded, the

excess (the larger excess if both limits are exceeded) is liable to CGT – see Example 8. To get this exemption, the let part must be lived in by someone, but must not be a completely separate home (e.g. not a self-contained flat with its own access from the street) and you should not have had more than minor alterations made to the home.
TCGA 1992 s223; SP14/80

EXAMPLE 8

Elizabeth Kerr bought a house in Belgravia in May 1988 and sold it eight years later in May 1996. Her gain, after deducting selling costs and her indexation allowance, was £200,000. Throughout this time the house was her main home for CGT purposes. For the first two years she lived in the whole house, but then she let out two-thirds of the house as living accommodation. The first two years of ownership (when she lived in the whole house) are exempt. The last three years of ownership are also exempt (see p. 221). Of the remaining three years, only one-third of the home is exempt (because she let out two-thirds). So the exempt part of the gain is 2 (first two years) + 3 (last three years) + 1 (one-third of three years) ÷ 8 = 6/8. £200,000 × 6/8 = £150,000. The non-exempt part of the gain is therefore £50,000. This is £10,000 more than £40,000, so £10,000 will be chargeable.

The first £6,300 of gains made in the 1997–8 tax year are exempt from CGT. Elizabeth will have to pay tax on £10,000 – £6,300 = £3,700. She is a higher-rate taxpayer, so the tax bill will be £3,700 × 40% = £1,480. She will also have to pay tax on any other chargeable gains in that tax year, as her annual exemption has been used up on her house sale.

If the letting counts as a business

If the let property counts as furnished holiday accommodation (see p. 234) or if income from the letting counts as earnings from a business because of services you provide, you may not have to pay tax when you sell the home even if a taxable gain arises. If you use the proceeds from selling the home (or from the part you let) to buy another property where you continue to provide similar accommodation and services, the new property can count as replacement of a business asset and the gain can be *rolled over* (see p. 291). If you don't use all the proceeds in this way, only the part you use can qualify.

Doing this only defers your tax bill, as you would normally have to pay CGT on rolled-over gains when you finally sell up and cease letting. However, if you don't do this until you reach 50 (or retire earlier through ill health) you qualify for *retirement relief*, which exempts part of the gains – see p. 292.

TCGA 1992 s152–s158 (Rollover relief), s163–2164, Sch 6 (Retirement relief); ICTA 1988 s503, s504 (2)–(9)

Employing someone in your home

If you employ someone, it's your responsibility to collect income tax and National Insurance contributions from them under the PAYE system – assuming that the amount of pay the employee gets will mean that tax and National Insurance are payable. This section tells you how to collect the money if you are employing someone in the home – e.g. a housekeeper, nanny and so on.

Another duty you have as an employer is to give your employee a payslip. This should show the amount of pay and the amount of the deductions – see p. 125. Payslip forms are available from office stationers.

If your employee earns £61 or more a week in the 1996–7 tax year, National Insurance will have to be deducted from his or her pay. Depending on his or her income and personal circumstances, tax may need to be deducted too.

The first thing to do is to get hold of Inland Revenue leaflet *IR53 Thinking of taking someone on?* from a tax office or tax enquiry centre (under *Inland Revenue* in the phone book). Complete form P223 at the end of the leaflet and return it to your local PAYE office (which may be different from the office that deals with your own personal tax affairs). You should also contact your local DSS office.

The local PAYE office will send you a *New Employer's Starter Pack*. This should give you all the information and forms you need, including

- P8 cards. These are a basic guide to PAYE for employers, with step-by-step instructions for straightforward cases. For more complex cases (e.g. if you are paying joint wages to a husband and wife), you will need to get the *Employer's further guide to* PAYE (booklet P7) from your PAYE office

- pay-adjustment tables. These show you how much of your employee's pay is tax-free each pay-day
- taxable-pay tables. These tell you how much tax to deduct from your employee's taxable pay
- deductions working sheets (P11). This is your record of how much you pay each employee and how much tax you deduct
- National Insurance Contributions tables, showing you how much National Insurance you should deduct each pay-day.

Board and lodging
There's no tax for the employee to pay on living accommodation provided, as long as the job is one in which accommodation is normally available – e.g. nanny, nurse, housekeeper. And there's no tax to pay on free or cheap meals if they're provided to all employees you may have.

Handing over the tax

You have to pay your Revenue accounts office what you deduct in tax and National Insurance from your employee's pay, and your own National Insurance as an employer. You have to pay at the end of each quarter (i.e. 5 July, 5 October, 5 January, 5 April), or at the end of every month if you expect the payments to average more than £600 a month.

You can deduct the cost of any statutory sick pay or statutory maternity pay you have incurred from the National Insurance you would otherwise be due to hand over.

When an employee leaves

You should complete the simplified deduction card up to the date of leaving and you will usually also need to complete a P45 (see p. 147), part of which you give to the employee and part you send to your tax office. Keep the deductions working sheet for at least three years after the end of the tax year to which it relates.

13 *Investments*

- Basic-rate taxpayers will pay only 20 per cent tax on most savings and investment income from 6 April 1996.
- Taxpayers are usually better off going for tax-free investments but, paradoxically, non-taxpayers may get better returns from taxable investments.
- There are special transitional rules in 1996–7 for some types of investment income – see p. 244.

There are two main taxes which apply to investments:

- **capital gains tax** If your investment is the sort where its value can fluctuate, there could be capital gains tax (CGT) to pay when you sell (or give away) the investment. But for the 1996–7 tax year, the first £6,300 of net chargeable gains is tax-free. Anything above that level is taxed at the same rate as if it were your income – 20, 24 or 40 per cent. For more on CGT, see p. 276.
- **income tax** Any investment income you get (such as interest or share dividends) is added to your earned income. You then deduct your outgoings (see p. 28) and your allowances (see p. 34), leaving your taxable income on which you pay tax. For the 1996–7 tax year, income tax is charged at 20 per cent on the first £3,900 of your taxable income, at the basic rate of 24 per cent on the next £21,600, and at the higher rate of 40 per cent on any of your taxable income above £25,500. However, the tax deducted at source on income from most savings and investments falls to 20 per cent from 6 April 1996. This brings the interest you get from banks, building societies and bonds such as UK gilts in line with the tax treatment of share dividends and share-based unit trusts. If your top rate of tax is 20 per cent you will no longer have to reclaim tax back. Basic-rate taxpayers will have no more tax to pay (even though the basic rate of

tax for other sorts of income is 24 per cent), but higher-rate taxpayers will continue to pay 40 per cent tax in total.
ICTA 1988 s833

How investment income is paid

Investment income can be paid in one of three ways:

- it can be tax-free (no tax to pay) – see list on p. 242
- it can be paid gross, i.e. before any tax has been deducted – see p. 242
- it can be paid with 20 per cent tax already deducted – see p. 245 for how this works.

Note that if you choose to have the income credited to your investment, the tax treatment is the same as if it's paid out to you. For tax purposes, you get income when it is paid or credited to you, even if the interest is worked out more frequently.

Husband and wife

A husband and wife are treated as individual taxpayers for both their investment income and investment (i.e. capital) gains. See Chapter 5 for more details of how married couples are taxed.

If you own an investment jointly, each of you is taxed on half the income or gains – unless you have made a declaration that you actually own the investment in unequal proportions. You must notify your tax inspector using form 17 within 60 days of the declaration.

It may be worth changing the proportions in which you own investments if

- one of you pays tax at a lower rate than the other
- one of you tends to use up the annual CGT exemption while the other does not.

You could, for example, make an outright gift of shares to a spouse who has no taxable income. But note that it must be a real gift. The donor can't keep control of the money.
FA 1988 s32

Which investment for which investor?

Here we give some guidelines on the types of investments which suit non-taxpayers and taxpayers. But don't consider tax alone anyway. Look at other aspects, too, e.g. the after-tax return you get, risk, and for how long you want to invest.

Non-taxpayers

You should consider:

- investments which can pay income gross, before any tax is deducted – bank and building society accounts, high-income British government stocks bought through the National Savings Stock Register, National Savings Investment accounts and National Savings Bonds
- investments where income is paid with tax already deducted but where the tax can be claimed back from the Inland Revenue, such as shares and unit trusts.

Taxpayers

You should consider:

- investments which are tax-free, e.g. tax-exempt special savings accounts (TESSAs), National Savings Certificates and personal equity plans (PEPs).

If you're prepared to take a risk, you can cash in up to £6,300 in capital gains free of tax in the 1996–7 tax year. Consider:

- investments which you hope will give a capital gain rather than income, e.g. low-income British government stocks and index-linked British government stocks (which are always free of capital gains tax), shares, unit trusts.

People receiving age-related allowances

If your income is in the region where each extra pound of 'total income' loses you age-related allowances (see p. 103), you should consider:

- tax-free investments – e.g. TESSAs, National Savings Certificates, PEPs.

Tax-free investment income

Income or proceeds from the following investments are tax-free:

- Save-As-You-Earn (SAYE schemes) – from 29 November 1994, no longer available to new savers except where linked to an employer's share-save scheme
- National Savings Certificates (and, in most cases, Ulster Savings Certificates if you live in Northern Ireland)
- National Savings Yearly Plan (withdrawn to new investors on 1 February 1995)
- National Savings Children's Bonus Bonds
- qualifying regular-premium investment-type life insurance (if held for at least 10 years, or three-quarters of the original term, whichever is shorter) – but the company pays tax
- proceeds from some friendly society plans
- Premium Bond prizes and lottery winnings (which don't really count as income)
- first £70 interest each year from a National Savings Ordinary account
- interest on a tax rebate
- interest to do with delayed settlement of damages for personal injury or death
- return on investments held in a PEP
- return on qualifying venture capital trusts
- the proceeds of a TESSA.

  ICTA 1988 s46, s325, s326, s329, s464, s487

Investment income not taxed before you get it

This type of income is paid to you *gross* – i.e. before any tax has been deducted. Examples of income paid this way include interest from bank and building society accounts if you're registered as a non-taxpayer, see p. 246, National Savings Investment accounts, National Savings Bonds and interest from deposits at non-UK branches of UK and overseas banks.

Any tax due on this sort of income must normally be paid by 31 January during the year of assessment (from the 1996–7 tax year). But if your interest isn't very substantial and doesn't vary much from year to year, and you pay tax under Pay-As-You-Earn (PAYE), the tax on it will probably be collected along with tax on your earnings – so you'll pay some of the tax sooner.

The rules in future

The way this sort of investment income is taxed is undergoing a major change. From the 1997–8 tax year onwards, it will all be taxed on a *current-year basis* – that is, your tax bill for 1997–8 will be based on the interest you actually receive between 6 April 1997 and 5 April 1998. If you acquire a new source of this type of investment income during 1994–5 or later tax years, it will be taxed on this basis immediately.

The old rules

If you've been getting income of this type for a few years, it will normally have been taxed on a *preceding year basis* – that is, your tax bill for the 1995–6 tax year will have been based on the income paid (or credited) to you in the 1994–5 tax year. The exception to this will have been if you had recently started or stopped getting income of this sort from a particular source, when special rules apply. For the first two and the last tax years of getting the income, it will normally have been taxed on a current year basis, although you may have some choice in the matter – see table on p. 244 for details.

For example, if you opened a National Savings Investment account between 7 April 1993 and 6 April 1994, in 1995–6 the interest will normally be taxed on a preceding-year basis, i.e. on income received between 6 April 1994 and 5 April 1995. You can opt to be taxed on a current-year basis, i.e. on income received between 6 April 1995 and 6 April 1996, providing you tell your tax inspector within six years of the end of 1995–6. But if you decide to stick with the preceding-year basis, you need to take account of the transitional rules for 1996–7, see below.

On the other hand, in the last-but-one tax year in which you get interest from one particular source of this type, when you tell the Revenue at the end of the next year that you've closed your account, your bill may be revised. Instead of the normal preceding-year basis, it will be based on the interest you actually got in the last-but-one tax year (current year basis) if this comes to more than your original bill.

If there is a big change in the amount of interest you get from a single source, e.g. if you greatly increase or decrease the size of your National Savings Investment account, your tax inspector may treat such interest as coming from a new source and apply the special rules. You won't need to worry about these rules if your interest is much the same from year to year. Note that if you get interest from more than one source which is paid without tax deducted, your tax inspector will normally apply the special rules to each source separately.

Transitional rules for 1996–7

If you are currently receiving income which is being taxed on a preceding year basis you will have to switch to a current year basis. By way of transition, your tax bill for 1996–7 will be based on the sum of half the interest you received in the 1996–7 tax year, plus half the interest you received in the 1995–6 tax year.

Taxation of investment income not taxed before you get it

Basis used to bill you for tax year	If interest starts to be paid in 1992–3 [1]	1993–4 [1]	1994–5 and later	If interest stops being paid in 1994–5	1995–6
1994–5	preceding or current – your choice	current	current	current	preceding or current – Revenue chooses
1995–6	preceding	preceding or current – your choice	current	–	current
1996–7	transitional	transitional or current (but it must be transitional if you chose the preceding basis for 1995–6)	current	–	–
1997–8	current	current	current	–	–

[1] Assuming income first arose after 6 April – if it arose on 6 April you move on to the preceding-year basis from the second year, although you can choose the current-year basis instead for the second year only.

Investment income taxed before you get it

Investments taxed in this way include share dividends, unit trust distributions and interest on some British government stocks. This type of income is taxed on a *current-year basis* – i.e. your tax bill for the 1996–7 tax year is based on the income paid (or credited) to you in that tax year. When you get the income, 20 per cent tax has already been deducted but basic-rate taxpayers do not have to pay any more tax.

Non-taxpayers

If you don't pay tax, even allowing for income of this type, you can (except with some types of shares – see p. 253) claim tax back. You can get the form (R40) from your tax inspector to claim back tax.

20-per-cent and basic-rate taxpayers

If you are liable for lower-rate or basic-rate tax only, tax due on this income is automatically met by the tax already deducted.

Higher-rate taxpayers

If you pay tax at the higher rate, you will have to pay extra tax, worked out on the gross (before-tax) income. Any extra tax due on interest received in the 1996–7 tax year is due on 31 January 1997. Tax may be deducted under PAYE, in which case you pay some of the tax earlier – but you can choose to pay in a lump sum instead.

Investment income will be treated as the top slice of your income, i.e. you won't be able to claim it falls within the basic rate band and pay only 20 per cent if you are a higher-rate taxpayer. For the 1996–7 tax year, any higher-rate tax is due on 31 January 1997.

Your tax return

On your tax return you should enter the gross (before-tax) amount of the interest received, the tax deducted and (unless no tax was deducted) the interest after tax. With share dividends and unit trust distributions, you enter the amount received and the amount of the tax credit.

How each type of investment is taxed

Alternative investments

If you invest in antiques, silver, gold coins or other tangible objects of this type, you will be hoping to make a capital gain. For how this is taxed, see p. 276.

Annuities

With annuities that you buy voluntarily, part of what you get back is treated as being a return of your original investment and is tax-free. For more details, see p. 110. The *whole* of income from annuities bought compulsorily, e.g. as part of a pension scheme, is taxable.
ICTA 1988 s619, s634, s656–658

Bank and building society interest

When you get interest from building societies, banks and other deposit-takers, you don't have to pay basic-rate tax on it. This is because these institutions pay tax direct to the Revenue before paying out the interest to you. If you pay tax at 20 per cent or at the basic rate, there is no more tax to pay.

If you pay tax at 40 per cent, you will have to pay extra tax on your interest. When working out your tax bill, the tax inspector will include the *grossed-up* amount of interest (see p. 37) as part of your income. If you got £400 interest, say, from a building society, this will be grossed-up to work out your taxable income. So if tax is deducted at 20 per cent, the grossed-up interest is £400 ÷ 0.8 = £500. You will have to pay tax at 40 per cent on this grossed-up amount of interest. But you are treated as having already paid 20 per cent tax on the interest – so you have to hand over only the difference, i.e. 20 per cent of the grossed-up interest. See the example below.

Non-taxpayers can have their interest from bank and building society accounts paid gross. To qualify, you need to tell each bank or building society with which you have an account by sending them a completed registration form (form R85 – available from post offices, banks, building societies and tax offices). Alternatively, you can reclaim the tax from the Revenue, see above.

There is no tax to pay on TESSA accounts (see p. 254) or Save-As-You-Earn (SAYE) accounts.
ICTA 1988 s477A, s480A, s480B

EXAMPLE 1

Charlie Carter gets £720 interest from his building society in the 1996–7 tax year. As he pays some higher-rate tax, he realises he'll have to pay extra tax on this interest. He works out the grossed-up amount of interest, i.e. £720 ÷ 0.8 = £900.

He adds this to his other income and finds he's liable for tax at 40 per cent on the £900 grossed-up interest, i.e. £360 tax in total. But he's treated as having already paid tax on this interest at 20 per cent, i.e. 20 per cent of £900 = £180. So he has to hand over £360 – £180 = £180 to the Revenue.

British government stocks

Interest on government stocks is paid with 20 per cent tax deducted, except for:

- interest on War Loan
- interest on any stock which gives you less than £2.50 gross interest each half year
- interest on stocks bought through the National Savings Stock Register
- the discount or profit on sale or maturity of Treasury Bills.

Note that with stock issued by certain nationalised industries and stock issued by certain foreign governments which pay interest in the UK, the interest is paid with 20 per cent tax deducted.

Index-linked British government stocks are treated in exactly the same way for tax purposes as other British government stocks.

Buying British government stocks can be a useful way of investing for a capital gain. If you buy at a price which is less than the price at which the stock will eventually be redeemed or sold you'll make a capital gain which is free of CGT. If you buy *low coupon* stocks – i.e. stocks which pay relatively low amounts of yearly interest – then you can invest for a return which is made up largely of a capital

gain. But don't let tax considerations force you into investments which would otherwise be unsuitable.
ICTA 1988 s18(3), s44–s52; TCGA 1992 s115

Business expansion scheme

The business expansion scheme (BES) was set up to encourage investment in new or small companies that find it difficult to raise money. The scheme ended on 31 December 1993 and was replaced by the enterprise investment scheme (see p. 249).

BES shares are free of CGT on the first occasion they are sold (or given away) if they were issued after 18 March 1986 and if you hold them for five years. But losses won't count for CGT purposes.

You could claim tax relief at your highest rate on up to £40,000 in any one year, but you must hold the shares for at least five years. If you sell the shares earlier, the relief is reduced by the amount of the sale proceeds. The relief is also lost if the sale is not at 'arm's length', e.g. the proper commercial price is not paid, or if you get 'value' from the company, e.g. fringe benefits, or if the company in which you invested ceases to qualify under the scheme in the first three years.
ICTA 1988 s289–s312

Company loans and loans to individuals

Interest on company fixed-income loan stocks or debentures is paid with 20 per cent deducted. But interest on loans to private individuals will be paid without tax deducted.

For company loans bought after 13 March 1984, the proceeds are free of CGT, provided the stock is a 'qualifying corporate bond'. Broadly speaking, a qualifying bond is a debt security issued on commercial terms whose value does not reflect any foreign exchange element. So securities denominated in foreign currency, or linked to foreign-currency assets, do not qualify. Nor, for disposals on or after 29 November 1994, do securities linked to a UK share index.

Note that if the loan is not repaid when it is due, and not likely to be repaid in future, you can set the loss off against gains for CGT purposes if the loan was a loan stock or a loan

or guarantee made to a UK-resident trader for use in his or her business. Otherwise you can't set the loss off.
ICTA 1988 s117, s234, s348; TCGA 1992 s115, s117, s251, s253

Commodities

How any profits you make from investing in commodities will be taxed depends on the circumstances.

Profits from buying and selling *physical* commodities are likely to be treated as trading profits, and so taxed as earned income. A loss might count as a trading loss and you could set it off against the total of your income from all sources, but not against capital gains.

Just one isolated venture into the commodity *futures* market is likely to be treated as giving rise to a capital gain (or loss). But if you make a profit from a series of transactions, or invest as a member of a syndicate run by brokers or by a professional manager, this is likely to be treated as investment income, which may mean that you don't benefit from your capital gains tax-free slice.
ICTA 1988 s128, s399; TCGA 1992 s143

Covenants

From April 1995, all payments received under a deed of covenant (except for those received by charities) are paid gross and are taxable. The more favourable tax treatment of pre-15 March 1988 covenants has now ceased.

Enterprise investment scheme

The enterprise investment scheme (EIS) allows you to claim tax relief of 20 per cent on investments of up to £100,000 each tax year in shares in unquoted companies issued after 1 January 1994. In addition, there is no CGT when the shares are first disposed of, so long as the tax relief has not been withdrawn because the investment has ceased to qualify under the scheme. Losses on disposal can be offset against an income tax or CGT bill. And if you make a chargeable capital gain when you dispose of *any* asset on or after 29 November 1994, you can defer the tax if you re-invest the money in EIS shares.

To get these tax advantages, one qualification is that shares must be held for at least five years. Another is that the CGT exemption is restricted if you receive value from the company in some form – e.g. if it makes you a loan, provides a benefit or transfers an asset to you at less than its market value. Qualifying companies include unquoted companies trading in the UK and companies quoted on the new Alternative Investment Market (AIM), regardless of whether they are based in the UK: see Inland Revenue leaflet *IR137* for more details.

To some extent, the precise rules on what qualifies need not overly concern investors. They will be able to find out whether an investment qualifies by contacting the sponsor of the share issue. In practice, qualifying issues will be marketed to investors as enterprise investment schemes. But it has to be said that a few sponsors of the business expansion scheme, the predecessor of EIS, tried to be too clever in manipulating the rules and found some share issues were not subsequently approved by the Revenue.

Half the amount of qualifying investments made in the first half of the tax year, i.e. before 5 October, can be carried back to the previous tax year, subject to a maximum of £15,000. But you must not exceed the overall maximum for the previous tax year of £100,000.

Friendly society policies

Some societies have tax advantages such as paying no income tax on a fund's income or CGT on any gains made in the fund. You can invest £25 in monthly premiums, £270 in yearly premiums, in a friendly society policy of ten years or more without paying tax on what you get back at the end.
ICTA 1988 s460

Income and growth bonds

These bonds are set up in different ways, often consisting of one or more life insurance policies and one or more annuities. The tax treatment of any bond will depend on how it's set up. Bonds can include various life insurance products, such as deferred annuities with a cash option, immediate temporary annuities, single-premium endowment policies or regular premium endowment policies.

Very briefly, the tax treatment is as follows:

- deferred annuity with cash option – proceeds are liable to tax at your highest rate on the profit you make (but you may be able to get top-slicing relief) – see p. 264

- immediate temporary annuity – the income you get is treated as income from a voluntarily purchased annuity. The company normally deducts 20 per cent tax before paying it out to you. Lower- and basic-rate taxpayers will not need to pay any more tax. Higher-rate taxpayers will need to pay a further 20 per cent tax
- endowment policies – at the end of the term, proceeds are taxed as a gain on a life insurance policy (if the policy is a non-qualifying one). Income from any bonuses cashed are treated as cashing-in part of a life insurance policy – see p. 267.

Investment trusts

Investment trust companies are companies quoted on the Stock Exchange. Their business is investing in the shares of other companies. The dividends they pay out are taxed in the same way as for any other company's shares.

Let property

In general, income from letting property is taxed as investment income. But the tax is worked out in the same way as for income from a business – see p. 230.

Life insurance policies

With regular-premium policies, there is normally no tax to pay on the proceeds as long as you don't cash the policy in before ten years or the first three-quarters of the term, whichever is the shorter. For more details, see p. 263. And for the rules on tax relief for policies taken out before 14 March 1984, see p. 271. With single-premium bonds, there's no basic-rate tax to pay when you cash them in, but there could be higher-rate tax – see p. 264.

Local authority investments

Interest on local authority loans made after 18 November 1984 is paid with tax deducted. Interest on local authority stock and yearling bonds is paid with 20 per cent tax deducted. Lower- and basic-rate taxpayers will not need to pay any more tax. Higher-rate taxpayers will need to pay a further 20 per cent tax. Any gain you make when you dispose of bonds is free of CGT.

National Savings investments

With National Savings Investment and Ordinary Accounts, and National Savings Capital Bonds, Income Bonds, Deposit Bonds and Pensioners Guaranteed Income Bonds interest is paid without deduction of tax. With National Savings Certificates and Yearly Plan (withdrawn to new investors on 1 February 1995), Children's Bonus Bonds and Premium Bonds, the proceeds are free of income tax. National Savings investments don't produce a capital gain and so are free of CGT.

With a National Savings Ordinary account, the first £70 of interest is tax-free – for husband and wife, it's £70 each. Anything more than that is taxed at 20 per cent and 40 per cent, if applicable. Any one person is allowed only £70 free of tax, however many National Savings Ordinary accounts he or she has. Note that if you and your spouse have separate accounts and you have, say, £100 interest and your spouse has £20, you will have to pay tax on £30 (i.e. £100 – £70) of your interest, even though the combined interest isn't more than 2 × £70 = £140. If you and your spouse have a joint account, however, you can have £140 interest free of tax.

With FIRST Option Bonds, interest is earned with 20 per cent tax deducted. If you're a non-taxpayer, you need to apply for a refund from your tax office. Lower- and basic-rate taxpayers will not need to pay any more tax. Higher-rate taxpayers will need to pay a further 20 per cent tax.
ICTA 1988 s18 (2–4), s46, s325, s326

Personal equity plans

These are a way of investing in shares in UK companies, unit trusts and investment trusts without having to pay tax on dividend or distribution income or on any capital gains. They are run by plan managers, e.g. banks or investment companies who take care of the administration.

You can put up to £6,000 in one general PEP and up to £3,000 in one single-company PEP each tax year. The range of investments you can buy through a general PEP includes:

- shares in UK or European Union (EU) companies
- certain corporate bonds and convertibles and preference shares issued by UK or EU companies – the bonds must have a minimum of five years to maturity at the time of

purchase, be denominated in sterling and carry a fixed rate of interest
- 'qualifying' unit and investment trusts i.e. those with at least half their investments in UK or EU shares and corporate bonds, etc.

In addition, you can use £1,500 of your £6,000 limit to invest in many (but not all) non-qualifying unit and investment trusts.

The money you place in a single-company PEP has to be invested in the ordinary shares of just one UK or EU company (investment trusts and corporate bonds are excluded).

If you don't invest the maximum, you can't carry your unused allowance forward to the next tax year. A husband and wife can each invest the maximum in their own PEP, but you have to be aged 18 or over and resident in the UK for tax purposes to qualify for a PEP.

Share dividends and distributions from unit trusts are usually paid with the equivalent of basic-rate tax already deducted. Whether or not that income is paid directly to you or reinvested in your plan, the plan manager will reclaim the tax for you. Any capital gain you make on your investments in the PEP is free of CGT. This is on top of the normal limit for exemption from CGT – £6,300 in the 1996–7 tax year. However, losses can't be set off against gains you make on other assets.

Cash may be deposited in a PEP to buy qualifying investments. The interest is paid gross if it is re-invested in the plan. You can also withdraw interest on cash of up to £180 a year without tax being deducted. But if you withdraw more than £180 in interest from cash on deposit, the whole lot becomes taxable and should be declared on your tax return. The plan manager is responsible for deducting and paying 20 per cent tax.

You can invest in shares, unit trusts and investment trusts in the same plan, and you can now transfer certain new issues of shares into your PEP (ask your plan manager).
ICTA 1988 s333

Shares

When you get dividends from UK companies there is no basic-rate tax to pay. With the dividends you get a tax credit. Your gross (before-tax) income is taken to be the amount of the dividend plus the amount of tax credit. The tax credit for the 1996–7 tax year works out at 20 per cent of the gross income. So if, say, the dividend is £80, the tax credit will be £20 and the gross income £100. A lower-rate or basic-rate taxpayer has no more tax to pay and a non-taxpayer can claim tax back, unless the dividend is either a stock dividend or a foreign income dividend. A stock dividend is one where you receive shares instead of cash; a foreign income dividend is one which companies with earnings from abroad have been able to issue since 1 July 1994.

If you pay tax at the higher rate, you will have to pay extra tax, but the tax credit counts as tax already paid.

When you sell your shares, any increase in value counts as a capital gain – see p. 295 for more details.

If the company gives you more shares as a result of a *bonus* (or *scrip*) issue, you are not liable to income tax unless you've chosen to have the shares instead of a cash dividend (a few companies give you the choice). If this is the case, you are liable to income tax on the cash equivalent of the shares.

If you hold your shares in a PEP, see p. 252. If your shares qualify for the BES, see p. 247. For the EIS – see p. 249. For details of share option or profit-sharing schemes, see p. 170.

ICTA 1988 s20, s231

Tax vouchers

You get a tax voucher from the company (or unit trust – see p. 255) showing the amount of the dividend (or distribution) and the amount of the tax credit.

With other types of income taxed before you get it, including distributions from unit trusts which specialise in British government stocks, you normally get a tax voucher or other document from the payer. This tells you the gross (before-tax) amount of income, the tax deducted and the actual sum you get.

Keep any tax vouchers as proof that tax has been credited or deducted.

TESSAs

Banks, building societies and other financial institutions offer tax-exempt special savings accounts to anyone over

18. Provided the savings are left in the account for five years, the interest earned on a TESSA is paid tax-free.

Most institutions will allow you to withdraw interest from your TESSA, but only an amount equivalent to the interest you'd receive after the deduction of 20 per cent tax. The remainder must stay in your account. If you withdraw too much interest (or any capital) the account will be closed. All the interest earned until then will be taxed as if it had been earned in the tax year the account is closed.

The most you will be able to invest in a TESSA is £9,000 over the five years – up to £3,000 in the first year, and up to £1,800 in each later year, provided you don't exceed the £9,000 overall maximum. Alternatively, you will be able to save a regular amount of up to £150 a month.

Once you have held a TESSA for its full five-year life, it has to be closed, but you can open a new TESSA account. And there's a more generous investment limit in the first year of a TESSA if it is opened within six months of an earlier one maturing. You can re-invest in the new TESSA all the capital you deposited (but not the interest earned) in the matured TESSA. In subsequent years the investment limit remains at £1,800 a year, and there is still an overall limit of £9,000.

ICTA 1988 s326A–s326C

Trust income

Trusts pay tax on their income – in the 1996–7 tax year, at 34 per cent if they are discretionary trusts, at the basic rate of 24 per cent otherwise. Trusts do not benefit from the 20 per cent rate of tax. This applies whether the income is kept by the trust or paid out to beneficiaries. With income paid out by the trust, you get a tax credit of the amount of tax deducted.

If you are a beneficiary of a discretionary trust, and the highest rate of tax you pay is less than 34 per cent, consider asking the trustees to pay out to you as much of the trust's income as possible. You'd be able to claim tax back from the Revenue. Trusts get only half the normal tax-free slice for CGT, i.e. £3,150 for 1996-7 as opposed to the £6,300 individuals have. For more on trusts, see p. 354.

ICTA 1988 s660–s670, s686, s687

Unit trusts

With distributions from most unit trusts, each distribution is accompanied by a tax credit of 20 per cent. The tax implications of this are the same as described for shares – see p. 253. Your gross (before-tax) income is taken to be the distribution *plus* the tax credit.

With the *first* distribution you get from a unit trust you're likely to get an *equalisation* payment. This is a return of part of the money you first invested, so doesn't count as income, has no tax credit and isn't taxable.

With an *accumulation* unit trust (where income is automatically re-invested for you) the amount re-invested – apart from any equalisation payment – counts as income and is taxable.

In your tax return you should enter the amount of the distribution and the amount of the tax credit.

If you buy unit trusts within a PEP, the income will be tax-free – see p. 252.
ICTA 1988 s20, s468, s469

Venture capital trusts

Venture capital trusts (VCTs) are a new sort of company quoted on the Stock Exchange. They operate like conventional investment trusts, but they invest in small unquoted trading companies which can include companies on the AIM (Alternative Investment Market). You can invest up to £100,000 a year in VCTs. They started on 6 April 1995 and have three tax advantages for investors:

- when you buy new ordinary shares in a VCT you can get income tax relief at 20 per cent, provided that the shares are held for at least five years. And, if you are re-investing money from the sale of an asset which is chargeable to CGT, you can defer any CGT due (see *Enterprise investment scheme* p. 249)
- dividends from VCTs are free of income tax
- gains you make when you dispose of your shares are free of CGT.

You need to balance these tax advantages against the intrinsic risk of investing in small unquoted companies. And to get the tax advantages there are, of course, conditions to be met. For example, at least 70 per cent of a VCT's investments must be in unquoted trading companies, with no more than 15 per cent in any one company or group of companies, and at least 30 per cent of a VCT's qualifying investments must be in ordinary shares. The definition of an 'unquoted trading company' will be broadly the same as for the enterprise investment scheme.

Which Schedules?

Investment income comes under the following Schedules:

Schedule A – income from letting property in the UK
Schedule D, Case III – interest, annuities or other annual payments
Schedule D, Case IV – income from foreign securities
Schedule D, Case V – income from foreign possessions
Schedule D, Case VI – income not assessable under any other case or schedule
Schedule F – distributions and dividends of a UK resident company.

Income regarded as yours during the administration period of a will

Any income which is regarded as yours during the administration period of a will or intestacy (i.e. while the details of who gets what are being worked out), will be paid to you with basic-rate tax deducted.
ICTA 1988 s695, s696

Tax on income from overseas investments

The tax treatment of income from abroad can be extraordinarily complicated, and if you have a substantial amount of such income you'll need to get specialist advice – and look at Inland Revenue leaflets *IR6* and *IR20*.

In general, if you're resident and ordinarily resident in the UK (see p. 173), all your income is liable to UK tax, whether or not it is brought into this country. However, income from overseas investments is often taxed in the country in which it originates – so two lots of tax could be charged on one lot of income. The UK government has made agreements with a wide range of countries to limit the extent to which income may be taxed twice. Under one of these *double taxation agreements*, the amount of tax which a foreign government deducts from income before it reaches you is reduced. The tax which is actually deducted is allowable as a tax credit against the UK tax on the same income.

Suppose, for example, that you're entitled to £1,000 in dividends from the US. Tax at 30 per cent, say, would normally be held by the US before paying over the dividends to non-US residents. However, because of our double taxation agreement with the US, only 15 per cent is withheld – i.e. you get £850. If, say, you're liable for tax in the UK at 40 per cent on your £1,000 gross dividends, there'd be £400 tax to pay. But the £150 you've paid in tax to the US would be allowed as credit against the £400 of UK tax you're liable for – so you'd have to hand over to the Revenue £250, not £400.

If you are liable for no UK tax (or less than has been deducted under a double taxation agreement) there'll be no further UK tax to pay – but you can't claim back the extra foreign tax you've paid.

How to get your relief

If your foreign income is paid to you through an agent (e.g. a bank) in the UK, who passes it on to you after deducting basic-rate tax, the agent should allow for any double taxation agreement when doing the sums. But if the income is paid direct to you from abroad, you have to apply for double taxation relief yourself. To get the foreign tax reduced, get an application form from the Financial Intermediaries and Claims Office (International)*. To get a credit for the foreign tax withheld, apply to your tax inspector.

When UK tax is due

From 6 April 1996, all foreign income you get will be taxed on a current-year basis.

Remittance basis

If this applies, you are taxed only on what income you bring into the UK. You can claim remittance basis if you're resident but not domiciled in the UK, or if you are a British

subject or a citizen of Ireland *and* you are resident but not ordinarily resident in the UK.
ICTA 1988 s65

Offshore funds

Any gain which you get when you sell an investment in an offshore fund is liable to income tax at your highest rate, unless the fund has *distributor status*. In this case only its income is liable to income tax and any gain will be liable to capital gains tax. An offshore fund can get distributor status if, for example, it distributes all its income.
ICTA 1988 s757–s763

14 *LIFE INSURANCE*

- Life policies, such as endowment policies, offer poor value if you cash them in early. Worse still, you could be hit with a tax bill if you are not careful – see p. 267.
- Some people enjoy tax relief on their life insurance premiums. They should take care not to lose it – see p. 271.
- You can still get tax relief on life insurance premiums which form part of a personal pension plan – see p. 272.
- Avoid inheritance tax by writing a life policy in trust – see p. 274.

Life insurance at its simplest is a way of providing for your dependants when you die. But as you can see from the table overleaf, policies have gone beyond this simplest form. Apart from insurance policies which pay out only when you die, there are policies which are mainly investments. Many of these were designed to make use of the premium subsidy available for qualifying policies – see p. 271. Though you can still get this subsidy on policies taken out on or before 13 March 1984, those issued after that date don't benefit.

Tax on the proceeds

You won't have to pay tax on the proceeds of *any* life insurance policy if (even with the policy gain added to your income) you pay tax at no more than the basic rate. And even if you're a higher-rate taxpayer there'll be no tax to pay on the proceeds of a *qualifying policy* if you keep it for long enough – see below. Otherwise you may have to pay higher-rate tax on any gain you make. How you work out the gain depends on whether the policy has come to the end of its term or you're cashing in all or part of it early.

There's normally no capital gains tax (CGT) to pay on the proceeds of a life insurance policy – but see pages 270 and 274.

In the 1994 Budget, the Chancellor announced that the tax treatment of life insurance as qualifying and non-qualifying policies would be reformed from 5 May 1996 onwards. However, a subsequent announcement said that reforms will be delayed pending further consultation. Details had not been announced as we went to press.

Qualifying policies

When a qualifying policy reaches the end of its term or pays out on the death of the person insured, the proceeds are free of income tax. So, for example, if you've kept a qualifying endowment policy till it matures there's no tax to pay. If you've kept the policy for at least ten years (or three-quarters of the term if this is less), there won't be income tax to pay either – see p. 266 for more details.

Broadly speaking, a life insurance policy is a qualifying policy if you pay regular premiums on it (e.g. monthly or yearly). There are other conditions about the length of the policy and how much the premiums can vary from year to year, but the insurance company will normally take care of these to make the policy qualify. Note that all policies taken out on or before 19 March 1968 are qualifying policies, whether they are regular-premium policies or not – as long as they haven't been altered since that date.
ICTA 1988 s266, s539, Sch 14–15

Non-qualifying policies

You may have to pay higher-rate tax on the proceeds of a non-qualifying policy when it matures. The gain you make counts as a taxable gain – see below for how to work out the gain and how it is taxed.

Tax the company pays

Though *you* pay no tax on the proceeds of a qualifying policy (and no basic-rate tax on the proceeds of a non-qualifying policy) it is wrong to think your return is tax-free. The insurance company has to pay tax on its profits, capital gains and income from investments. The company's tax bill is seen by the Inland Revenue as taking care of the

Finding your policy

Policy type	Term	Whole-life
investment or protection?	protection	either or both
qualifying policy? [1]	yes, if term one year or more	yes
how you pay	regular premiums	regular premiums
the benefits	**level-term** – pays out a lump sum if you die before a fixed date. If you don't die, nothing is paid out normally **decreasing term** – as with level term but cover decreases over the years. Commonly used to pay off a mortgage if you die *(mortgage protection policy)* **family income benefit** – pays out a tax-free income to your dependants (if you die) over the remaining years of the term **flexible term insurance** – as with term insurance but you have various options (e.g. to increase the cover each year, to renew the policy, to convert it to an investment-type policy) without further medical checks. But watch out if you get the premium subsidy, as you could lose it if you take up an option – see p. 271	**whole-life** – pays out a lump sum when you die, however far in the future. Policies can be *without-profits* which guarantee a fixed sum, or *with-profits* where the amount paid out increases over the years as the company adds bonuses. With some policies you stop paying premiums at a certain age (65, say). You can cash in the policy before you die **unit-linked whole-life** – your premiums buy units in funds run by the life insurance company. Some of the units are cashed each month to pay for a whole-life policy – units left are your investment. You can cash in the policy before you die With *flexible cover plans* you can choose the amount of life cover you get and therefore how much of your premiums are used for investment
what the policies are useful for	• protecting your dependants from suffering financially if you die during the term of the insurance • paying a large inheritance tax bill if the giver dies within seven years – see p. 363	• protecting your dependants from suffering financially when you die – however far in the future • possibly, building up a lump sum. If for your heirs, see p. 273 • paying inheritance tax when you die – see p. 363

[1] Individual policies may not meet all the qualifying requirements even where we say yes – check with your insurance company

Endowment/friendly society	Other investment type
either or both	investment (level of life cover may be low)
yes, if term ten years or more	no – but see *the benefits* (below)
regular premiums	single premium
all pay out a lump sum at a fixed date or if you die before then **endowment** – policies can be with or without profits (see *whole-life*). You can cash in the policy early **unit-linked savings plans** – part of each premium goes to buy term insurance, the rest buys units in one or more investment funds. The level of life cover may be low. You can cash in the policy early **friendly society savings plans** – the level of life cover is low, and you can't pay more than £270 a year in premiums (10 per cent of the premiums are ignored if premiums are paid more often than once a year). You can cash in the policy early.	**unit-linked single-premium bonds** – pay out a lump sum when you cash them in, or when you die. Your premium buys units in a fund run by the insurance company. You can cash in early. See p. 270 for more details **income bonds** – pay out a fixed income for a set number of years, and then return your original investment. Bonds are based on *annuities* and maybe *endowment policies* (which can be qualifying). Bonds will pay out if you die before a fixed date. With some bonds you can't cash in early. See p. 250 **growth bonds** – pay out a lump sum at a fixed date, or if you die before then. Bonds are based on *annuities* and/or *endowment policies* (which can be qualifying). With some bonds, you can't cash in early. See p. 250 for more details
• building up a lump sum (but watch out for low surrender values if you cash in the policy in the first few years). If for your heirs, see p. 273 • paying off a mortgage	**unit-linked bonds** • taking 5 per cent a year tax-free from your investment – see p. 267 **unit-linked bonds and growth bonds** • deferring income until you pay lower rate of income tax **income bonds** • providing an income

basic-rate tax on what you get from the policy.

Note that some of the business done by friendly societies is *tax-exempt*. So they don't have to pay corporation tax, or tax on investment income or capital gains which come from this business.

Working out the gain on a non-qualifying policy

When a policy comes to an end, the gain is normally the amount you get *less* the total premiums paid (but see p. 268 if you've cashed in part of your policy earlier). If the gain arises because the person dies, the gain is the cash-in value of the policy immediately before death (if this is less than the sum insured) *less* the premiums paid.

How the proceeds are taxed

The gain is added to your investment income for the year in which the policy comes to an end. You're liable for higher-rate income tax on the gain (but *not* basic-rate tax). So if you pay tax at the higher rate of 40 per cent, as the basic rate is 24 per cent, you'd have to pay tax at 40 – 24 = 16 per cent on the policy gain – see the example below. But if adding the gain to your income means that you'd be paying tax at a higher rate than you would otherwise have done – because it pushes part of your income over the higher-rate threshold – the Revenue should apply *top-slicing relief* to reduce your tax bill.

Top-slicing relief

Top-slicing relief, in effect, spreads the gain you make over the years that the policy has run. To work out your tax bill with top-slicing relief, first work out your *average yearly gain* by dividing the total gain by the number of *complete* years for which the policy ran. Then add this average yearly gain to your income for the tax year, and work out the higher-rate tax on the average yearly gain. To get your tax bill on the whole gain, multiply the tax bill on your average yearly gain by the number of complete years you have spread the gain over. See Example 1 below.

But note that cashing in *part* of a non-qualifying policy could create a *chargeable event* – see p. 268. If there has been a chargeable event before the policy came to an end, top-slicing relief uses only the number of years since the chargeable event.

ICTA 1988 s266, s539, Sch 15 (qualifying policies); ICTA 1988 s540, s541, s547, s550 (tax on proceeds)

EXAMPLE 1

Harris Granby bought a £20,000 single-premium bond in February 1992. He cashed it in for £30,000 in June 1996, making a gain of £10,000. He already has taxable income for the 1996–7 tax year of £23,500. If his tax bill were worked out in the normal way he would have to pay tax on his gain as shown below.

Rate of tax	Income on which Harris pays this rate of tax	Gain on bond	Amount of tax
20 per cent	£3,900		£780
24 per cent	£19,600		£4,704
24 per cent		£2,000	£480
40 per cent[1]		£8,000	£3,200
total gain on bond		£10,000	
basic- and higher-rate tax on gain			£3,680
subtract tax at basic rate on gain (24 per cent of £10,000)			£2,400
total tax bill on gain			**£1,280**

[1] Higher-rate tax paid on taxable income over £25,500 in the 1996–7 tax year.

But Harris gets top-slicing relief. With this, the *average yearly gain* of £2,500 (i.e. the £10,000 total gain divided by the four complete years the policy ran for) is added to his investment income for the year. His total tax bill on the gain is the higher-rate tax he'd pay on this average yearly gain, times the number of complete years he held the bond. Top-slicing relief saves Harris £1,280 – £320 = £960.

Rate of tax	Income on which Harris pays this rate of tax	Gain on bond	Amount of basic and higher-rate tax
20 per cent	£3,900		£780
24 per cent	£19,600		£4,704

24 per cent	£2,000	£480
40 per cent	£500	£200
total gain on bond	£2,500	
total tax on average yearly gain		£680
subtract tax at basic rate on average yearly gain (24 per cent of £2,500)		£600
so tax bill on average yearly gain is		£80
total tax bill on gain (£80 × 4)		**£320**

Age-related allowances

Although when you cash in all or part of a non-qualifying policy any gain is free of basic-rate tax, the whole gain (i.e. without top-slicing relief) is counted as part of your income for the year. For most people this has no effect on their allowances. But if you're aged 65 or over during the tax year, increasing your income can reduce the *age-related allowances* you get (see p. 103).

Age-related allowances are reduced by half of the amount by which a person's 'total income' exceeds a certain limit – £15,200 for the 1996–7 tax year. So if the gain from an insurance policy (or the excess if you cash in part of a policy) means a reduction in your age-related allowances, you'll in effect pay more income tax, whether or not you're liable for higher-rate tax.
ICTA 1988 s257

Cashing in a policy early

Life insurance policies with an investment element have some value – the *surrender value* – even before the policy comes to an end. How much tax you have to pay (if any) depends on whether or not the policy is a qualifying one.

Cashing in a qualifying policy
If you've been paying regular premiums for at least three-quarters of the term of the policy, or ten years, whichever is less, the gain you make remains tax-free. So with a 25-year term, there'd be no tax to pay if you surrendered after 10 years; with a 10-year term, there'd be no tax after 7½ years. But if you cash in the policy before this, you'll be taxed on the gain in the same way as when a non-qualifying policy pays out. So you'll be liable for higher-rate tax if it applies to you and will get top-slicing relief if this would cut your tax bill. You pay tax on the difference between the surrender value and the *gross* premiums paid (i.e. the premiums you've paid *plus* any premium subsidy – see p. 271).

Cashing in a non-qualifying policy
If you cash in a non-qualifying policy before the end of its term you pay tax on the surrender value in the same way as if it had run for its full term – see p. 263. So you may have to pay higher-rate tax (but not basic-rate tax) on the amount by which the cash-in value exceeds the premiums you've paid. You'll get top-slicing relief if this would reduce your tax bill.
ICTA 1988 s540

EXAMPLE 2

Ernest Strident has a ten-year unit-linked savings plan for which the premium is £50 a month. After five years he decides to cash in the policy. The total premiums to date are £3,000 and the surrender value is £3,500, so he's made a gain of £500. As he is a higher-rate taxpayer, he has to pay tax at 40 – 24 = 16 per cent on the £500 gain, i.e. £80 in all.

Cashing in part of a policy

You may want to cash in part of your policy, rather than the whole of it. Or, if bonuses are added, you could surrender a bonus. This is treated in the same way as cashing in part of your policy.

Cashing in part of a qualifying policy
If you cash in part of a qualifying policy after ten years (or

after three-quarters of its term if this is less), the gains you make are tax-free. But if you cash in part of the policy before this, you'll be taxed in the same way as for non-qualifying policies – see below.

Cashing in part of a non-qualifying policy

If you cash in part of a policy rather than the whole of it, you may be able to avoid paying tax straight away. What happens is that you get a tax-free allowance for each *complete* year that the policy has to run. So long as the allowance you're due is more than the total amount you get from the policy, there's no tax to pay at the time. But when the term of the policy finally comes to an end or you cash the rest of the policy in, there may be tax to pay.

For each of the first 20 years of the term of a policy the allowance is 1/20 (i.e. 5 per cent) of the premiums paid so far. For each year after the 20th year the allowance is 1/20 of the premium paid in that year and the previous 19 years. So, if you pay £1,000 a year in premiums, your allowance after the first year will be £50, after the second £100, after the third £150, and so on. Allowances not used each year are carried forward. Complete years are calculated from the date the policy is taken out – but you don't get an allowance until the first complete year starting after 13 March 1975.

If you exceed your total allowances, this creates a *chargeable event*. The difference between your total allowances and what you've had from the policy (the *excess*) is counted as a gain. This gain is treated in the same way as if you cash in a whole policy, so is subject to higher-rate tax, but not basic-rate tax. You'll get top-slicing relief if this reduces your tax bill, with the gain spread over the number of years you've had the policy, or the number of years since the last chargeable event, if there's been one already. When an excess is added to your income, the allowances you've taken into account are cancelled, and you start building up allowances again.

ICTA 1988 s546

EXAMPLE 3

Harvey Redbridge pays tax at the higher rate of 40 per cent. He has bought a single-premium bond for £10,000 and wants to withdraw as much as he can without paying tax at the moment.

For each of the first 20 years Harvey gets an allowance of $\frac{1}{20}$ of the total premiums paid so far – i.e. $\frac{1}{20}$ of £10,000 = £500. He can cash in £500 each year without paying tax in that year. For the 21st year onwards his allowance is $\frac{1}{20}$ of the premiums paid in that year and the previous 19 years – zero in Harvey's case as he paid for the policy all at once in the first year. So if he uses up his allowances in the first 20 years he won't be able to cash in any more of his policy without paying tax at the time (unless he's a basic-rate taxpayer by then).

Paid-up policies

Making a policy paid-up means that you stop paying the premiums but don't take your money out. Making part of a policy paid-up means you can reduce your premiums.

If you make a policy paid-up, the same rules apply as if you were to cash it in. However, you won't have to pay any tax until the policy finally pays out.
ICTA 1988 s540

When the policy comes to an end

If you've cashed in part of a policy before it finally comes to an end, the total gain on which you may have to pay tax is:

- the amount you get at the end *plus* any amounts you've had in the past, *less*
- the total premiums paid, any excesses you've already had (see p. 268) and any pre-14 March 1975 gains on the policy which the Inland Revenue was told about (either by you or the insurance company).

If after making these deductions you're left with a negative figure, you can subtract this from your 'total income' to reduce your higher-rate tax bill. But you can't subtract more than the total of the excesses you've made from partial surrenders and pre-14 March 1975 gains.
ICTA 1988 s540, s541, s547, s549

EXAMPLE 4

When Harvey's single-premium bond comes to an end (see Example 3), he's still paying tax at 40 per cent and so he'll have to pay tax on his gain. If Harvey used up his £500 allowance for each of the first 20 years, he'd have had 20 × £500 = £10,000 from the policy. If he got another £10,000, say, when the policy ended, his total gain would be £20,000 *minus* the £10,000 premium = £10,000, which would be added to his income for the year. Harvey would pay higher-rate (but no basic-rate) tax on the proceeds, i.e. 40 – 24 = 16 per cent × £10,000 = £1,600.

Capital gains and unit-linked policies

With a unit-linked policy, the insurance company invests your premiums in units in one or more investment funds. However, you don't own the units – the insurance company does. And so while you can get a tax-free return, the company has to pay tax on its investment income and on the capital gains it makes. In practice, the company doesn't have to sell units every time a policy is cashed in. So, in effect, the rate at which it pays any tax on capital gains can be lower than the full percentage – say, 10–20 per cent. This is deducted either from the investment fund or from the proceeds of the policy when you cash it in. So if you see that a deduction has been made for tax on capital gains, it's not tax on *your* gains but on the company's. You can't claim it back as being part of your £6,300 CGT exemption or by setting losses against it. (If you're not likely to pay CGT, you might consider investing in unit trusts rather than unit-linked life insurance.)

Single-premium bonds, which are invariably non-qualifying policies, are often unit-linked. The life insurance element of these bonds is usually tiny and what's paid on death will generally be the surrender value of the units. In a High Court case (*Fuji Finance Inc v Aetna Life Insurance Ltd*) in 1994, it was ruled that these bonds are really pure investment and not life insurance contracts at all. If the ruling stands, the special tax rules for non-qualifying life insurance policies would not apply to these bonds, and CGT could be payable on the proceeds.

The case was due to go to appeal as we went to press and the judgment could be altered. However, the government has announced that legislation will be passed if necessary to ensure that unit-linked insurance bonds sold in the past as life insurance contracts will be treated as life insurance contracts. Legislation will depend on the outcome of the court case, and the position of bonds sold in future remains unclear.

Cluster policies

With some policies, instead of your premiums buying just one insurance policy, they can be used to buy several policies. For example, if your premium was £50 a month you might get a cluster of ten policies, each with a premium of £5 a month. The advantage of cluster policies is that you don't have to treat all the policies in the same way. If you're a higher-rate taxpayer and you cash in part of a non-qualifying policy, you will be taxed on any *excess* that arises (see p. 268). You could end up paying less tax at the time if you have a cluster of policies, and cash in one (or more) of them. (But if you're paying tax at the same rate when you finally cash in the rest of the proceeds, you'll pay the same amount of tax in the long run.)

Tax relief on premiums

If you took out a qualifying policy before 14 March 1984, you are almost certainly getting a 12½ per cent subsidy on the premiums (whether you pay tax or not). You get the subsidy by paying lower premiums: if your premium is £100 a year (*gross*) you hand over £87.50 (*net*); the insurance company claims the extra £12.50 from the Revenue. But there's a limit on the amount of premiums you can get the subsidy on: the maximum is £1,500 a year of *gross* premiums or one-sixth of your 'total income', whichever is greater. In general, your 'total income' is your before-tax income (including the taxable gains from insurance policies) *minus* your outgoings – see p. 28.

This means that if your 'total income' is £9,000 or less, the subsidy stops when your *net* premiums reach £1,312.50 (£1,500 *less* the 12½ per cent subsidy). Premiums for a deferred annuity (see p. 272) also count towards this limit. A husband and wife can each have premiums up to the limit (before 6 April 1990, the limit applied to their combined 'total income'). A divorced couple go on getting the subsidy on premiums for policies on each other's lives, provided the policy was taken out before the divorce and after 5 April 1979.
ICTA 1988 s266, s274, Sch 14

Hanging on to your subsidy

The subsidy continues for policies taken out before 14 March 1984. But if you vary the terms of such a policy and the benefits are increased or the term extended (whether or not this is by exercising an option already in the policy), you'll lose all your subsidy. However, benefits which increase automatically as part of the original contract will not affect the subsidy.

If you're thinking of changing a policy which gets the premium subsidy, check with the insurance company to see if your planned change would affect the subsidy.

Life insurance with a personal pension

If you're self-employed or an employee not in an employer's pension scheme, you may be able to get tax relief at your highest rate of tax on premiums for special term insurance sold with personal pension plans. You can claim full tax relief on premiums of up to 5 per cent of your *net relevant earnings* – i.e. your taxable profits from being self-employed or your earnings from a job where you're not in the employer's pension scheme. But what you pay in such premiums reduces the maximum amount you can pay in to a personal pension.
ICTA 1988 s637, s640

Death and superannuation benefits

You can still get tax relief on certain combined sickness and life insurance policies issued by friendly societies. You'll get tax relief on the life part of your premium, at half your top rate of tax – so if you're paying tax at 40 per cent, you'll get tax relief at 20 per cent.

You can get tax relief at the same rate for the part of a trade union subscription which is for superannuation (i.e. pension), funeral or life insurance benefits.
ICTA 1988 s266

Premium subsidy for deferred annuities

You get a 12½ per cent subsidy on premiums used to buy a *deferred annuity*. You get this on gross premiums of up to £100 (i.e. premiums you pay of up to £87.50). There's also tax relief at the basic rate on premiums for deferred annuities which will pay an income to your dependants after your death, providing you *have* to pay the premiums either under an Act of Parliament or under the rules of your job.
ICTA 1988 s266, s273, s274

Dealing with the proceeds

A life insurance policy will usually pay out to your estate, if you die. But you may want the proceeds to go to someone else. You could do this on your death by simply leaving the money in your will. But in that case, the proceeds of the policy will be added to your estate, and there might be an inheritance tax to pay – see Chapter 18. You could instead *assign* the policy to someone else during your lifetime. You can do this by completing a *deed of assignment* and sending a *notice* to the life insurance company (ask the company or a solicitor for details). You may want to assign the policy for a number of reasons:

- to make a gift
- to avoid inheritance tax by writing the policy in trust
- to raise cash
- to get a loan.

Assignment and subsidy

If you get the premium subsidy and assign your policy, you can still get the subsidy while you continue to pay the premiums. But if the premiums are paid for by someone else (other than your husband or wife) they won't qualify for the subsidy.

Gifts

If you give a policy away (by assigning it to somebody else) it counts as a gift for inheritance tax purposes. The value the Revenue puts on the gift is either the market value of the policy *plus* any amounts paid out earlier, or the total amount paid in premiums up to the time you give the policy away, whichever is higher. The market value will often be close to the cash-in value. But, for example, the market value of a policy on someone close to death will be almost as high as the amount the policy would pay out on death. If you continue to pay the premiums after you've given the policy away, the amount you pay also counts as a gift. But there shouldn't be any inheritance tax to pay as the payments will normally come into one of the tax-free categories – see p. 341. If you die, the proceeds won't form part of your estate.

If you've been given somebody else's life insurance policy, you are liable for any tax that's due when the policy pays out or is cashed in – see p. 260 for how much (if any) tax you'll have to pay.
ICTA 1988 s540; IHTA 1984 s167

Trusts

By getting the policy *written in trust*, you may be able to avoid inheritance tax as the proceeds are not added to your estate. The proceeds can then also be paid to the beneficiaries without waiting for probate.

If you want the policy to pay out to your wife (or husband) or children, the simplest way of setting it up in trust is to get a suitable trust wording from the insurance company involved. Most companies are happy to recommend the appropriate trust for your needs. As a gift, the proceeds of policies written in trust will not form part of your estate, but the premiums may count as gifts for inheritance tax purposes unless they come into one of the tax-free categories – see p. 341. If the policy pays out while you're still alive (e.g. a growth bond), you'll have to pay any income tax that's due, though you will be able to claim it back from the trustees. For more about trusts, see p. 354.
ICTA 1988 s547, s551

Selling your policy

If you sell a non-qualifying policy, it's treated in the same way as though you had cashed it in – see p. 267. You may have to pay higher-rate tax on the amount that you sold the policy for *less* the premiums you've paid.

If you sell a qualifying policy you'll be taxed as above if you do so in the first 10 years or within three-quarters of its term if this is shorter (this also applies if you made it paid-up in this period and then sold it later on). If you buy a policy, there may be CGT to pay if you eventually make a gain on it (as with other assets – see Chapter 15).

Note that you can't avoid paying the income tax that's due by selling your policy and buying it back – in the hope that you'd be liable for CGT instead. If you've had your own policy reassigned to you, you'll have to pay income tax, not CGT, on the gain.
ICTA 1988 s540, s544

Security for a loan

You may be able to use your insurance policy as security for a loan either from the life insurance company or from somewhere else, e.g. a bank. A loan from the insurance company is treated as a partial surrender (for the amount of the loan) if the policy was taken out before 26 March 1974 and is non-qualifying, or if it's qualifying and the money is lent at less than a commercial rate of interest. Any repayment (other than interest) of the loan you make to the life insurance company is treated as a premium when working out the tax bill at the end. If you're still alive when the policy pays out, you'll be liable for any extra tax that's due.

Note that it won't be treated as a surrender if the loan is to a person over 64 borrowing the money to buy an annuity, nor if the loan is from somewhere else, e.g. a bank or building society, rather than the insurance company.
ICTA 1988 s540

15 *Capital Gains Tax*

- Everyone can make capital gains of £6,300 in 1996–7 tax-free.
- You can make use of any unused tax-free amount by 'bed-and-breakfasting' investments – see p. 305.
- Gains made in line with inflation are tax-free – see p. 282.
- You can delay a capital gains tax bill if you re-invest your money in certain ways – see p. 288.
- From the 1996–7 tax year, the age at which you can dispose of a business and claim retirement relief for capital gains tax has gone down to 50 – see p. 292.

The simplest example of making a capital gain is *selling something you own at a profit.* For example, you buy a Victorian etching for £10,000, and sell it a couple of years later for £12,000. Your capital gain (ignoring any allowance for inflation) is £2,000, or a bit less if you can claim some expenses of buying and selling.

But you can make a capital gain even when no buying or selling is involved, e.g. if you give something away. So here are the basic rules:

- you can make a capital gain (or loss) whenever you *dispose of an asset,* no matter how you come to own it
- broadly, anything you own (whether in the UK or not) counts as an asset, e.g. houses, jewellery, shares, antiques
- you dispose of an asset not only if you sell it, but also if you give it away, exchange it or lose it. You also dispose of an asset if you sell rights to it, e.g. grant a lease, or if it is destroyed or becomes worthless, or if you get compensation for damage to it, e.g. insurance money, and don't spend all the money on restoring it
- not every gain you make will be taxable, nor will every loss be recognised by the Inland Revenue

- there is no capital gains tax (CGT) to pay when you die
- for rules if you dispose of a business asset see p. 291
- if you re-invest in some unquoted companies see p. 288
- for some gifts (including those to your husband or wife), you can avoid an immediate tax bill (see p. 288).
  TCGA 1992 s1, s2, s15, s21–s24

Note: nearly all statutory references are to the Taxation of Chargeable Gains Act 1992. We haven't, in all cases, given the full reference – so *s222* = *TCGA 1992 s222*. Other statutes are mentioned individually.

Overseas

If you are domiciled in the UK (see p. 174), CGT applies to gains you make anywhere in the world – i.e. overseas as well as in the UK (*s1*). If the gains cannot be remitted to the UK (because of exchange or currency controls operated by the country the gain is made in), you can ask the Revenue to defer bringing them into the tax net until they can be remitted (*s279*).

If you are living abroad, CGT still applies to you for any tax year in which you are *resident* or *ordinarily resident* in the UK (see p. 173) – even if only for part of that tax year (*s2*). But if you are not domiciled in the UK (see p. 174), gains made abroad are liable to CGT only if remitted to the UK (*s12, s16*).

A person who goes abroad for longer periods of time may cease to be resident and ordinarily resident. If you cease to be both, you won't be liable for UK CGT on disposals from the day after you leave the UK until 5 April before you come back. If you've been away for more than three years, this exemption continues until the day before you return. You could take advantage of this to dispose of assets which would produce chargeable gains (if you still want to hold the assets, you could buy them back the next day, establishing a higher initial price for when you return to the UK).

Tax-free gains

Gains on some assets are free from CGT. (The other side of the coin is that *losses* on these assets can't normally be used to reduce your taxable gains for tax purposes.)

The main assets on which gains are tax-free are:

- your only or main home – see p. 219 (*s222*)

- motor vehicles. This rule normally favours the Revenue since you usually sell your car for a loss. But if you sell, say, a vintage or classic car, bus or traction engine at a gain, that will be tax-free unless you make a habit of doing this, in which case you could be taxed as though you were trading in cars (*s263*)
- National Savings investments – none is liable to CGT, though some are liable to income tax (*s121*)
- British money including post-1837 gold sovereigns (*s21*)
- currency for personal use abroad. Normally, foreign currency is an asset for CGT purposes. But gains on currency for the use of your family and yourself abroad, e.g. on holiday or to maintain a home abroad, are tax-free (*s269*)
- betting and lottery winnings (*s51*)
- British government stocks (or options in them), though income tax might be due on any accrued interest. This exemption now extends to many types of corporate bond, as long as you acquired them after 13 March 1984 (*s115, s117; FA 1984 s64*)
- shares, unit trusts, investment trusts and corporate bonds held in a personal equity plan (PEP) – see p. 252 (*s151; ICTA 1988 s333*)
- shares in qualifying venture capital trusts (see p. 256)
- shares issued after 18 March 1986 under the business expansion scheme (see p. 248) sold more than five years after you bought them – on their first disposal only (*s150C*)
- shares issued under the enterprise investment scheme (see p. 249)
- life insurance policies. The proceeds – whether on maturity, surrender or sale – are free of CGT provided you didn't buy the policy from a previous holder, but note the insurance company will have paid CGT on gains before you get the proceeds (*s210*)
- damages for any wrong or injury suffered by you in your private or professional life, e.g. damages for assault or defamation (*s51*)
- settled property. If you have been given an interest under a UK settlement (but not the underlying property), the proceeds if you sell it are tax-free (*s76*)
- timber. A gain on the disposal of timber – whether growing or felled – is tax-free provided that you're not taxed as carrying on a forestry trade (in which case the disposal will be liable for income tax as a trading

transaction). The exemption does not apply to the land on which the timber was growing (*s250*)

- decorations for valour. A gain on the disposal of an award for valour or gallant conduct is tax-free, e.g. your father's Victoria Cross or George Cross, provided that you did not buy the award (*s268*)
- gifts to charities or certain national institutions (*s257*)
- a gift of *heritage property* is tax-free if it satisfies certain conditions (for what *heritage property* is, see p. 342) (*s258*)
- 'wasting assets', i.e. any chattel which had a predictable useful life of no more than 50 years when you first acquired it, provided that you have not used the asset in your business so that it qualified for capital allowances. This covers electronic equipment and racehorses, say, but also machinery (including antique clocks) (*s45*)
- for chattels with a predictable life of more than 50 years, gains may be partly tax-free – broadly speaking, the rules are as follows:

  If the *disposal proceeds* are less than £6,000, any gain is tax-free. So if you buy a watercolour for £1,500 and sell it for £5,750, the gain is tax-free.

  If the *disposal proceeds* are more than £6,000, your taxable gain is *either* your actual gain *or* 5/3 of the excess over £6,000, whichever is the lower.

  If the disposal proceeds are less than £6,000, and you've made a loss, you're assumed to have received £6,000. So if you buy a picture for £7,000 and sell it for £5,000, your loss, for tax purposes, is £1,000.

  If you sell a set of articles, e.g. a set of matching chairs, separately, but in effect to the same person, the Revenue is likely to treat the sales as a single sale. So if you sold six chairs for £2,000 each, you'd be taxed as though you'd made a single sale of £12,000, not six sales of £2,000. (*TCGA 1992 s262*)

Working out your gains or losses

To work out your chargeable gain (or loss) on assets which aren't tax-free, this is what you do:

Step one Take the *final value* of the asset. This will be:

- the *disposal proceeds* if you sold it
- its *market value* if you gave it away
- the *insurance proceeds* if it is destroyed. For damaged assets, see p. 305.

Step two Subtract the *initial value* of the asset to get the *gross capital gain* (or loss). The initial value is:

- *what you paid for it* if you bought it
- its *market value at the time of the gift* if you were given it (though see p. 288 for special rules about gifts)
- its *probate value* if you inherited it.

If you acquired the asset before 31 March 1982, use the market value on that date as the initial value (but there is an alternative – see p. 281).

Step three Deduct any *allowable expenses* which you incurred in acquiring or disposing of the asset, or in increasing its value – this gives you the net capital gain (or loss). You can include:

- legal and valuation fees, stamp duty, commission, advertising
- the legal cost of defending your title to the asset
- money spent on the asset which has increased its value (but not maintenance or normal repairs).

TCGA 1992 s38

With assets acquired before 31 March 1982, you don't normally include any expenses incurred before that date (but see p. 281).

A gain can be reduced, or eliminated by *indexation* which is explained fully on p. 282. Disposals after 29 November 1993 can no longer be turned into a loss by applying indexation. Indexation increases the amount of your initial value and allowable expenses in line with the Retail Prices Index (RPI) since March 1982 and prevents you being taxed on gains made purely because of inflation. Gains after indexation are called *chargeable gains*.

EXAMPLE 1

Larry Beaulieu bought a second home in January 1987 for £55,000. He paid legal fees of £450 and stamp duty of £550. In July 1988, he added an extension costing £10,000. In May 1996 he sells the home for £110,000, with agents' fees of £2,000 and legal fees of £300.

Larry works out his capital gain (before any indexation allowance – see Example 3, p. 283 for how indexation works):

	£
sale proceeds	110,000
less **purchase price**	55,000
less **allowable expenses:**	
costs of acquisition	1,000
costs of improvement	10,000
expenses of disposal	2,300
net capital gain	**41,700**

Assets acquired before 31 March 1982

Indexation began in March 1982, so gains before that date are not indexed. Normally, only gains made since that date are chargeable, and indexation takes account of inflation since that date.

So when working out the gain on an asset bought before 31 March 1982, you now use its market value on that date, not the cost when you originally acquired it. You also ignore any expenses incurred before 31 March 1982 in working out the net gain (or loss). Indexation allowance applies to the market value on 31 March 1982 and to any expenses incurred since that date.

In some cases, using the March 1982 value could mean a bigger tax bill, as the following example shows.

EXAMPLE 2

Roger Wiley bought shares in XYZ Telephones Plc in January 1980, at a cost of £10,000. By March 1982, their value had fallen to £5,000, though they then recovered. Roger sold them for £15,000 in June 1996. Ignoring indexation allowance, Roger had made a net gain of £15,000 – £10,000 = £5,000 on the shares.

But the gain is much bigger if Roger uses the March 1982 value for assets acquired before 31 March 1982:

	£
sale proceeds	15,000
less **value on 31 March 1982**	5,000
net capital gain	**10,000**

Where you've owned something before 31 March 1982 which fell in value up to that date and has risen since, using the March 1982 value will artificially inflate your gain. The opposite is true if you bought something before 31 March 1982 which rose in price up to that date and has since fallen in value – the loss you make is artificially inflated.

Where either of these things would happen, the gain or loss will be worked out using the original cost. This means that the initial value is what you paid for the asset; and you can claim expenses incurred before 31 March 1982. In this case, both initial value and pre-31 March 1982 expenses are indexed from 31 March 1982.

If in Example 2 Roger had sold the shares in June 1996 for £8,000, then using the March 1982 value there would have been an unindexed gain of £8,000 – £5,000 = £3,000; using the actual purchase price in January 1980, there would have been a loss of £10,000 – £8,000 = £2,000. If you make a gain under one set of rules and a loss under the other, it will be treated as though you had made neither a gain nor a loss on disposal.
TCGA 1992 s35

All seems too complicated?
You can elect for all assets acquired before 31 March 1982 to be treated as if you'd acquired them on that date, and only expenses incurred since then can be deducted from gains. You must make the election within two years of the end of the first tax year after 5 April 1988 in which you dispose of an asset bought before 31 March 1982. Once you make this election, you can't change your mind. You'll be no worse off if all or most of your assets were worth more on 31 March 1982 than when you acquired them.
TCGA 1992 s35(5)

Indexation allowance

Indexation allowance gives some protection against being taxed on paper profits. It works like this: your initial value and allowable expenses are linked to the RPI (Retail Prices Index) and increased in line with the index. The effect is that your taxable gain is reduced or eliminated. See p. 367 for a list of the RPI figures since March 1982, when indexation started.
TCGA 1992 s53–s55

How to work out the indexation allowance

First work out your net gain or loss in the normal way, taking no account of the indexation rules: take the asset's *final value* and subtract the *initial value* and *allowable expenses* (see p. 280).

Then, for the initial value and each allowable expense, you must work out the indexation allowance. Multiply the initial value or expense by the following (worked out to three decimal places):

$$\frac{RD - RI}{RI}$$

where RD = the RPI for the month in which the asset is disposed of, and RI = the RPI for the month in which the initial value or expense became 'due and payable'.

So if, for example, you buy something for £5,000, and the RPI for the month in which you buy it is 105, and the RPI for the month in which you sell it is 120, your indexation allowance for the initial value is worked out like this:

$$£5,000 \times \frac{120 - 105}{105}$$

$$= £5,000 \times 0.143$$
$$= £715$$

EXAMPLE 3

Larry Beaulieu works out the indexation allowance due on the gain he made selling his holiday home in May 1996 (see Example 1 on p. 280).

The relevant RPI figures are as follows:

January 1987 (when he bought the home)	100.0
July 1988 (when he built the extension)	106.7
RPI when he sells the home	151.7

(Note: the selling RPI has been estimated for the purposes of this calculation – see p. 369 for details of where to find actual figures.)

He can work out the indexation allowance on the initial value (£55,000) and costs of acquisition (£1,000) together, since they were incurred in the same month of January 1987. The indexation allowance on these January 1987 costs of £55,000 + £1,000 = £56,000 is as follows:

$$\pounds 56{,}000 \times \frac{151.7 - 100.0}{100.0} = \pounds 56{,}000 \times \frac{51.7}{100.0}$$
$$= \pounds 56{,}000 \times 0.517$$
$$= \pounds 28{,}952$$

The indexation allowance on the cost of the extension is:

$$\pounds 10{,}000 \times \frac{151.7 - 106.7}{106.7} = \pounds 10{,}000 \times \frac{45.0}{106.7}$$
$$= \pounds 10{,}000 \times 0.422$$
$$= \pounds 4{,}220$$

total indexation allowance	= £28,952 + £4,220	
	= £33,172	
net chargeable gain on sale of home	= £41,700 – £33,172	
		= £8,528

Working out the tax bill

The first step in calculating your CGT bill is to add together all your *chargeable gains* (gains after indexation) for the tax year and deduct your *allowable losses* for the year. The result is your *net chargeable gains* for the tax year. The first slice of chargeable gains (£6,300 in 1996–7) is tax-free. And you may be able to set off losses from earlier years against your gains this year.

If your chargeable losses exceed your chargeable gains (including those covered by the tax-free slice of £6,300 in 1996–7), you will have made a *net chargeable loss.* This can be used to reduce your CGT bill in future years.
TCGA 1992 s2

The tax-free slice

The first slice of net chargeable gains in any tax year is free of CGT. The size of this tax-free slice is set for each tax year.

For the 1996–7 tax year, the tax-free slice is £6,300. A husband and wife get a £6,300 tax-free slice each, which they can set against only their own net gains.

If your net chargeable gains are less than the amount of the tax-free slice, there will be no CGT to pay. But you can't carry any unused part of the tax-free slice forward to future years.
TCGA 1992 s3, Sch 1

EXAMPLE 4

Nerys Peacock has made a chargeable gain on her holiday flat of £15,000 in the 1996–7 tax year. In the same year, she sold shares, with a chargeable loss of £12,475.

Nerys has a net chargeable gain for the tax year of £15,000 − £12,475 = £2,525. The tax-free slice for the year of £6,300 will wipe out this net chargeable gain, and there will be no CGT to pay.

However, it's worth noting that Nerys has 'wasted' losses of £3,775, because her net chargeable gains were less than the tax-free slice. She needed only £8,700 of losses to reduce her net chargeable gains to the level of the tax-free slice, and the extra £3,775 which brought the total below £6,300 can't be carried over to another year.

Losses from previous years

If your net chargeable gains come to more than the tax-free slice, any losses you have left from previous years can be deducted from the total.

Note that losses from previous years are deducted after the tax-free slice, so they aren't wasted by reducing your net chargeable gains below £6,300. If you don't use all the losses carried over from previous years, they can be carried forward to future years.
TCGA 1992 s2, s3

EXAMPLE 5

In the 1995–6 tax year, Gregor Knight lost £6,000 on some shares he had sold. He had no gains in that tax year to set the loss off against, so the loss was carried forward for future years.

In the 1996–7 tax year, Gregor made a net chargeable gain of £9,750 on selling some more shares (and no other gains or losses). His tax-free slice for 1996–7 is £6,300, so he would pay CGT on £9,750 − £6,300 = £3,450. However, he can set off some of the carried forward from the previous year to reduce this taxable gain to zero.

This leaves £6,000 – £3,450 = £2,550 in losses to be carried forward to future years.

How much tax

If there's anything left of your net chargeable gains after you have deducted the tax-free slice and losses carried over from previous years, there will be CGT to pay. The remaining total is added to your taxable income and taxed as if it were the top slice of your income – at 20 per cent, 24 per cent or 40 per cent.

This may not be as straightforward as it sounds because investment income with tax of 20 per cent deducted at source is also taxed as the top slice of your income. (Remember to take account of gross investment income.) Here's how capital gains and income use up the different tax rates.

The 20 per cent tax rate covering up to £3,900 is first used for non-investment income, then for capital gains, then for investment income. But with the 24 per cent rate covering the next £21,600 (i.e. £25,500–£3,900) the order is varied. First it taxes non-investment income, then investment income, and finally capital gains. Any capital gains (and income) which takes you over £25,500 is taxed at 40 per cent.

To work out whether any gains will be taxed at 20 per cent, deduct non-investment income from £3,900. The balance, if any, will be used to tax capital gains. To work out whether any gains will be taxed at 24 per cent, deduct from £21,600 any remaining non-investment income and investment income. The balance, if any, will be used to tax gains at 24 per cent.

Any gains still not taxed will be taxed at 40 per cent. See Examples 6 and 7 for how this works in practice.

EXAMPLE 6

Lily Brooke has net chargeable gains of £11,500 in 1996–7, £5,200 after deducting the tax-free slice of £6,300. She has no unused losses from previous years. Her taxable income is £21,200: £19,500 from investments, £1,700 from non-investment income.

Here's the tax on Lily's capital gains:

		CGT
20 per cent tax on the first £3,900 –		
1 Non-investment income	£1,700	
2 Capital gains	£2,200	**£440**
3 Investment income	–	
Total	£3,900	
24 per cent tax from £3,901 to £25,500		
1 Non-investment income	–	
2 Investment income	£19,500	
3 Capital gains	£2,100	**£504**
Total	£21,600	
40 per cent tax on £25,501+		
1 Non-investment income	–	
2 Investment income	–	
3 Capital gains	£900	**£360**
Total	£900	**£1,304**

EXAMPLE 7

Lily's son Linford also has net chargeable gains of £11,500 in 1996–7, £5,200 after deducting the tax-free slice of £6,300. He has no unused losses from previous years. His taxable income is £21,200: but unlike his mother, £19,500 is non-investment income, and £1,700 from investment.

Here's how Linford's CGT is worked out.

		CGT
20 per cent tax on the first £3,900 –		
1 Non-investment income	£3,900	
2 Capital gains	–	
3 Investment income	–	
Total	£3,900	
24 per cent tax from £3,901 to £25,500		
1 Non-investment income	£15,600	
2 Investment income	£1,700	
3 Capital gains	£4,300	**£1,032**
Total	£21,600	

40 per cent tax on £25,501+		CGT
1 Non-investment income	–	
2 Investment income	–	
3 Capital gains	£900	**£360**
Total	£900	**£1,392**

Gifts

When you give something away, you're usually treated as disposing of it for what it is worth, even though you get nothing for it. So if you buy a picture for £20,000 and give it away a few months later when it's worth £25,000, you'll make a gain (ignoring indexation) of £5,000.

The person who receives the gift is treated as having paid what the property is worth. So, with the gift of the picture, if the person receiving the picture sells it later for £28,000, the gain (ignoring indexation) is £28,000 – £25,000 = £3,000.

TCGA 1992 s17

Re-investment relief

Any chargeable gain made after 29 November 1993 from a disposal of any shares or other assets can be deferred if the gain is re-invested in a qualifying unquoted trading company, enterprise investment scheme company or venture capital trust. This includes companies quoted on the Alternative Investment Market (AIM). The re-investment must take place between one year before and three years after the chargeable gain was made.

Re-investments in companies such as subsidiaries and certain financial concerns are excluded as are investments where you are guaranteed a return of your investment at the outset. The gain will also become chargeable if you re-invest in a company which ceases to meet the qualifying conditions within three years of your investment being made, or if you emigrate within three years.

CGT and the family

If you dispose of an asset to a *connected person,* you are treated by the Revenue as disposing of the asset for its market value at the time of the gift. A *connected person* includes your wife or husband *and:*

- a relative. *Relative* means brother, sister, parents, grandparents and other ancestors or lineal descendants (but not uncle, aunt, cousin, nephew or niece)
- the wife or husband of a relative
- your wife or husband's relative
- the trustees of a settlement which you have set up
- a company which you control
- a person with whom you are in partnership or their wife or husband or relative.

So if you don't sell for the proper commercial price, you'll be taxed as if you had, even if you didn't intend to make a gift.

More important still is that if you make a loss on a disposal to a connected person, you can set that loss off only against a gain from another disposal by you to that person. This is the case even though your loss is a proper commercial one – i.e. based on the market value. So if you sell shares at a loss to your son, the loss cannot be used to reduce your general taxable gains for the year.
TCGA 1992 s18, s286

Gifts between husband and wife

The following applies to gifts between a husband and wife who are not separated.

- Whether or not any money changes hands, there is no tax to pay at the time of the disposal, and there is no gain or loss for tax purposes.
- The recipient gets the giver's initial value plus the giver's allowable expenses, plus any indexation allowances up to the time of the gift.
- The recipient gets any further indexation allowance due until the asset is disposed of.
  TCGA 1992 s58

Death

There is no CGT to pay on death. This has profound implications on whether you should make gifts in your lifetime, or wait until you die. This is because:

- rates of *inheritance tax* (IHT) for gifts made on death are higher than for gifts made more than three years prior to death – see p. 340
- for *CGT* there is often a tax liability on gifts made during life.

There is, therefore, often a 'trade-off' between the two taxes. If your estate is likely to be liable for a lot of IHT on death, it may be worth giving now – paying CGT on any gains you realise and cutting down IHT on your death. The alternative is to hang on, avoiding CGT altogether, but risking a higher IHT bill.

- In general, the less well off you are, the better it is to hang on to things until you die.
- Remember that you can pass property gradually from your estate without tax, by making use of the £6,300 tax-free slice of CGT, and by using the exemptions for IHT.
- If you can claim a large indexation allowance, and lots of allowable expenses (and, in the case of homes, various periods where the gain is ignored – see p. 221), the CGT bill may be little or nothing, so then it may be worth giving something away before you die.
  TCGA 1992 s62

CGT and executors

On death, your estate passes to your personal representatives. The Revenue regards them as acquiring the property at its *market value at the date of your death.* The effect is that the value of everything you own is given a 'free uplift' to its value at the date of death. The beneficiaries of your estate acquire the assets at the market value as from the date of death (this is the probate value). Indexation applies from the date of death.

Allowable losses in the tax year of your death (made before your death) are set off first against your taxable gains for that period. If there are still losses left over they can be set against your taxable gains for the three tax years before the tax year of death, taking later years first (but the losses are needed only to reduce the chargeable gains to the level of the tax-free slice – see Example 5 on p. 285). This is the only time when allowable losses can be carried back.
TCGA 1992, s62

CGT and business

Replacing business assets

If you dispose of a *qualifying business asset* and invest an amount equal to the disposal proceeds in another qualifying business asset during the period of one year *before* the disposal or within three years *after* the disposal, you can claim *roll-over relief* on your taxable gain on the disposal of the old asset.

Qualifying assets are:

- land and buildings occupied and used for the purpose of your trade
- plant or machinery which is fixed but which does not actually form part of a building, e.g. heavy engineering equipment bolted to the floor of the workshop
- ships, aircraft and hovercraft – but not vehicles
- goodwill.

  TCGA 1992 s152–s159

How it works

The gain is usually rolled over by reducing (for tax purposes) your acquisition cost for the new asset by the amount of the chargeable gain. So when you dispose of the new asset, its initial value (in working out your gain) is reduced. You can roll over your tax liability again by investing in another qualifying asset.

If you re-invest in a *wasting asset,* i.e. in an asset with a predictable life not exceeding 50 years when you acquire it, or in an asset which will become a wasting asset in the next 10 years, your gain is deferred until the earliest of the following:

- you cease to use the new asset for the purposes of the trade
- the tenth anniversary of your acquisition of the new asset
- you dispose of the new asset without re-investing the proceeds in a new qualifying asset. If you *do* re-invest in a non-wasting asset before selling the old asset, the original gain is rolled over into the new asset, and the deferred gain is cancelled.

Other points

- Any indexation allowance available on the old asset is taken into account in determining the size of the gain rolled over.

- If you have more than one business, the re-investment need not be in the same business as the one in which the old asset was used.
- If the asset you disposed of was used for private purposes as well as business purposes, or if you do not spend an amount equal to the whole of the disposal proceeds on the new asset, only a proportionate part of your taxable gain is deferred.
- You may even be able to claim roll-over relief if you dispose of an asset which you own personally but which is used for the purposes of the trade carried on by the company in which you work if you then purchase a new qualifying asset which is used for the purposes of the trade carried on by the same family company. Roll-over relief is available in this situation even if you charge the company a full market rent for the asset.

Retirement relief

If you are aged 50 or over or have to retire before then due to ill-health, and you dispose of a business (or shares in it), part or all of your gain may be tax-free. This relief is available for any kind of disposal including sale, gift and selling off assets after the business has ceased. You don't actually have to retire to get the relief. You will be able to claim the relief if:

- you are 50 or over, *or*
- you are retiring due to ill-health. In this case, you'll need to satisfy the Revenue that you are incapable of carrying on your work and that your incapacity is likely to be permanent.

The disposal requirements are:

- you must be disposing of the whole or part of a business which you have owned for at least one year in most cases (but see p. 294), *or*
- you must be disposing of shares which you have owned for at least one year (but see p. 294) in a company or a holding company for the business you worked in. To satisfy this condition, you must be entitled to at least 5 per cent of the voting rights *and* you must be a *full-time* working officer or employee of the company or a subsidiary. 'Full-time' generally means that you spend substantially the whole of your working hours in the job.

Relief is also available where trustees dispose of shares or assets in which you have an interest (though not if your interest is only for a fixed period of time).
TCGA 1992 s163, s164, Sch 6

How much tax relief?
You get the maximum retirement relief if you have owned the business for ten years:

- the first £250,000 of capital gains is free of CGT altogether
- half the gain between £250,000 and £1m is taxable.

If the gain is more than £1m, then £250,000 plus half of £1m – £250,000 = £750,000 (i.e. £375,000) is tax-free. This is a maximum tax-free gain of £250,000 + £375,000 = £625,000.

If you have owned the business for less than ten years, you get 10 per cent of the maximum relief for every complete year of ownership. So if you have owned the business for just one year, gains up to 10 per cent of £250,000 are tax-free (i.e. gains of up to £25,000). And 10 per cent of half the gain betweeen £250,000 and £1m is tax-free (a maximum of 10 per cent of £325,000, or £32,500). You must have at least one complete year of ownership (but see opposite) – for the period of ownership. After that, you're entitled to relief in proportion to the period. So if you have owned the business for 8 years and 3 months, your relief is 82.5 per cent.

The relief applies to the permanent capital assets of the business – it doesn't apply to the value of trading stock. Similarly, if you dispose of shares, the relief will apply only to the value of the shares that represents chargeable business assets. You don't have to have owned every asset for the whole time that you have owned the business – you can still get the full relief on assets owned for less than ten years if you have owned the business for more than ten years.

You get only one lot of retirement relief, but you need not use it on one disposal – you can claim it bit by bit as you divest yourself of the business. A husband and wife can each claim it, in effect doubling the amount of relief if they each qualify.
TCGA 1992 s163, s164, Sch 6

Owned several businesses? The last one for under a year?
The period that qualifies for retirement relief can be extended if you have carried on two or more qualifying businesses in succession, provided that the gap between businesses is two years or less. The different periods of business in the ten years before the date for which you want to claim relief can be added together. In this case, you can include the last period of business even if it was for less than one year.
IR Press Release, April 1994

EXAMPLE 8

Bill Whitsock bought a newsagent's shop in March 1990 when he took early retirement. In July 1995, he sold the shop as a going concern at the age of 65 – his chargeable gain was £45,000.

Bill had owned the business for five years four months (5.3 years), so is entitled to 5.3×10 per cent = 53 per cent of the maximum retirement relief. This means that 53 per cent of the first £250,000 of gain can be tax-free – a total of £132,500 tax-free. So Bill's whole gain is tax-free.

Gifts of business assets

If you give business assets (or sell them at an undervalue) to an individual or trust you can claim roll-over relief (see p. 291) as long as the recipient isn't resident overseas.

There is a special roll-over relief for a gift of business assets by an individual to a company resident in the UK. The relief applies to the disposal of a business asset which you have used in your business for the period you have owned it. It also applies to shares in your family trading company.

If you claim the relief, the gain you make on the disposal is held over and deducted from the acquisition cost of the asset for the company. If you charged the company a special low price for the asset but still made some gain, that gain is chargeable. But the rest of the gain is rolled over.
TCGA 1992 s165

Retirement relief or roll-over relief?

Ideally, you should go for retirement relief, rather than for roll-over relief, because roll-over is only a deferral of tax, not exemption from tax.

If retirement relief is not available, or is insufficient, the general roll-over relief for gifts or the special relief for gifts of business assets can be very useful in passing on your business in your lifetime. But rolling over your gain is likely to reduce the other person's acquisition cost and increase his or her gain.

Shares and unit trusts

Special rules for shares are necessary because of their uniform nature. One share of a particular class in a given company is just the same as another share of the same class in that company, e.g. one ordinary share of £1 in ICI is worth just as much as any other £1 ordinary share in ICI.

Rules are straightforward if all the shares you own of a particular type were acquired by you at the same time, and disposed of all together. In this case, you calculate CGT in the same way as for any other asset – see Example 9 below.

Problems begin if you have acquired shares of the same description at different times. When you come to dispose of the shares, special rules decide *how much the shares cost you; which shares you've disposed of;* and *what your indexation allowance is* (if any). The rules are explained below.

Investment trusts and unit trusts

The same rules apply to shares in an investment trust as for quoted shares in any other type of company. The rules for shares also apply to units in a unit trust. But see p. 302 for regular purchases through a savings plan.

EXAMPLE 9

Don has a holding of 2,500 £1 ordinary shares and 500 7 per cent £1 preference shares in European Plastics plc. He acquired the ordinary shares for £2,100 in August 1982 and he acquired the preference shares for £250 in May 1973.

In the 1996–7 tax year he disposes of all the ordinary shares for £5,250 and all the preference shares for £360. The gross gain on each disposal, ignoring incidental costs, is:

Ordinary shares	£	**Preference shares**	£
proceeds	5,250	proceeds	360
less cost	2,100	less cost	250
gross gain	3,150	gross gain	110

In each case, Don is entitled to an indexation allowance:
RPI for month of disposal (for this example) 151.7
RPI for March 1982 is 79.44
RPI for August 1982 is 81.90

The indexation allowance is:

Ordinary shares

$\frac{151.7 - 81.90}{81.90} = 0.852$

$= 0.852 \times £2,100 = £1,789$

The chargeable gain on the ordinary shares =
£3,150 – £1,789 = £1,361

Preference shares

$\frac{151.7 - 79.44}{79.44} = 0.910$

$= 0.910 \times £250 = £228$

The chargeable gain on the preference shares =
£110 – £228 = minus £118,
i.e. there is no chargeable gain

If Don had sold only half of his holding of ordinary shares and only half of his holding of preference shares, his allowable costs for each disposal would have been half the allowable costs shown.

Which shares do you sell?

If you have acquired shares of *the same class in the same company* at different times, the Revenue has special rules for deciding which shares you've disposed of. They decide:

- the price you paid for the shares (or their *initial value* if you didn't buy them)
- when you acquired the shares
- how much indexation allowance you have, if any.

Example 10 on p. 299 shows how the rules work in practice.

Shares listed on the Stock Exchange or dealt in on

the Unlisted Securities Market (USM) are valued at the *lower* of:

- the lower of the two quoted closing prices shown in the Stock Exchange Daily Official List for that day, plus *one-quarter* of the difference between the lower and the higher closing price
- half-way between the highest and lowest recorded prices for the day of valuation.

If you dispose of shares in stages, the Revenue looks at an earlier disposal before a later disposal in seeing which shares you have disposed of.

The Revenue will say that you have disposed of the shares in the following order:

Batch one: shares acquired on the same day as disposal

If you acquire and dispose of (or *vice versa*) shares of the same type on the same day, the disposal will be matched to the acquisition made on that day.
TCGA 1992 s105

Batch two: shares acquired within ten days of the disposal

Next, the Revenue looks at all the shares of the same type which you acquired at any time within ten days before the disposal. There is no indexation allowance for shares owned for ten days or less. This is to prevent you buying shares at the end of one month and selling them at the beginning of the next to get one month's indexation allowance.
TCGA 1992 s107(3), (4), (5)

Batch three: shares acquired on or after 6 April 1982

Shares (except those disposed of on the same day or within ten days) are pooled. The cost of each share is the average cost of acquiring the shares in the pool. So if you bought 2,000 shares for £5,000, 2,000 for £6,000, 2,000 for £7,000, the average is £18,000 ÷ 6,000 = £3 a share. You have a separate pool for each type of share you hold in a company. Any more shares of that type which you acquire are added to the pool, unless disposed of on the same day or within ten days. The total acquisition costs of pooled shares are treated as expenditure on a single asset.
TCGA 1992 s107(8), (9), s108

Batch four: shares acquired before 6 April 1982

If you bought several lots of the same share at different times they are put into the 1982 pool. The cost of each share is its market value on 31 March 1982 (or the original cost if this is to your advantage and you have not made the rebasing election – see p. 281). Indexation runs from March 1982.
TCGA 1992 s109

Batch five: shares acquired on or before 6 April 1965

The Revenue will match the shares you dispose of with shares bought later rather than earlier – see p. 304 for how they are valued. However, you can elect for all such shares to be treated as if they had been acquired on 6 April 1965 and pooled with your Batch four shares instead. In most cases, this will not only greatly simplify the calculations, but will also mean you pay less CGT – tell your tax inspector within two years of the end of the first tax year after 5 April 1985 in which you dispose of such shares.
TCGA 1992 s35, Sch 2

Rights and bonus issues

Shares you get under a rights or bonus issue belong to the same batch as the original shares to which they relate.

Rights issues give you the right to buy new shares in proportion to your existing shareholding. When you come to sell shares, you take the cost of the original shareholding *plus* the cost of the rights issue, apply the index-linking rules to them separately, divide by the number of shares in the whole shareholding and multiply by the number of shares you've sold. This is your acquisition cost for the shares you've sold.

Bonus issues give you free shares to tack on to existing shares. Your acquisition cost (or your pool cost) will be affected – e.g. if you buy 2,500 shares for £5,000, and get a bonus of 1,500 shares, your cost per share falls from £2 to £1.25. This adjusted cost is indexed from the same day as the original shareholding was indexed.
TCGA 1992 s126–s128, s131, s132

EXAMPLE 10

Sue Shearson built up a holding of Worldwide Pharmaceuticals 50p ordinary shares over 25 years :

1 August 1962	1,500 shares for £1,250
1 May 1964	500 shares for £375
1 May 1968	2,000 shares for £1,600
4 September 1972	1,000 shares for £850
13 June 1979	1,500 shares for £1,300
26 November 1982	2,500 shares for £2,350
1 April 1985	1,250 shares for £1,800
16 July 1985	2,000 shares for £3,200

She has begun to sell parcels of shares since 1985, as follows:

25 June 1987	2,000 shares for £4,500
19 May 1996	5,000 shares for £12,400

Notes

1. The market value of the shares on 31 March 1982 was 92p.
2. The relevant RPI figures are as follows: March 1982 – 79.44; November 1982 – 82.66; April 1985 – 94.78; July 1985 – 95.23; June 1987 – 101.9; May 1996 – 151.7 (estimated: the figure is to be published after we go to press).

The 1987 sale The first lot of shares that Sue sold were the 2,000 in June 1987. Sue hadn't bought any shares in Worldwide Pharmaceuticals that day or during the previous ten days, so these shares are taken to come from her pool of shares bought since 5 April 1982. The shares in this pool were acquired in three lots:

2,500 for £2,350 in November 1982
1,250 for £1,800 in April 1985
2,000 for £3,200 in July 1985
Total: 5,750 for £7,350

The first step is to work out the value of the pool at the time the shares were sold, incorporating indexation. This means working out the indexation allowance at the time shares were bought compared to when there was a previous addition to the pool:

April 1985: indexation allowance on November 1982 shares

$$= £2{,}350 \times \frac{94.78 - 82.66}{82.66}$$

$= £345$

So the value of the pool including the indexation allowance in April 1985 was the new shares at £1,800 + £2,350 + £345 = £4,495

July 1985: indexation allowance on existing pool

$$= £4{,}495 \times \frac{95.23 - 94.78}{94.78}$$

$$= £22$$

So the value of the pool including the next indexation allowance in July 1985 was the new shares at £3,200 + £4,495 + £22 = £7,717

In June 1987 when the first sale takes place: indexation allowance on existing pool

$$= £7{,}717 \times \frac{101.9 - 95.23}{95.23}$$

$$= £540$$

So the 'indexed value of the pool in June 1987 is £7,717+ £540 = £8,257.

If Sue sold all 5,750 of her post-April 1982 shares on 25 June 1987, she could have subtracted from the proceeds the indexed value of the pool, i.e. £8,257. But she sold only 2,000 of the shares, so she can deduct from the £4,500 proceeds:

$$\frac{2{,}000}{5{,}750} \times £8{,}257 = £2{,}872$$

So the chargeable gain on the June 1987 sale is:

£4,500 – £2,872 = £1,628

The value of the remaining 5,750 – 2,000 = 3,750 shares in the pool on 25 June 1987 is:

$$\frac{3{,}750}{5{,}750} \times £8{,}257 = £5{,}385$$

This figure can now be used as the initial cost of calculating the gain on subsequent disposals from the pool, indexed to June 1987.

The May 1996 sale Sue sold 5,000 shares in May 1996 for £12,400. Of these shares, 3,750 are the remainder of the post-April 1982 shares and 5,000 − 3,750 = 1,250 come from the pre-April 1982 shares.

The gain on the 3,750 post-1982 shares can be worked out using their value at the June 1987 sale, worked out above (£5,385). The sale proceeds are:

$$\frac{3{,}750}{5{,}000} \times £12{,}400 = £9{,}300$$

The net gain is £9,300 − £5,385 = £3,915.

Indexation allowance on this net gain runs from June 1987 (RPI = 101.9) to May 1996 (estimated RPI = 151.7):

$$£5{,}385 \times \frac{151.7 - 101.9}{101.9} = £2{,}633$$

The chargeable gain on 3,750 post-April 1982 shares:

£3,915 − £2,633 = £1,282

The remaining 1,250 shares sold in May 1996 brought in £12,400 − £9,300 = £3,100. These shares come from the 1982 pool, which is made up of shares bought before 6 April 1982 and after 5 April 1965 as follows:

2,000 at £1,600 in May 1968
1,000 at £850 in September 1972
1,500 at £1,300 in June 1979
total: 4,500 at £3,750

The initial value of this pool is taken as £3,750 if the actual cost is used. But there is a choice between using the actual cost and the market value on 31 March 1982 of 92p. 4,500 shares at 92p is £4,140, so Sue decides to go for rebasing to 31 March 1982 – this higher initial value means a lower capital gain. The initial value of the 4,500 shares becomes £4,140, with indexation allowance running from March 1982.

The indexation allowance on this pool if all the shares had been sold in May 1996 would be:

$$£4{,}140 \times \frac{151.7 - 79.44}{79.44} = £4{,}140 \times 0.910$$
$$= £3{,}767$$

So if Sue had sold all 4,500 of the 1982 pool shares in May 1996, she could have subtracted from the proceeds the initial cost of £4,140 and indexation allowance of £3,767 – a total of £7,907. But she has sold only 1,250 of these shares, so she can deduct from the £3,100 proceeds:

$\frac{1,250}{4,500} \times £7,907 = £2,196$

The chargeable gain on the 1982 pool shares = £3,100 – £2,196
= £904

The total chargeable gains on shares sold in May 1996
= £1,282 + £904
= £2,186

For Sue's records, she still has 4,500 – 1,250 = 3,250 shares in her 1982 pool. Their value at May 1996 is:

$\frac{3,250}{4,500} \times £7,907 = £5,711$

This figure can be used when calculating the cost of subsequent disposals from this pool, indexed to May 1996.

Finally, there are also 2,000 shares from before 6 April 1965. These will not be touched until all the shares in the 1982 pool have gone. When, finally, Sue starts to dispose of the pre-1965 shares, it will be 'last in, first out' (the May 1964 purchase will go before the August 1962 shares) unless she opts to add them to her 1982 pool. Putting them into the 1982 pool would give them an initial value of 92p a share (their market value at 31 March 1982). Since this is higher than the 75p–83p they actually cost, Sue would be well advised to go for this option.

Regular savings plans

With unit trust or investment trust monthly savings plans, working out your gains and losses could be very complicated. You would have to work out the gain and indexation allowance for each instalment when making a disposal from the pool.

If you want to avoid the detailed calculations, you can opt for a simplified way of working out the initial costs and indexation allowances. This assumes that all 12 monthly instalments are made in the seventh month of the year (the year is the accounting year of the fund). If you have made small one-off investments or re-invested the income, the amounts are added to the total of monthly instalments. On the other hand, small withdrawals are subtracted from the total.

Special rules will apply if:

- you add a one-off lump sum of more than twice the monthly instalment in any month (this is treated as a separate investment)
- you increase the monthly instalments after the seventh month (the extra is added to next year's fund)
- you withdraw more than a quarter of the amount invested in the year by regular instalments (you will have to calculate the gain and indexation allowance on each investment).

To opt for this simplified method, you must write to your tax office within two years of the end of the first tax year after 6 April 1988 in which you dispose of the units or shares *and* any of the following applies:

- you face a CGT bill
- the disposal proceeds are more than twice the amount of the tax-free slice for the year (£6,300 for 1996–7)
- your other disposals in the year create net losses.

SP 3/89

EXAMPLE 11

Hugh Jacks invests £100 a month in a unit trust regular savings plan. The distributions are re-invested. Hugh opts for the simplified method of calculating the initial costs and indexation allowance for the investment.

The unit trust's accounting year runs from 1 January to 31 December. In the 1996 accounting year, distributions to the value of £100 were re-invested. Using the simplified method, Hugh is taken to have invested the 12 instalments of £100 plus the £100 reinvested distributions, i.e.:

£100 × 12 + £100 = £1,200 + £100
= £1,300

This investment will be indexed from the seventh month of the accounting year, i.e. July 1996.

Payment by instalments

Newly issued shares are often paid for by instalments. With a privatisation issue, indexation allowance on the total paid runs from the date you acquire the shares. With other share issues, indexation allowance depends on when the instalments are paid:

- if paid within 12 months of when the shares were acquired, indexation allowance on the instalments runs from when the shares were acquired
- if paid more than 12 months after the shares were acquired, indexation allowance runs from when the payments were made.
  TCGA 1992 s113

Takeovers, mergers and reconstructions

If you exchange your existing shares for new shares on a takeover or merger, or if the company is being reconstructed, the exchange will not normally give rise to a disposal. As far as *time of acquisition* and *cost* are concerned, the new shares will be in the position of the old.

But if you exchange your old shares for new shares and cash, you are taken to have disposed of a proportion of your old shares. The gain or loss which you make on the disposal is a proportion of the gain or loss you would have made if you had disposed of the shares entirely for cash. That proportion is the percentage of the exchange represented by cash. So if the exchange is one-fourth cash, three-fourths new shares, your gain or loss will be one-fourth what it would have been if you had taken all cash.
TCGA 1992 s126–s138

Quoted shares acquired before 6 April 1965

The Revenue assumes that these shares were disposed of by you on 6 April 1965 and immediately re-acquired by you for what they were worth on that date. The normal rule for calculating the market value of quoted shares (see p. 297) is *not* used. Instead, the Revenue makes a calculation which is more favourable to you, using the greater of:

- the lower of the two quoted prices shown in the Stock Exchange Official Daily List for that day, plus half the difference between them

- the price half-way between the highest and lowest prices at which bargains were recorded on that day, excluding bargains at special prices.

These shares are *not* pooled with shares of the same type which you acquired after 5 April 1965 unless you have chosen this option. Instead, your chargeable gain (or loss) on a disposal of the shares is the difference between market value at 6 April 1965 and the disposal proceeds (less any indexation allowance).

This calculation is then compared with the 'truth' – i.e. the Revenue sees whether you would have made a gain, or a loss, using the initial value of the shares when you first acquired them (in most cases, what you actually paid for them).

If the first calculation would have the effect of increasing a real loss (or gain), the Revenue takes the actual loss (or gain) instead.

If one calculation shows a gain, and the other shows a loss, you are treated as having made neither a gain nor a loss for tax purposes.
TCGA 1992 s35, Sch 2 paras 1–7

Bed-and-breakfasting

You 'bed-and-breakfast' shares by selling them, and then buying them back the following day. The purpose is as follows:

- if you have made a gain on the shares, and your net chargeable gains for the year are below the £6,300 tax-free slice, you could sell enough shares to bring your gains for the year up to, but not beyond, the tax-free slice. This would create a higher acquisition cost for the shares, so your taxable gain on a later disposal would be reduced
- if your chargeable gains for the year look like being more than the tax-free slice, and you own shares which are standing at a loss, you could sell enough shares to bring your gains for the year down to the tax-free slice.

Insurance proceeds

If you receive insurance proceeds for damage to, or the loss of, an asset, you may have to pay CGT, unless the proceeds of disposal of that asset are tax-free. So if you receive insurance money in compensation for theft of your jewellery, you may have a tax liability – but not if you get insurance money when your main home burns down.

However, there's no liability on the proceeds if you spend them in restoring or (generally within one year of the loss) replacing the asset. The rules work like this. For restorations:

- the proceeds are deducted from your allowable costs for the asset
- if you spend the money on restoring or replacing the asset, and if this is an allowable expense for CGT (it normally is), the figures balance – i.e. what you spend is added back to your allowable expenses.

For replacements:

- the proceeds are deemed to be equal to your allowable costs for the original asset including any indexation allowance
- any excess of the proceeds (plus any remaining value in the original asset) is deducted from the allowable cost of the replacement asset.

There may be difficulty where insurance proceeds are spent restoring a damaged item which was badly in need of repair at the time of the damage, since part of the expense will be for repair (not allowable) rather than for restoration (allowable). You also have to be a little careful about what constitutes replacement: if you 'replace' your stolen necklace with a watercolour, the Revenue is unlikely to be co-operative.
TCGA 1992 s23

16 *Stamp Duty*

- Stamp duty is a tax that's hard to avoid, but some homebuyers may save money with a bit of fine-tuning – see p. 308.

Stamp duty – brought in nearly 300 years ago – is a tax on *documents* required for the change of ownership of property. What is taxed is not, for example, the actual sale of a house or shares, nor the person doing the buying or selling, but the document associated with that transaction. If there's no document, there's no tax – and all quite legal, too. This feature of the tax is one that, in theory at least, gives great scope for tax-avoiders. But in practice it's usually impossible to avoid documents: the ownership of houses, for example, has to be transferred by a written document.

There are two main types of stamp duty:

- *ad valorem duties*, which are charged as a percentage of the price of the house, shares or whatever – the higher the price, the higher the duty
- *fixed duties*, where the duty is fixed – often in pennies rather than pounds – and not related to the value of the transaction.

Transfers of houses and land

Sales or exchanges of houses, land and other property are liable for *ad valorem* duty of 1 per cent, with the exception that transfers up to £60,000 pay no tax. Although there is nothing in the legislation to say who should pay the tax, it is normally the buyer.

Once the price of a house goes over £60,000, stamp duty becomes payable on the *whole* price. To take an extreme, if unlikely, case, the tax on a purchase price of £60,000 is nil, but on a price of £60,001 the tax would be £601.

It is not possible to avoid stamp duty by splitting the purchase of a house or land into two or more parts, each part for £60,000 or less. To qualify for exemption from tax, the solicitor or you (if doing-it-yourself) have to submit a certificate which says: '*It is hereby certified that the transaction hereby effected does not form part of a larger transaction or of a series of transactions in respect of which the amount or value of the consideration exceeds £60,000.*'

> If you're buying a home priced at a little more than £60,000, it's going to pay you handsomely if you can get the price down to £60,000. If bargaining won't do the trick, and if you are buying carpets, curtains and other fittings, try to get agreement to pay for these separately – duty is charged only on the price of the house. This could well save you some £600 in tax.

Tenants buying their houses at a discounted price under the Right-to-Buy Scheme pay stamp duty on the discounted price.

Exchanges of property

With an exchange of property there can be stamp duty to pay even if no money changes hands. For example, if two houses worth £100,000 each are exchanged, it counts as two property transfers and stamp duty of £1,000 (1 per cent) is charged for each property. If both houses were worth £50,000 there would be no stamp duty because each of the transfers is below £60,000.

If you are swapping one property plus cash for a more valuable property (e.g. you exchange your current property worth £80,000 for one worth £100,000 and hand over the extra £20,000 in cash) make sure that the contract makes clear the cash will be paid as *equality* money. If your contract does not make this clear, stamp duty will be charged on £100,000 for each of the two transfers. If you specify that the cash is equality money, duty will be charged only on £80,000 for the lower-value property.

The rules are different if you are buying a new property from a builder who accepts your old property (plus some cash). In this case, you would pay stamp duty only on what you pay for the new property (if it exceeds £60,000) i.e. the value of your old house plus the cash. Handing over your old property as part payment for the sale would not be regarded as a separate sale, so there'll be no stamp duty on that part of the transaction.

The rules for swapping can be complicated. To get advice contact a stamp office.*
FA 1994 s239

Leases
What you pay for an *existing* lease on a flat or house is taxed in exactly the same way as transfers of houses and land (including the £60,000 tax-free exemption).

But *new* leases – such as a long lease on a new or refurbished flat – are treated differently, and often taxed twice over. The premium on a long lease (that is, the lump sum you are paying for the lease) is taxed in the same way as a transfer of a freehold house (except that you do not benefit from the £60,000 exemption if the yearly ground rent is over £600). But the yearly payments you have to make under the lease (excluding the service charges) are also taxed. The amount of tax depends on the length of the lease and the average amount of the yearly payments. Sometimes neither the lease nor the annual rent is expressed in actual cash amounts. In this case stamp duty will be based on the open market value of the property, or the market rent in the case of a new lease.

Transfer of shares

Transfers of shares are currently liable for *ad valorem* duty of 0.5 per cent. This is rounded up to the nearest 50p. The stockbroker adds the tax to the cost of the shares, and it's the buyer of the shares who normally pays the tax. There is no tax-free amount – i.e. all of the transaction, whatever the amount, is liable for tax. However, if you give shares away – i.e. you transfer ownership and do not receive money or other 'consideration' in exchange – there is no stamp duty to pay.

In October 1986, stamp duty reserve was introduced to catch purchases of shares for which no document was produced and which therefore escaped stamp duty, e.g. shares bought and resold in the same Stock Exchange account. In the 1995 Budget, it was proposed that stamp duty reserve tax (SDRT) would be payable on all 'paperless' share transactions at a flat rate of 0.5 per cent. This is in preparation for the introduction of paperless share transfers under the Crest system, which the Stock Exchange expects to be up and running in the summer of 1996.

17 BUILDING UP A PENSION

- A pension scheme or plan is one of the best ways to save for retirement – you get tax relief on your contributions, and the investments grow tax-free.
- If you are in a scheme at work, consider making additional voluntary contributions – see p. 320.
- If you are paying into a personal pension plan, make the most of the maximum contributions you can, including unused relief from earlier years – see p. 330.

During your working life, you will probably be building up an income from various sources for your retirement. You may well build up rights to a state pension through your National Insurance contributions. And you may also get pensions from employers' pension schemes you've belonged to and from your own personal pension plans. In addition, you are likely to have some income from savings and investments, or perhaps you'll have created some ready cash by moving to a smaller home or selling a business.

Although a state retirement pension provides a basic income which is currently kept in line with inflation, few people would want to have no other income. The real advantage of employers' pension schemes and personal pension plans over other forms of savings is the tax concessions. You get full tax relief on the contributions you make into the scheme up to certain limits. No tax is charged on investment income or capital gains made by a pension fund. And you can normally take part of the proceeds as a tax-free lump sum. Details of how income from pensions is taxed are given in Chapter 5. In this chapter we'll look at the tax implications of your pension choices, and the limits on contributions and benefits available in each case. At the end of the chapter we'll look at how to make use of unused tax relief from past years.

The state pension scheme

Basic retirement pension

You qualify for a basic state retirement pension by paying (or being credited with) enough National Insurance contributions of certain types during your working life. The contributions which count are:

- Class 1 contributions – paid by people who work for an employer, although reduced-rate contributions paid by some married women and widows don't count towards a pension
- Class 2 contributions – paid by the self-employed
- Class 3 contributions – voluntary payments to make up gaps in your contribution record
- flat-rate contributions made before 6 April 1975 – the predecessors of Class 1 and Class 2 contributions.

Class 4 contributions paid by the self-employed don't carry any entitlement to a pension.

Additional pension (SERPS)

Since 1978, during periods spent working for an employer, you have been able to build up the right to the additional state pension known as the state earnings related pension scheme (SERPS). Like the basic state pension, your SERPS pension will be increased each year in line with the Retail Price Index, but will be related to your average pay between certain limits (adjusted for increases in average earnings) and the number of years you have been making the relevant National Insurance payments into the scheme.

Many employers' pension schemes are 'contracted out' of SERPS. This means you pay less National Insurance, but you don't build up any SERPS pension. Instead, if your employer's pension scheme is based on your *final pay*, it currently has to guarantee that your pension is broadly equivalent to (or better than) the SERPS pension you would have earned during the same period. If your employer's scheme is based on the value of your share of the investments in the pension fund (a *money purchase* scheme), it must guarantee to make certain payments to the fund, and you get *protected rights* (see below).

Another substitute for SERPS is a personal pension plan. This also gives you some protected rights, including a widow's or widower's pension. Plans used as an alternative to SERPS are often referred to as *protected rights* plans and *rebate* plans. If you take out one of these, some of the National Insurance contributions paid by you and your employer will be rebated to the plan provider (a life insurance company, friendly society, unit trust, bank or other authorised provider) together with basic-rate tax relief on your National Insurance rebate. The government will also make an extra contribution to the plan as an added incentive if you are aged 30 or over. If you are young and not in an employer's scheme (or in an employer's scheme which is not contracted out), it might be worth considering contracting out through a personal plan in the hope of getting a better pension than SERPS would give you. If you are older, staying in SERPS – or contracting back in – will be the better option, given the current level of rebates. But it's unlikely to be worth leaving an employer's scheme simply in order to rejoin SERPS.

Graduated pension

Graduated pensions are a relic of the state scheme which existed from 1961 to 1975. They were built up by people who earned more than £9 a week. The Department of Social Security (DSS) keeps records of the pension each person has earned, and you'll get a small index-linked pension at retirement.

National Insurance for the state pension

Class 1 contributions for employees (1996–7)

National Insurance contributions are worked out on your weekly or monthly earnings *before* deducting payments to an employer's pension scheme or personal pension plan. You don't pay contributions on fringe benefits or expense payments that you get, but payments in kind which can be easily sold (such as shares, gilts, commodities and gold bullion) are subject to National Insurance.

- You pay 2 per cent of your pay on the first £61 each week – the lower earnings limit (but nothing if you earn less than this).
- You pay 10 per cent of your pay between £61 and £455 each week – the upper earnings limit – or 8.2 per cent if you are contracted out through your employer's scheme.
- You don't pay any National Insurance on pay over the upper earnings limit.

Class 2 contributions for the self-employed (1996–7)

- You pay £6.05 a week. You can claim exemption from making these payments if your earnings are no more than £3,430 in the 1996–7 tax year, but then you won't be building up a state pension entitlement.

Class 3 (voluntary) contributions (1996–7)

- You pay £5.95 for each week.

Employers' pension schemes

An employer's pension scheme is an effective way of saving for your retirement. The employer normally pays most or all of the cost – a valuable tax-free fringe benefit. If the scheme is contributory, you get tax relief at your highest rate of income tax on your own contributions, so the cost to you is less than the amount invested in the fund. Each time you're paid, your employer subtracts the amount of your pension contributions (including any additional voluntary contributions, AVCs, you make – see p. 320) from your gross pay and uses the Pay-As-You-Earn (PAYE) system to work out the tax that's due on the pay that's left.

In addition, the pension fund doesn't have to pay any tax on its investment income or capital gains, so the return on its investments is likely to be higher than from other ways of saving. At retirement, you are allowed to receive a substantial tax-free lump sum. The pension you get is taxed as earned income, not investment income.

To qualify for these tax concessions a pension scheme must either be set up under an Act of Parliament (as many schemes for public employees are), or be *exempt approved* by the Inland Revenue. Approval is automatic if the scheme meets all the statutory conditions, but the Revenue has the power to approve schemes which don't entirely conform.

Your employer doesn't have to offer membership of a pension scheme and can't make you join one.
ICTA 1988 s590–594

Benefits from employers' pension schemes

The benefits you get will vary from scheme to scheme, but common benefits are:

- a pension payable to you on retirement
- the right to swap some of your pension for a tax-free lump sum (in some schemes you always get a tax-free lump sum – there is no choice)
- a pension for your widow, widower or dependants
- a pension if you choose to retire early, or have to do so because of ill health
- life insurance.

The maximum benefits you can get are restricted by the Revenue and by the rules of the scheme, which may not be as generous as the Revenue allows. With a few exceptions, the Revenue limits apply to all types of pension scheme – i.e. money-purchase schemes too, not just final pay schemes.

The basic Revenue limits allow for a maximum pension of 1/60 of your final salary for each year you have been in the scheme up to 40 years – i.e. a maximum pension of two-thirds of your final salary. They also allow part of this pension to be swapped for a lump sum building up at a rate of 3/80 of final salary for each year up to 40 – i.e. a maximum lump sum of 1½ times final salary.

However, the tax rules also let you build up pension and lump sum at a faster rate. This is useful where you will be a member of a scheme for less than 40 years and your employer is willing to agree more generous pension terms, or where the pension fund built up is enough to buy more than the basic benefits allowed. These more generous limits are applied to the benefits from your present pension scheme *plus* retained benefits, which means pension and other benefits that you've built up through previous employers' schemes and personal plans. And the absolute maximum two-thirds pension and 1½ times salary lump sum continue to apply. How the faster build-up rates work depends on when the scheme you belong to was set up and when you joined it.

Your pension

If you joined your pension scheme before 17 March 1987, you can build up the maximum two-thirds pension over just 10 years. The fastest rate at which it can build up is as follows:

Years of service before retirement age	Proportion of 'final salary'
1 to 5	$\frac{1}{60}$ for each year
6	$\frac{8}{60}$
7	$\frac{16}{60}$
8	$\frac{24}{60}$
9	$\frac{32}{60}$
10 or more	$\frac{40}{60}$

If you joined a scheme after 17 March 1987, you need at least 20 years' service to qualify for the maximum pension. The quickest rate at which the pension can build up is $\frac{1}{30}$ of final salary for each year of service.

If your scheme was set up after 13 March 1989 or, if set up before then, you joined it on or after 1 June 1989, there is also a cash limit on the maximum pension you can get. This is set by putting an *earnings cap* on the final salary which can count for pension purposes. In the 1996–7 tax year, the earnings cap is £82,200, meaning that the maximum pension you can get after 20 or more years' service is £54,800 ($\frac{2}{3}$ × £82,200).

If you take part of your benefits as a lump sum (see p. 317), the maximum pension you can have under the Revenue limits is reduced accordingly.

The scheme can define 'final salary' in any way it chooses, as long as it's not more favourable than either:

- your pay in any of the five years before normal retirement date, *or*
- your average pay for any three or more consecutive years in the 13 years before normal retirement date.

Note that a controlling director's 'final salary' must not be more than would be allowed by the second definition.

'Pay' can mean your salary plus bonuses, commission, director's fees and the taxable value of any fringe benefits. If the first definition is used, payments apart from salary must be averaged over at least three years. If the pension is based on the amount you earned in years before the final one, the scheme is allowed to increase the figure in line with any increase in the cost of living from the end of that earlier year until your retirement (known as *dynamisation*).

You may want to check the precise rules of your scheme to find out what your pension might be; there are many variations within the limits allowed by the Revenue.

These rules apply to your pension in the first year of retirement, but the scheme can provide for your pension to be increased (within limits) each year to compensate for inflation. Under the Pensions Act 1995, from an appointed day – expected to be in April 1997 – pension schemes will have to increase your pension, once it starts to be paid, by the rate of inflation up to a maximum of 5 per cent a year.

Your lump sum

Scheme rules may allow or require part of the maximum pension to be exchanged for a tax-free lump sum. The maximum lump sum allowed depends on the number of years you've worked for the employer before normal retirement age, and your 'final salary'.

If you joined your employer's scheme before 17 March 1987, the following limits apply:

Years of service before retirement age	Proportion of 'final salary'
1 to 8	3/80 for each year
9	30/80
10	36/80
11	42/80
12	48/80
13	54/80
14	63/80
15	72/80
16	81/80
17	90/80
18	99/80
19	108/80
20 or more	120/80

If you joined on or after 17 March 1987, your lump sum can be increased by the same proportion as any increase in your pension. However, if you joined between 17 March 1987 and 13 March 1989 or 31 May 1989 (see below), there is a maximum cash limit on the lump sum of £150,000.

If you joined the scheme after 31 May 1989, or the scheme was set up after 13 March 1989, your lump sum can't be more than 1½ times your final pay up to the earnings cap – see p. 316 – or 2¼ times your initial annual pension, including dependants' benefits and benefits gained by AVCs.

Widow's and widower's pension

If you die, your widow's or widower's pension is restricted to two-thirds of your final pension, but most schemes offer less than this. Some schemes enable you to take a lower pension when you retire, and leave a higher pension for your surviving partner, but you won't be allowed to leave a pension greater than the one you took when you retired.

Death in service benefits

Some employers give death in service benefits to all employees, others restrict it to pension scheme members. Your dependants can get a tax-free lump sum of up to four times your final salary (subject to the earnings cap – see p. 316 – if it applies to you) to share and each can get a pension. The total pension payable to any individual cannot be more than two-thirds of the maximum pension you could have got had you continued working until retirement on your present salary. The total of all the pensions paid cannot be greater than the maximum pension. In practice, few schemes are this generous.

Early retirement

Employers' schemes set a normal pension age. Nowadays, many schemes have the same age for men and women and this is often 65. However, it is possible to start your pension at a much lower age. Whether or not early retirement will affect your pension will depend on when you joined the scheme.

If you joined a pension scheme set up after 13 March 1989, or joined any pension scheme after 31 May 1989, the *tax* rules allow you to take your pension at 50 and there's no requirement for the pension to be reduced (but your scheme's rules may not allow this).

If your present employer's scheme was set up before 14 March 1989, you can receive your pension at 50 if you're a man or 45 if you're a woman within ten years of retirement. Unfortunately, your benefits must be reduced if you take early retirement. Your pension will be the greater of:

$\frac{1}{60}$ of your final pay × number of years' service

or

$$\frac{\text{number of years with employer}}{\text{total possible years with employer (up to 40)}} \times \text{the maximum pension you could have got}$$

Your maximum lump sum will be worked out in a similar way, and will be the best of:

$\frac{3}{80}$ of your final pay × number of years' service

or

$$\frac{\text{number of years with employer}}{\text{total possible years with employer (up to 40)}} \times \text{the maximum lump sum you could have got}$$

Many employers' schemes pay less than the maximum and may not allow early retirement, and these limits apply to the sum of all the pensions you may be entitled to, not the individual schemes themselves.

You can choose to be bound by the new rules and get a full pension if you want and if your scheme allows it, but then the earnings cap of £82,200 will also apply if you do.

Early retirement due to ill health

The definitions of ill health relevant to early retirement vary widely among schemes. You won't be allowed to get a pension of more than you would have got if you had retired at the normal time with your present salary, but most schemes will give you less than the maximum.

How much can you pay in?

The employer must contribute more than a token amount to the pension scheme. There is no set limit on an employer's contributions, as long as they are reasonable compared with the benefits provided. An employer can also make special payments to provide additional benefits for selected members (e.g. an employee who joined the company late in life and hasn't earned much pension entitlement).

Basically, it's the employer who decides whether to pay

the full cost of the scheme or whether the scheme is to be contributory. If it's contributory, your employer decides how much you will pay, but to satisfy Revenue rules it can't be more than 15 per cent of your before-tax earnings. If your scheme was set up after 13 March 1989, or you joined your present scheme after 31 May 1989, there is also a cash limit on contributions – £12,330 in the 1996–7 tax year.

Additional voluntary contributions

In addition to any regular contributions, an employee may make additional voluntary contributions (AVCs) to the scheme, or to a free-standing additional voluntary contribution plan (FSAVC) from an authorised pension provider (the same people who sell personal pension plans). This is particularly useful in the years before retirement if the total benefits you'll get from your employer's pension scheme fall short of the maximum allowed by the Revenue. You get full tax relief on these contributions, and there is no tax charged on income or capital gains your invested money earns, so AVCs are very tax-efficient.

At retirement, you can normally decide which of the possible retirement benefits you want your AVCs to top up, e.g. your pension (the extra provided by AVCs does not have to be inflation-proofed – see p. 317 – but you can choose to use AVCs to provide protection against inflation), your dependants' pensions, or a combination of these. (Note: if you started making AVCs after 7 April 1987, you can't use them to boost your tax-free lump sum.) You must keep within the individual limit for each benefit. Consult your pensions manager if you want to make AVCs. Things you'll need to consider are:

- what benefits the scheme would provide in return for your AVCs. There is no point in paying contributions which would earn you more pension or other benefits than the maximum you're allowed
- you're not allowed to pay more than 15 per cent of your earnings in any tax year in pension contributions *including* any AVCs.

EXAMPLE 1

John Friar is 62 and due to retire when he's 65. Because he's changed jobs several times in his working life, his total pension will be a lot less than the maximum allowed. So he arranges to pay £100 a month in AVCs. As he's a basic-rate taxpayer, he gets tax relief of £24 on each £100 he pays in – so the true cost to him is only £76 a month. The money is paid into a special AVC fund invested with an insurance company. The fund has grown by around 14 per cent a year tax-free over the last five years.

Leaving a scheme

When you leave a job, the money or pension rights that have built up for you may be *preserved*, so that you get a pension when you retire. In a money purchase scheme, the money already invested will simply grow as before. In a final pay scheme, preserved pensions must be increased by at least 5 per cent a year, or the rise in the Retail Price Index (RPI) if lower. Alternatively, pension rights from both money purchase and final salary schemes can be *transferred* to your new employer's scheme if the new scheme agrees to accept them, or you can buy an insurance policy (known as a section 32 policy) which will provide retirement benefits. You can also transfer your pension rights into a personal pension plan.

If you have been a member of a contributory employer's pension scheme for less than two years, the scheme has the right to give you a refund of your own (but not your employer's) contributions. Equally, it has the right to give you a preserved pension and is not obliged to give a refund. It all depends on what's written in the scheme's rules. If you do get a refund:

- normally, 20 per cent tax will be deducted by the trustees from contributions you withdraw, but there's no further tax to pay
- at present if the scheme is *contracted out*, there will almost always be a deduction from your refund to buy you back into the state scheme
- getting a refund means that you forfeit the right to a preserved pension from the scheme – something you might regret later in life. However, you can use the rules about unused tax relief (see p. 330) to make a payment into a personal plan for the period no longer covered by membership of an employer's scheme.

In a non-contributory scheme, you can't get a refund, and there is no obligation to give a preserved pension.

Unapproved employers' schemes

Your employer might offer you membership of a pension scheme which is not approved by the Revenue and does not fall within the rules outlined so far. Although such schemes don't qualify for favourable tax treatment, they can be more flexible than an approved scheme because you don't have to take the benefits in the form of a pension and there's no set retirement age. But unapproved schemes are mainly useful as *top-up schemes* if your earnings are significantly above the earnings cap (see p. 316). There are two types of unapproved schemes:

- **unfunded schemes** With these, your employer simply pays you a pension and/or lump sum at retirement which is taxed at that time as part of your earnings
- **funded unapproved retirement benefit schemes (FURBs)** Your employer pays contributions into a fund which is invested and used to provide you with a pension and/or lump sum at the time you retire. The contributions count as a taxable fringe benefit at the time they are made on which you are taxed. Income and gains earned by the fund will normally be taxable. But, by setting up the fund as a trust, tax can be limited to the basic rate and the fund can claim a capital gains tax (CGT) allowance of £3,150 in the 1996–7 tax year. You pay no tax when the benefits are paid out and you can take them all as a lump sum if you like.
  ICTA 1988 s155(4), 595 and 686(2)

Personal pension plans

The National Insurance paid by self-employed people (including partners in a partnership) qualifies them for the basic state pension but not a SERPS pension. If you are self-employed, you'll almost certainly need to make additional provision for retirement. A personal pension plan makes this possible, with full tax relief on your contributions (up to certain limits) and with the money invested in a tax-free fund.

If you are in a job but not a member of the employer's scheme (either because there isn't one, you aren't eligible, or you've chosen not to join), you can take advantage of a personal pension plan to top up your basic and additional state pensions. The basic rule is that you can't belong to an employer's scheme (even if it's a non-contributory scheme) and have a personal pension at the same time. But you can belong to an employer's scheme and pay into a personal plan if:

- the personal plan is used only for contracting out of SERPS, and you are not already contracted out through your employer's scheme, *or*
- the personal plan covers earnings which are otherwise non-pensionable earnings, e.g. from freelance earnings, *or*
- you take out an FSAVC plan; in fact, an FSAVC plan is *not* technically a personal plan, and the rules on contributions and benefits are very different (see p. 320).

You're not disqualified from taking out a personal pension just because your employer provides you with some life insurance cover which will pay out a lump sum if you die, or provides a pension only for your spouse or dependants. You'll still be entitled to take out a personal pension as well.

Every five years, the company running your pension plan will send you a form to fill in to check that you are still eligible to have a personal pension plan. It's important that you complete and return this form, otherwise your pension will be made paid up and no more contributions to it will be accepted.
SI 1988/1013

Planning with personal pension plans

Personal pension plans provide benefits for you by investing your contributions to build up a fund. When you retire, part of your fund can be taken as a tax-free lump sum, but the remainder must be taken as a pension. It is impossible to predict how well your investments will do, or how much pension you'll be able to take, so you won't know what your pension will be until you actually retire.

The tax limits which apply to your contributions and benefits depend on when you took out your plan. If you took out a plan before 1 July 1988, it is an old-style plan (called a *section 226 plan, section 620 plan* or *retirement annuity contract*). Modern plans are those taken out on or after 1 July 1988. You cannot take out an old-style plan now, but you can continue paying into an existing old-style plan.

How much can you pay in?

The rules about how much you can pay into personal pension plans each year are complicated and depend partly on how much you have paid in previous years. Companies may refuse to accept premiums which are above the Revenue limits. If you do pay too much into an old-style plan, you won't get tax relief on the excess.

If you pay too much into one of the modern personal pension plans, your contributions must be refunded – you won't be allowed to leave them invested.

ICTA 1988 s619, s626 (Retirement annuity policies), s639, s640 (Personal pension policies)

Net relevant earnings

The maximum you can pay into personal pension plans in a tax year depends on your *net relevant earnings* for the tax year. A husband and wife each have their own net relevant earnings. If you're self-employed, these are your *taxable profits* being assessed for the tax year, and will normally relate to a particular accounting year. For how tax years relate to accounting years, see p. 183 for businesses started on or after 6 April 1994, and p. 186 for businesses started before that date. Taxable profits normally means your business takings (including money owed to you) for your accounting year, less allowable business expenses, capital allowances and any losses from earlier years of the business which haven't been set off against other income.

If you're in a job, your net relevant earnings for the tax year are your salary, plus the taxable value of fringe benefits, less any allowable expenses. For freelance work, net relevant earnings are the fees you've received less any allowable expenses. The table below gives more details.

If you're paying into a modern plan, earnings above the earnings cap (£82,200 in the tax year 1996–7) don't count towards net relevant earnings. The earnings cap is usually raised each year in line with the RPI. The earnings cap doesn't apply to old-style plans. If your earnings are substantially above the cap, you may be able to contribute more towards your pension if you stick with an old-style plan.

ICTA 1988 s646

	Income taxed on	Net relevant earnings for 1996–7 tax year
If you're in a job	current-year basis	pay from that job in 1996–7 tax year
If you have freelance earnings	current-year basis [1]	taxable profits in 1996–7 tax year
If you're self-employed and started up before 6 April 1994	transitional basis [2]	half the sum of your taxable profits [3] for the two consecutive accounting periods ending in 1996–7
If you're self-employed and started up on or before 6 April 1994	current-year basis [4]	taxable profits [3] for accounting period ending in the tax year

[1] If a substantial part of your income comes from freelance work, you may be taxed as if you were self-employed
[2] If you started up during 1993–4, opening year rules may still apply – see p. 186.
[3] If your business makes certain payments (patent royalties, covenant payments, annuities), they must be deducted from your taxable profits when working out your net relevant earnings
[4] Current-year basis will be the norm, but in the first year or two special opening rules apply – see p. 183.

EXAMPLE 2

Harry Hook has been self-employed for some years and his accounting year ends on 31 December each year. His profits for the calendar years 1995 and 1996 are £14,500 and £15,700 respectively. His tax bill for 1996–7 is worked out according to the transitional rules (see p. 186) and is based on taxable profits of £15,100, i.e. half of £14,500 + £15,700. Harry also has a part-time lecturing job. There is no pension with that job, and in 1996–7 he earns £3,200. Harry's nct rclcvant carnings arc £15,100 + £3,200 – £18,300.

Limits on your contributions

The amount you can pay in will depend on your age at the start of the tax year (6 April) and the type of plan you are contributing to.

Maximum percentage of net relevant earnings

Age	Old-style plan %	Modern plan %
up to 35	17.5	17.5
36 to 45	17.5	20.0
46 to 50	17.5	25.0
51 to 55	20.0	30.0
56 to 60	22.5	35.0
61 to 74	27.5	40.0
75 and over	You cannot make further contributions	

ICTA 1988 s640(2) (Personal pension policies); s619(2), s626 (Retirement annuity policies)

The contribution limits are based on your income, even if your employer makes some or all of the contributions. Your contributions can be spread over as many different plans as you like. If you have a mixture of old-style and modern plans, the overall limit is that for the modern plans, but you won't be able to put more into an old-style plan than the limit for the old-style plan.
ICTA 1988 s655(1)

How much tax relief?
You get tax relief at your highest rate of tax on personal pension premiums up to your contribution limit each year. Husband and wife each have their own limit worked out on their own net relevant earnings. Tax relief on associated life insurance policies is limited to premiums of not more than 5 per cent of net relevant earnings. This limit is part of the overall limit, not additional to it.

If you're an employee taking out one of the new personal plans and decide to contract out, the minimum contribution paid by the DSS (and the government's incentive, if you qualify) will not count towards the overall limit. If your employer pays into your plan, this does count towards the limit.

If you're self-employed, premiums you pay in, say, the 1996–7 tax year will normally reduce your tax bill for that year, even if you're using up unused relief from earlier years (see p. 330). But if you backdate a premium (see p. 330), you reduce the tax bill for the year it's backdated to – so you get a tax rebate if you have already paid tax for that year.

If you are an employee taking out a new-style plan you

pay your premium for the current year with basic-rate tax deducted – so for every £100 you wished to invest, you would hand over only £76. The Revenue pays the balance directly to your plan. Higher-rate taxpayers should claim the higher-rate tax relief from the Revenue.

EXAMPLE 3

David Lloyd is an employee who wants to build a large pension but doesn't have an employer's scheme to which he can contribute. His net relevant earnings for the 1996–7 tax year are £32,000. He is aged 50, so he can get tax relief on up to 25 per cent of £32,000, that is £8,000.

David has both an old-style plan and a modern plan, and wants to use the maximum £8,000 of his contribution limit. He could put it all in his modern plan, but he could not put it all in his old-style plan as this would exceed the 17.5 per cent limit on old-style plans. He decides to put the maximum of £5,600 (17.5 per cent of £32,000) into his old-style plan, and contribute the remaining £2,400 into his modern plan.

He will pay his contributions to the modern plan net of basic-rate tax, so he will only pay £1,824. His plan provider will claim the tax rebate of £576 and pay it into the plan. Contributions to the old-style plan will be made without deducting tax, so he will have to hand over the full £5,600 but he will claim his tax relief through PAYE.

Benefits from personal pension plans

Your pension

Neither old-style plans nor modern plans have upper limits on the pension you can get. There is no minimum pension either – so you could lose out if your investments do badly.

You can choose within a wide age range when you want to start taking a pension. In the past, starting your pension meant immediately buying an annuity – i.e. swapping your pension fund (less any tax-free lump sum) for a lifetime income. This was fine if annuity rates were high at that time, but if annuity rates were low you would be stuck with a low pension for your whole retirement.

You are allowed to put off buying an annuity if you want and your plan allows it, though you have to buy an annuity by the age of 75. In the meantime, you can take your tax-free lump sum and (within limits) draw an income direct from the pension fund. The income you can draw will be reviewed every three years to make sure that your pension fund isn't being run down too far.

Your lump sum

If you took out your plan before 17 March 1987, your lump sum can be up to three times your remaining pension, but subsequent rules have been less generous.

If you started your modern plan before 27 July 1989, you are allowed to take a quarter of your fund after you have provided for dependants' pensions. If you started your plan on or after 27 July 1989, you can take a quarter of the fund remaining after any *protected rights* or *contracted out* pension has been provided, for plans which have been partly used to contract-out of SERPS.

For personal plans taken out between 17 March 1987 and 26 July 1989, there is also a cash limit on the lump sum of £150,000. But, in practice, the limit is easily avoided. First, it applies per plan, so you could have several plans each with a £150,000 limit rather than just one. Second, you can switch at retirement or earlier to a current modern personal plan without any cash limit. You'll do this automatically, if at retirement, you exercise an *open market option* which lets you switch from your original plan provider to another in order to get a higher annuity.

Widow's and widower's pension

A contracted-out pension plan will pay a widow's or widower's pension as part of your protected rights. But with other pension plans a surviving spouse or any other dependant is not automatically entitled to a pension if you die after retirement.

Any provision for a spouse has to be made at retirement when you purchase annuities with your accumulated fund. In addition to your initial pension, you can buy a guarantee that the pension will continue for up to ten years – even if you die before then – and you can ensure a widow's or widower's pension is paid after your death by choosing a joint life annuity. You can also arrange pensions for other dependants. All these provisions will reduce your initial pension.

There is no upper limit for any widow's, widower's or dependants' pensions, but their sum cannot be greater than the pension you are getting when you died.

If you die before you draw the pension

A plan used to contract out of SERPS must provide for a widow's or widower's pension to be paid if you die before retirement and your spouse is aged 45 or more, or is younger but has dependent children to care for. If these conditions are not met, and in the case of plans which are not used for contracting out, a lump sum will be paid out. This will usually be the value of your invested fund or may be a return of your contributions with interest or bonuses. There are no restrictions on who can receive the lump sum. It can be used to buy a pension for a dependant, but does not have to be used in this way. With an old-style plan there is no overall limit on dependants' pensions.

You can use up to 5 per cent of your net relevant earnings to provide a tax-free lump sum (or a series of tax-free lump sums in the form of income) in the event of your death by linking your plan to a term life insurance policy – see p. 272.

Early retirement by choice

The Revenue does not impose an upper limit on a pension taken early from a personal plan, but your accumulated fund will be less than it would have been if you had contributed to the fund for longer. And your annuity (or equivalent income, if you defer buying an annuity) will be less (for the same amount of money) if you retire early because it will be paid for more years. With old-style plans, the earliest age at which you can withdraw your pension is usually 60; with modern plans, it is 50.

Some plan providers charge penalties if you stop contributions before the retirement date agreed when the plan was taken out.

Early retirement due to ill health

You can receive your pension as soon as you are too sick to continue working, regardless of your age, but it could be worth little if you have not paid contributions for very long, or your fund has not had time to accumulate.

Many pension plan providers will let you buy a *waiver of premium* benefit, which allows the fund to accumulate as though you were still paying premiums. Plan providers are also allowed to offer *permanent disability insurance*, which guarantees you a minimum income if you become incapable of working for health reasons, but few if any providers offer this benefit. Up to 25 per cent of your contributions can be used to provide these sickness benefits, but these premiums will reduce the amount invested for your main pension benefit.

Unused relief from the last six years

You can get tax relief on premiums above your allowance (up to the whole of your net relevant earnings for the year) if you didn't pay the maximum premiums allowed in any of the previous six tax years. You have to use up the earliest unused relief first.

With modern plans you would get tax relief for a previous year only if you were not a member of an employer's pension scheme in that year. You won't count as having been a member if you belonged to a scheme but left it without any preserved pension rights.

To work out if you've got any unused relief you have to use the limits that applied in the relevant tax year. To claim *carry forward relief* you will need to complete form PP42, available from your tax office.

Provided you are eligible for relief, the contributions themselves do not have to be made out of earnings, but could instead use savings or, say, a redundancy payment or inherited money. This means that carrying forward relief can be a useful way of boosting your pension payments if you have a sudden windfall.
ICTA 1988 s642

Backdating contributions

You can ask in any tax year to have all or part of the premiums you pay in that year treated for tax purposes as if you'd paid them in the previous tax year (as long as you have sufficient unused relief for that year). And if you didn't have any net relevant earnings in the previous tax year, you'll be able to get the premiums treated as if you'd paid them in the year before that.

This means that if you can't afford to make payments this year to use up all the tax relief available to you (including any unused relief from previous years) you may be able to catch up next year. It also means that if your top rate of tax was higher last year, it will be worthwhile asking for some of the premiums you have paid this year to be treated as if you'd paid them in the previous year. That way you'll get more tax relief (and you'll get part of your tax relief sooner).

Lloyd's underwriters can ask for a premium they have paid in the tax year to be treated as though it were paid up to three tax years before, as long as in that year they have sufficient unused relief resulting from Lloyd's underwriting activities.

To elect to carry back contributions, get form PP43 from your tax office.
ICTA 1988 s641

Making the most of available relief

Backdating premiums and using up unused relief from past tax years can be combined to give even greater benefit. If, say, you have £1,000 of unused relief from seven years ago, you can ask to have £1,000 of the premiums you pay this year treated as though you'd paid them last year. As long as you've used all last year's available relief, the premiums can then use the relief carried forward from six years earlier.

If you had no net relevant earnings last year, you can backdate part of this year's premium to the year before and use up unused relief from six years before that – i.e. eight years ago.

The two facilities can also be usefully combined for someone approaching retirement (or even shortly after retirement as long as he or she is under 75) who has had non-pensionable earnings for a number of years. It can be very worthwhile withdrawing other savings in order to pay the maximum contributions into a personal pension plan in order to use up all the available relief.

If you are near retirement and not making any pension contributions, but you have other savings for your retirement (say, in a building society account), it *may* be sensible to transfer some or all of your money to a pension plan. You would do this by claiming unused tax relief from the past six or seven years. You would then get a tax rebate at your highest rate on all your contributions – but you won't be able to get all your capital back, as only part can be taken as a lump sum.

EXAMPLE 4

Arnold Chippendale is a self-employed cabinet-maker. He took out an old-style plan in 1980, paying £15 a month (£180 a year). He has never increased his premiums and has savings of £30,000 in his building society account. With just over ten years to go before retirement, he wonders if it's worth putting some of his savings into his pension plan.

Arnold will be able to use all his unused tax relief for the last six years, but if he backdates some of his premiums to last year he can reclaim relief from seven years ago.

Year	Net relevant earnings £	Maximum contribution £	Premium paid £	Unused tax relief £
1989–90	10,000	1,750 (17.5%)	180	1,570
1990–1	10,000	1,750 (17.5%)	180	1,570
1991–2	11,000	1,925 (17.5%)	180	1,745
1992–3	12,000	2,400 (20.0%)	180	2,220
1993–4	17,000	3,400 (20.0%)	180	3,220
1994–5	18,000	3,600 (20.0%)	180	3,420
1995–6	20,000	4,000 (20.0%)	180	3,820
1996–7	20,000	4,000 (20.0%)	180	3,820
		22,825	1,440	21,385

Arnold decides to put £21,385 into his pension plan, i.e. the maximum contribution of £22,825 less the premiums already paid of £1,440. This is the full amount of his available unused tax relief since 1989–90 for an old-style plan. In order to get the unused relief for 1989–90 he asks the Revenue to treat part of this payment (£10,000) as though it were paid in 1995–6. Arnold gets a tax rebate of £5,232. He decides to put this back into his building society account which, along with the remaining £8,615, still leaves him £13,847.

Unused tax relief from longer ago

If an assessment becomes final for a tax year more than six years ago and means that there's some unused tax relief, you can use it as long as you pay the premiums within six months of the assessment becoming final, *and* pay the maximum amount allowable for the current tax year.
ICTA 1988 s625, s642

18 *INHERITANCE TAX*

- The threshold at which taxable estates become liable to inheritance tax was increased substantially to £200,000 in April 1996 – making this tax much less of a worry for many people.
- From April 1996, shares in qualifying unquoted companies may avoid inheritance tax when you pass them on – see p. 349.
- You can take action while you are alive to save your heirs inheritance tax – but don't leave yourself short.

When you come to pass your money on – whether as a gift in your lifetime or as a legacy when you die – there could well be a bill for inheritance tax (IHT). And this can be

A voluntary tax?

Don't be misled. Careful planning can greatly reduce – or even wipe out – any liability to IHT. No planning at all can mean a heavy bill. But remember that if you don't plan, you yourself will be no worse off. It just means that there's less for your heirs. So don't gamble with your own financial security just to save tax for others.

Domicile

We're assuming that everyone who reads this is domiciled in the UK. Your domicile is, broadly, the country where you've chosen to end your days. It can be quite different from the country where you're living – though if you've been resident in the UK for 17 out of the last 20 tax years you'll have UK domicile (so far as IHT is concerned) whether you like it or not. If you're not domiciled in the UK, rules are different. For example, if you *are* domiciled in the UK, gifts to a non-UK-domiciled husband or wife are exempt only up to £55,000.
IHTA 1984 s267, s18(2)

the case even if you don't think of yourself as being rich. This chapter explains the basic rules, and tells you how to work out an IHT bill. It explains the straightforward ways of saving tax and gives an introduction to more complex schemes, including the use of trusts.

IHT is a tax on what you leave on death (your estate). But it may also cover gifts you make in your lifetime, especially if you die within seven years of making them.

Gifts in your lifetime

For IHT purposes there are three types of gifts you can make during your lifetime:

- **tax-free gifts** (also known as *exempt transfers*) This includes gifts between husband and wife, gifts to charity and small gifts of up to £250 a year to anyone else – see p. 341 for a full list of tax-free gifts
- **gifts which may become tax-free** (also known as *potentially exempt transfers*) They are taxable only if you die within seven years of making them – the tax is collected after your death. This includes all gifts to people which aren't tax-free (such as gifts to children) and gifts to some types of trust
- **chargeable gifts** (also known as *chargeable transfers*) Gifts which aren't tax-free or potentially exempt – and tax may be due at the time of the gift. Chargeable transfers are largely gifts to companies and certain types of discretionary trust.

It's only with a very narrow range of gifts that you might have to pay IHT in your lifetime. If you're not involved with trusts or companies, you can miss out the next section and go straight to *What happens when you die* on p. 336.
IHTA 1984 s2, s3A; FA 1986 s101

Tax on chargeable lifetime transfers

If you make a gift which is liable to IHT in your lifetime, you begin to clock up a *running total* of chargeable transfers. The IHT bill depends on the amount of your running total of chargeable transfers over the most recent seven years. The rates for the 1996–7 tax year are as follows:

Running total	**Rate of IHT**
£0–£200,000	nil
over £200,000	20 per cent of the excess over £200,000

When you make your first chargeable transfer, there will be no IHT to pay if it falls in the nil-rate band. If it is more than the amount of the nil-rate band, then IHT is due on the excess at 20 per cent. When you make your next chargeable transfer, it is added to the first, and if the running total is more than the nil-rate band, tax is due.

Further chargeable transfers will be added to your running total to see if tax is due on them. But any chargeable transfer made more than seven years before drops off the running total.

Note that if you had a running total of gifts made before 18 March 1986 under capital transfer tax (which was replaced by IHT in the 1986 Budget), this is included in your running total for IHT until the seven years are up.
IHTA 1984 s7

How large is the gift?
IHT is charged on the *loss to the giver,* not on the gain to the recipient of a gift. With chargeable transfers, it's normally the giver who pays the IHT at the time of the gift, so the tax paid is part of the gift. This means that the tax bill is worked out on the *grossed-up* value: the amount which after deduction of IHT would leave you with the amount you actually hand over.

Suppose, for example, you gave £80,000 in a chargeable transfer, and your running total meant that the whole gift was liable to tax at 20 per cent. The tax bill is *not* 20 per cent of £80,000 (£16,000), but £20,000. This is because, to have £80,000 after deduction of 20 per cent inheritance tax, you'd have to give a grossed-up gift of £100,000 – making a tax bill of £20,000 (20 per cent of the £100,000 grossed-up value).

If the receiver of the gift agrees to pay the tax, then the gift does not have to be grossed up.
IHTA 1984, s3

EXAMPLE 1

Marion Jones regularly uses up her £3,000 tax-free gift each year (see p. 344). In addition, she gave £100,000 to a discretionary trust in March 1993, with a further £150,000 in June 1996. The gifts were not tax-free and count as chargeable transfers (the trustees agreed to pay the IHT, so there is no need to gross-up the value of the gifts). Marion had made no previous chargeable transfers in the seven years before March 1993.

Until the March 1993 gift, Marion's running total was nil: the £100,000 gift in March 1993 gave her a running total of £100,000. However, this was within the nil-rate band for IHT, so no tax was due on this gift.

When Marion made the second gift of £150,000 in June 1996, that took her running total to £100,000 + £150,000 = £250,000. This is over the top of the nil-rate band for the 1996–7 tax year of £200,000, so IHT is paid on the excess:

£250,000 – £200,000 = £50,000
tax at 20 per cent of £50,000 = £10,000

Any further gifts Marion made to the trust in the next few years would be added to the £250,000 running total, and taxed at the rates in force at the time of the gift. Seven years after the March 1993 gift – in March 2000 – the £100,000 would drop out of the running total.

What happens when you die

On your death, the whole of your estate – roughly speaking, what you own when you die – is liable to IHT, as are any gifts made in the previous seven years.

For IHT purposes, your running total at death comprises:

- all property you owned at the time of death
- the proceeds of any insurance policies paid into your estate (unless *in trust* to your dependants – see p. 274)
- the value of any potentially exempt gifts made in the seven years before death (they become chargeable transfers on death)
- the value of any chargeable transfers made in the seven years before death

  less
- debts (e.g. an outstanding mortgage), though the amount deducted may be restricted if the debts arise from gifts you made previously
- reasonable funeral expenses (including the cost of a headstone).

  IHTA 1984 s4, s5, s172; SP7/87

Tax on death

Some of the bequests in your will may be tax-free, e.g. those to your spouse or to charity (see p. 342 for a list).

If there is no will, what you have left will be distributed according to the rules of intestacy, and again some of the resulting transfers may be tax-free.

The value of the tax-free gifts is deducted from your estate to give its taxable value. The IHT depends on the total taxable value – the rates for the 1996–7 tax year are as follows:

Running total	**Rate of IHT**
£0–£200,000	nil
over £200,000	40 per cent of the excess over £200,000

So if the total value of the estate is less than the amount of the nil-rate band (£200,000 for 1996–7), there is no IHT to pay. If the total is more than the nil-rate band, IHT is due at 40 per cent of the excess only.
IHTA 1984 s7

EXAMPLE 2

Gerald Finch dies leaving an estate worth £160,000. His will donates £5,000 to charity, makes bequests of £5,000 each to his son and daughter, and leaves the rest to his wife. He has made no other gifts while alive.

Bequests to charity and spouses are tax-free gifts. Only the two gifts to his children are taxable, and at £10,000 they are well within the nil-rate band. No IHT is due on his estate.

EXAMPLE 3

When widow Susan Bailey died in July 1996, she left £10,000 to charity and the remaining £220,000 of her estate to be divided between her two children. She had made no other gifts.

The £10,000 bequest to charity is tax-free, but the £220,000 left to her children is liable to IHT:

- the first £200,000 isn't taxed
- that leaves £220,000 – £200,000 = £20,000 to be taxed at 40 per cent: 40 per cent of £20,000 = £8,000. The £8,000 is deducted from the £220,000 to give £212,000, and this is divided equally between the two children, who get £106,000 each.

EXAMPLE 4

Roger Ferguson gave his son John £110,000 in June 1993, his daughter Margaret £110,000 in July 1993 and his youngest child Brian £110,000 in March 1994. He died in May 1996, leaving £160,000 to be divided between the three children.

The three gifts made in 1993 and 1994 were initially exempt from the tax, but because Roger has died within seven years of making them, they must be added to what he has left (on his death), to find the value of his estate for IHT purposes. Roger had already used up his £3,000 annual exemption for gifts (see p. 344). That means the total value of his estate for IHT is £160,000 + £110,000 + £110,000 + £110,000 = £490,000. The total tax bill is as follows:

- the first £200,000 isn't taxed
- that leaves £290,000 (£490,000 − £200,000) to be taxed at 40 per cent: 40 per cent of £290,000 = £116,000.

Some of this tax bill comes from the estate and some from Roger's children – see Example 5 opposite.

Who pays the tax?

Chargeable gifts and potentially tax-free gifts made during the seven years before death are reassessed when you die, and there may be tax to pay on them. Any tax due is, in the first instance, payable by the person who received the gift, but, if they are unwilling or unable to pay, your estate will be billed. But you can specify in your will that tax which becomes payable on lifetime gifts will be paid by your estate.

To work out how much tax is due from each person, you must work out the tax on each gift as it is added to the running seven-year total at the time the gift was originally made (i.e. possibly taking into account gifts made up to 14 years before your death). But you use the tax *bands and rates* which apply at the time of death. Any tax which was paid on chargeable transfers when they were made is deducted from the recipient's new tax bill (but there's no refund if the new bill comes to less).

Tax due on the estate itself may be paid either by the estate or by your heirs depending on the types of bequests which you make. You can specify that a bequest is *subject to tax*, in which case it is treated as a gross gift out of which the

recipient must pay the tax due. More commonly, bequests will be *free-of-tax* (not to be confused with tax-free gifts), in which case, the recipient gets the amount you specify and tax on its grossed-up value is paid from the remaining estate. The apportioning of the overall tax bill on the whole estate to the various bequests can be complicated.
IHTA 1984 s199–s201

EXAMPLE 5

The total tax bill for the Fergusons in Example 4 is £116,000 – but not all of that comes from Roger's estate. To see where the tax comes from, we must consider the various gifts in the order they were made.

1 The first gift was £110,000 to John. Since there were no previous gifts, this creates a running total of £110,000. This is within the nil-rate band, so no tax is due.

2 The next gift was £110,000 to Margaret. This is added to the running total of £110,000 to give a new cumulative total of £220,000. This is over the nil-rate band, so tax will be due:

- tax on the first £200,000 isn't taxed
- tax on the next £20,000 (£220,000 – £200,000) is at 40 per cent: 40 per cent of £20,000 = £8,000. So Margaret will have to pay £8,000 in IHT.

3 The next gift was £110,000 to Brian. This is added to the running total of £220,000 to give a cumulative total of £330,000. The tax due on this running total is worked out as follows:

- the first £200,000 isn't taxed
- tax on the next £130,000 (£330,000 – £200,000) is at 40 per cent: 40 per cent of £130,000 = £52,000. This £52,000 is the total tax due so far: Margaret is already responsible for paying £8,000 of this total, so Brian has to pay £52,000 – £8,000 = £44,000 of IHT.

4 The final 'gift' is what Roger left on death: £160,000. This brings the running total to £330,000 + £160,000 = £490,000, on which tax is due of £116,000. £52,000 of this has already been paid by Margaret and Brian, leaving £116,000 – £52,000 = £64,000 to come from the estate.

After paying the tax, the estate is worth £160,000 – £64,000 = £96,000. This is divided between the three children, who each get ⅓ of £96,000 = £32,000.

Note that if Roger had intended to give equal benefit to all three of his children, he failed: the gifts of £110,000 to each of the three children end up being worth very different amounts:

- John paid no IHT on his, so it's worth the full £110,000
- Margaret paid £8,000 on hers, so it ends up worth £102,000 (i.e. £110,000 – £8,000)
- Brian faced a tax bill of £44,000, so his gift is worth just £66,000 (i.e. £110,000 – £44,000).

The children could have covered themselves against this eventuality by taking out a special life insurance policy which would pay out enough to cover the IHT if Roger died within seven years of making the gifts to them. Alternatively, Roger could have made provision in his will for any IHT on the lifetime gifts to come from his estate.

Gifts more than three years before death

The IHT on gifts made more than three years before death is reduced on the sliding scale below:

Years between gift and death	Percentage of the 40 per cent rate payable	Bill for each taxable £1,000
Up to 3 years	100	£400
More than 3 but not more than 4	80	£320
More than 4 but not more than 5	60	£240
More than 5 but not more than 6	40	£160
More than 6 but not more than 7	20	£80
More than 7	tax-free	tax-free

IHTA 1984 s7

EXAMPLE 6

Harry Patel gave his son Sammy a gift of £210,000 four and a half years before he died (having already used up his £3,000 tax-free allowance). Harry left all of his estate to his wife Sonia, so there was no tax to pay on it. But the gift to Sammy became chargeable because Harry died within seven years of making it.

Harry had made no other gifts in the seven years before the gift of £210,000 – i.e. there was no running total of gifts. The tax on the £210,000 was (at 1996–7 rates) worked out as follows:

- the first £200,000 isn't taxed

- that leaves £210,000 − £200,000 = £10,000 to be taxed at 40 per cent: 40 per cent of £10,000 = £4,000.

However, the gift was made more than three years before Harry died, so Sammy's tax bill of £4,000 is reduced on the sliding scale. Only 60 per cent of the tax is payable, as the gift was made more than four but not more than than five years before Harry's death. So Sammy must pay 60 per cent of £4,000 = £2,400 in IHT.

When a gift is made

It's usually easy to decide when a gift is made. For example, if you give your son £100,000 by cheque, it will be the date on which the cheque is cleared by your bank and your account is debited.

If you make a gift with some strings attached (known as a *gift with reservation*) the gift will not be made, for IHT purposes, until it becomes a completely free gift (i.e. the benefit ceases to be reserved). For example, if you gave your home to your son, but continued to live there, this would be treated as a gift with *reservation of benefit*. If you were still living there on your death the house would be counted as part of your estate, even though it would actually belong to your son. You could avoid the problem if you paid your son a full market rent for the property, but this might not be sensible if your son had to pay tax on the rent.

The rules for gifts with reservation of benefit apply only for gifts made after 17 March 1986, so a gift made before then is unaffected. The rules are complicated: if you are considering a gift with a possible reservation of benefit, get professional advice.

FA 1986 s102, Sch 20

Tax-free gifts

Tax-free gifts are ignored by the Revenue. If a gift is tax-free:

- there's no tax to pay on it, by you or by anyone else
- the gift isn't added to your running total, so it doesn't eat up your nil-rate band.

If you're going to make gifts, it's clearly sensible to use the opportunities you have to make gifts tax-free. Tax-free gifts fall into three categories:

- gifts which are tax-free whenever they are made – i.e. regardless of whether they're made during life or on death
- gifts which are tax-free only if made on death
- gifts which are tax-free only if made during life.

Gifts tax-free whenever they are made

- Gifts between husband and wife of any amount. These can be in cash, property, or anything else. There's no limit at all – even if you're separated. (For divorce, see p. 96.) If the person who receives the gift isn't domiciled in the UK but the donor is, gifts above a total of £55,000 will count as a potentially exempt gift.
- Gifts to UK charities of any amount. Special anti-avoidance rules can apply if you give part of a property (e.g. a share in land or a business) to a charity and keep the rest yourself.
- Gifts of any amount to British political parties.
- Gifts of any amount to certain public institutions, e.g. the National Gallery, the British Museum, the Victoria and Albert Museum, local authorities and universities.
- Gifts of heritage property to a non-profit-making body, provided Treasury approval is obtained. *Heritage property* is outstanding land or buildings, and books, manuscripts or works of art of special interest.
- Gifts of land in the UK made to registered housing associations after 13 March 1989.
- Gifts of shares or securities to a trust for the benefit of all or most of the employees of a company provided that the trustees hold more than half of the ordinary shares in the company and have voting control.
  IHTA 1984 s18, s23–s26, s28

Gifts tax-free on death only

- The estate of a person whose death was caused or hastened by active military service in war or of a warlike nature. This would include the estates of servicemen killed in Northern Ireland. It can also include people wounded in earlier conflicts who die earlier than they otherwise would have done.
- A lump sum paid under an employer's pension scheme to your dependants if you die before reaching retirement age, provided the trustees have discretion as to who gets the money (they usually do). Because they have discretion, the lump sum never forms part of your estate, so there's

no gift for tax purposes. Within set limits you can say who you want to get the money, and your wishes will normally be respected. The total lump sum can be up to four times your salary at the time of your death together with a return of your contributions to the scheme.

- A lump sum paid to your dependants on your death at the discretion of the trustees of your personal pension plan.
  IHTA 1984 s151, s152, s154, SP10/86

Gifts tax-free in life only
The following gifts are tax-free in your lifetime. But if you exceed the limits (e.g. give more as a wedding gift than the tax-free limit – see below), that doesn't mean you have to pay any tax when you make the gift. Unless the gift is a chargeable lifetime transfer (see p. 334), it will become chargeable only if you die within seven years.

- Wedding gifts. Each parent of the bride or groom can give up to £5,000 tax-free (it doesn't have to be to their own child). A gift by either the bride or the groom to the other in anticipation of the marriage is tax-free up to £2,500, though once they are married they can normally make tax-free gifts of any amount to each other. A grandparent or more distant ancestor can give up to £2,500 tax-free. Anyone else can give up to £1,000. Gifts don't need to be in cash. Strictly speaking, wedding gifts have to be made *in consideration of the marriage,* and *conditionally on the marriage taking place.*
- Gifts up to any amount made as normal expenditure out of income. This allows you to give money away year after year without an IHT liability. The gifts must be part of a pattern, though not necessarily to the same person each time. If your giving has just begun, the first gift will be covered by the exemption if it's clear a pattern of gifts will follow, e.g. you start to pay regular premiums on a life insurance policy for someone's benefit. Gifts must come out of income, so anything other than cash won't usually be covered. (Note that part of some annuity payments is return of capital, and does not count as income.) Your gifts must leave you with sufficient income to maintain your normal standard of living. If you resort to capital, e.g. sell shares, in order to live in your usual way, you will lose the exemption unless you make up the lost capital out of income in a later year.

- After divorce, transfers of property to an ex-husband (or ex-wife) will usually be exempt from tax. This is because there won't usually be any *donative intent* – i.e. any intention to make a gift. In other words, the transfer is made as part of the divorce settlement.
- Gifts for the maintenance of your family. A gift for the maintenance of your spouse or ex-spouse is tax-free. So is a gift for the maintenance of a child of one or both of you (including an adopted child) if the child is under 18 or is still in full-time education or training. The exemption also covers gifts for the maintenance of a child you have been taking care of for some time in place of either of his parents.
- Gifts to meet the regular needs of a relative of either you or your spouse are tax-free if the relative is unable to support himself or herself owing to age or infirmity. Gifts to your mother or mother-in-law are covered even if she is able to support herself, provided she is widowed, separated or divorced.
- Small gifts. You can give an unlimited number of people gifts of up to £250 (each) a year. You won't need to use this exemption if the gift is tax-free for another reason. If you give more than £250 to anyone, the exemption (for that person) is lost *even for the first £250.*
- Any gifts of up to £3,000 in a single tax year which aren't tax-free for any other reason. These gifts don't have to be in cash. If you don't use up the exemption in one year, you can use the rest of it in the following year, provided you've used up that year's exemption first. Any part of the £3,000 still unused at the end of the following year is lost – i.e. it can't be carried any further forward. *IHTA 1984 s10, s11, s19–s22*

EXAMPLE 7

In the 1995–6 tax year, Simon Ryland used up £1,000 of his £3,000 exemption. In the 1996–7 tax year, he makes gifts of £4,500 which aren't tax-free for any other reason. The Revenue will say that the first £3,000 (of the £4,500) came out of the 1996–7 allowance. The other £1,500 of the gift comes out of the unused 1995–6 allowance. But the remaining £500 unused allowance from 1995–6 can't be carried forward to 1997–8.

Valuing a gift

The next few pages deal with how to value (for IHT purposes) something which is given away. This is the first step in working out the tax on a gift. Remember that it's the loss to the giver, not the gain to the recipient, which counts. Also bear in mind that it's the value of the gift at the date it's made on which tax will be charged if you do not survive seven years. If you are going to make a gift of land, antiques, paintings, a business, or unquoted shares or securities, get a professional valuation first:

- it's useful evidence when you're negotiating a value with the Revenue
- you're less likely to get an unexpectedly high tax bill.

If property counts as *business property* or *agricultural property* there are special rules for valuing it which can reduce the tax – see pages 349 and 350.

'Market value'

In the normal case, *value* equals *open market value*. This means that the value of an asset is taken to be the price which it would fetch if it were sold in the open market at the time of the gift.

For gifts of money, there's no problem. The value of the asset is the amount of money. For a gift of a car or furniture, the value is what you could expect to have sold it for. (So when you're valuing an estate on death, you should use the *second-hand* value of furniture, fridges, etc.)

The rest of this section deals with exceptions to the normal rule.

IHTA 1984 s160

Value of property on death

The Revenue assumes that any piece of property, e.g. land, or a holding of shares, is sold in one lump. So it won't speculate as to whether your property could have been broken up for sale in parts to get a higher or a lower price, unless the division would have been a natural and easy thing to do.

No account is taken of the difficulty (or impossibility) of putting the property on the market at one time. The Revenue will assume that there's a ready market, and that the sale itself won't affect the market value. This can cause severe probems where shares in a private company are

involved: the value, for tax purposes, can be higher than the price you could get.
IHTA 1984 s160

Joint interest in land
If you have a joint interest in land, e.g. you're a co-owner of a house, the starting point is to take the open market value of the land as a whole, and allocate to you your share of that value. Your share is then discounted (i.e. reduced in value for IHT valuation purposes – by 15 per cent, say, to reflect the lack of demand for property without vacant possession).

Unit trusts
Units in a unit trust scheme authorised by the Department of Trade and Industry are valued at the manager's buying ('bid') price on the day concerned, or the most recent day before that on which prices were published.

Quoted shares and securities
The market value of shares and securities quoted on the Stock Exchange and the Unlisted Securities Market (USM) is the lower of *either:*

- the lower closing price on the day of the gift plus a quarter of the difference between the lower and higher closing prices for those shares for the day (known as the *quarter up* rule), *or*
- half-way between the highest and lowest recorded bargains in those shares for the day.

Unquoted shares and securities
Valuing these can get you into murky waters. It's very much a matter for negotiation with the Revenue. Some clues are:

- if the Revenue has recently decided for someone else what your particular type of shares are worth, that value will probably apply to your holding
- the fictional 'purchaser' of the shares will be assumed to possess information about the company confidential to the directors at the time of the gift. This could put the value up or down
- the Revenue will probably try to compare your unquoted shares with quoted shares in a company of equivalent size in the same line of business (if there is one)

EXAMPLE 8

You hold £1 ordinary shares in XYZ Plc whose ordinary shares are listed on the Stock Exchange. You need to know their market value on 1 June 1996. The Stock Exchange Official Daily List, which is published after that day but which records prices on that day, shows that a £1 ordinary share in XYZ Plc was quoted at 175–181 with bargains marked at 176, 176½ and 179. The quarter up valuation gives 176½ and the mid-way valuation gives 177½. So the market value is taken to be 176½ a share.

- if you own 75 per cent of the ordinary shares you will usually have the power to put the company into liquidation. This could mean your holding is worth 75 per cent of the underlying assets of the company
- if you have a bare majority of the ordinary shares, you will be able to decide what dividends are paid, so the after-tax earnings of the company must be a better guide to the value of your shares. The value of the assets will probably still be the starting-point – *less* a discount, because you can't put the company into liquidation
- if you are a minority shareholder (and not a director), the dividends paid will be a good guide to the value of your shares
- for securities other than shares, e.g. loan stock, the rate of interest and the likelihood of its being paid are important. If you have a right to repayment of your principal at any time and the company is in a position to repay you, the value of your securities should be increased.
  IHTA 1984 s168

Life interests and reversions
If you give someone, e.g. your spouse, the right for life to all the income from particular property or the exclusive right to occupy or enjoy certain property, for IHT you will put her in the same position as if she owned the property – see p. 355. So there is no tax advantage in giving your spouse just a *life interest*. However, from a practical point of view, you may wish to give a person no more than a life interest so that you can be sure that your capital will find its

way to your children or grandchildren, for example, once the *life tenant* has died.

But make sure that your trustees have a wide power to apply capital for the benefit of the life tenant in case of emergencies.

Because the person with the life interest is treated as owning the whole property, a gift of the *reversion* (i.e. rights to the property when the life interest ends) is normally valued at *nil* – provided it's never been bought or sold.
IHTA 1984 s4, s5, s48, s49

Related property
Property is *related*, for tax purposes, if it is owned by your spouse (either directly or through trustees), or if it is now, or has been in the previous five years, owned by a charity to which you or your spouse gave it.

Where property is related to other property, and its value as part of the combined properties is greater than its value on its own, the higher value may be taken as the actual value.
IHTA 1984 s161

EXAMPLE 9

Suppose you own 55 per cent of the ordinary shares in ABC Ltd and your wife owns 45 per cent. The value of your holding on its own is £70,000 and the value of your spouse's is £40,000. Suppose the value of a 100 per cent holding is £160,000. The value of your holding for IHT is 55 per cent of £160,000, i.e. £88,000 – and not £70,000.

Related property disposed of after your death
Suppose that on your death you own 45 per cent of the ordinary shares of a family company, your wife owns 35 per cent and your son 20 per cent. Your 45 per cent will be valued as 45/80 of an 80 per cent holding (i.e. your share of your and your spouse's combined holding). However, if your executors make an actual sale of your 45 per cent and your spouse does not sell at the same time, and if the sale is

to a complete outsider – at a price which is less than the holding's related value – within three years of your death, your executors can claim that the valuation on your death should be readjusted to a valuation on an unrelated basis.
IHTA 1984 s176

Other sales after death: quoted shares or securities; interests in land

- If quoted shares or securities, or units in an authorised unit trust, are part of your estate on death and the person who is liable to pay the IHT on them sells them within a year of your death for less than their value immediately before your death, the later (lower) value may be substituted to re-calculate the tax liability.
- If your estate on death includes an interest in land which is later sold – by the person liable to pay the IHT on the property – within four years of your death, and the sale price is less than the value at the date of your death (*less* by at least 5 per cent or £1,000), that later value may be substituted for the value on your death and the tax re-calculated.
  IHTA 1984 s178–s198

Business property

If certain conditions are met, business property is valued at less than its market value for IHT purposes. This *business property relief* cuts the tax bill on a gift or bequest:

- an unincorporated business (e.g. a solicitor's practice or a corner shop) receives 100 per cent relief, i.e. IHT on a transfer is nil
- from 6 April 1996, 100 per cent business relief is extended to all unquoted shares in qualifying companies regardless of the size of holding or voting entitlement. Prior to this, if you held 25 per cent or less of the voting rights, you would receive only 50 per cent relief if you transferred your shares
- shares dealt on the Unlisted Securities Market and the Alternative Investment Market are treated as unquoted
- quoted shares with a controlling interest receive 50 per cent relief
- land, buildings or equipment you own which are mainly or wholly used by a business you control or a partnership of which you are a member (the rules are complicated) receive 50 per cent relief.

In all these cases, to get the relief, you must have owned the property for at least two years immediately before the gift or your death. If you've owned it for less than this, you may still qualify if the property replaces other property which you acquired more than two years before.

You won't, in any case, get the discount if the business consists wholly, or mainly, of:

- dealing (but not acting as a market-maker) in securities, stocks or shares, land or buildings
- the making or holding of investments.

Property for personal use doesn't qualify for the discount. So if, for example, you control a company which owns cars used mainly for private purposes, the relief won't apply to the cars.

If the person giving the property dies within seven years, business relief may be lost if, for example, the property has been sold or unquoted shares have been floated on the Stock Exchange. Get professional advice before handing on your business.
IHTA 1984 s103–s114

Agricultural property
If you own agricultural land or buildings (which, from 6 April 1995, includes land used for short rotation coppice), they can be valued at less than their market value for inheritance tax if certain conditions are met. You can get *agricultural property relief* at:

- 100 per cent if you have vacant possession or can get it within 24 months
- 50 per cent if the land is tenanted and you haven't the right to vacant possession within two years. But relief is increased to 100 per cent for land which is let after 31 August 1995, i.e. the rule requiring vacant possession within 24 months will not apply to new lets.

You need to have either owned the land for seven years while someone else has used it for agriculture, or to have farmed it yourself for two years.
IHTA 1984 s115–s124B

Basic tax planning

There are no universal rules of IHT planning which dictate what everyone should do and should not do. It all depends on your personal circumstances. IHT is not just a tax on the rich. On the other hand, many people who are no more than comfortably off – worth up to £220,000, for example – worry too much.

If you don't plan for IHT, it's no skin off your nose. It simply means that there's less for your heirs. So don't dive into complicated schemes just to give your children slightly more than they would otherwise get. Above all, don't risk your own – or your spouse's – financial security by giving away more than you can afford while you're still alive.

All that apart, it does of course make a lot of sense to take account of the tax rules when you're planning your gifts. You may not necessarily go for the biggest tax-saving: IHT planning is a mixture of knowing the rules and applying common sense. Below we tell you how.

First principles

- Make use of your exemptions – in particular, the annual exemption of £3,000 and the *normal expenditure out of income* exemption.
- Watch out for capital gains tax (CGT) on lifetime gifts. Gifts of cash and certain other assets are not liable to CGT, but gifts of things like shares, holiday homes and valuables to anyone other than your spouse may mean a CGT bill – see Chapter 15.
- If you can afford to make substantial gifts – more than the nil-rate band – make them sooner rather than later. If you survive for three years after making the gift, the tax is reduced on a sliding scale (see p. 340), and if you survive seven years there is no tax at all.
- If you have a stable marriage, make gifts to your spouse so that he or she can make tax-free gifts to other people. (The gifts to your spouse must be genuine. If he or she *must* hand it on, the husband and wife exemption won't apply and the whole gift may become chargeable if you die within seven years.)

Estate spreading

Estate spreading means giving away wealth now. The idea is to reduce the amount you're worth, so that there will be less tax to pay when you die. Estate spreading can make sense if:

- it doesn't destroy your financial independence *and*

- IHT on death would be substantial, *or*
- the person receiving the gift needs it now.

For a married couple the first step in estate spreading is often said to be the equalisation of their estates – i.e. their total wealth is divided equally between them. Because gifts between husband and wife are normally exempt, this can usually be done tax-free.

This can have a number of advantages, particularly if one spouse had little personal wealth before. For example, both may be able to make use of the annual exemption, the small gifts exemption (see p. 344), and the nil-rate band (see p. 337), whereas, if the family wealth had remained largely in the hands of one spouse it would have been possible for only that spouse alone to make use of these exemptions. If the joint wealth is fairly substantial it may be possible for each spouse to make gifts of more than the exemptions available. These will be totally tax-free after seven years.

The other major advantage is in the amount of IHT payable on death. As each spouse now has wealth in his or her own right, each can leave at least part of their estate to the children or grandchildren. Without equalisation, there might be no tax at all to pay on the first death, but a very high bill on the second.
IHTA 1984 s18

Estate freezing

You can use various techniques for 'freezing' the value of some of your wealth now and allowing the increase in value which would otherwise come to you (and raise the value of your estate) to go to someone else. There are various ways of doing this for a family business, for example, so that future growth goes to your children – you should take professional advice if you think you could benefit.

One common way of freezing your estate is to put investments into trust for your children or grandchildren. This reduces the value of your estate, though it may involve an IHT bill at the time of the gift – see p. 334. But the gift can be set up to take advantage of the nil-rate band (i.e. up to £200,000 in 1996–7). And any growth in the investments accumulates in the trust and is no longer part of your estate. There's more about trusts on p. 354.

A simple way of setting up a trust for your children or

grandchildren is to use life insurance policies. Provided the premiums can be paid out of your *normal expenditure*, they will be tax-free gifts (see p. 344). But you must make sure that the proceeds don't form part of your estate – see p. 336.

Unit trusts can also be put into trust for your children or grandchildren in this way, using a regular savings plan. Some unit trust managers can help set up the trust.

The family home

This is most people's largest single asset, and can, on its own, push you over the nil-rate band. You can't give it away and continue to live in it to save IHT – it could count as a *gift with reservation* (see p. 274). If the person you give it to lives in the property with you and pays a fair share of the expenses you might save IHT – get advice.

A couple may be able to save some IHT if they jointly own the home, depending on the form of ownership (in England and Wales):

- *joint tenants* share ownership of the home. But they both (or all if there are several owners) own the whole home and have identical interests in it. If one dies, their share automatically goes to the other, and can't be given to anyone else. But it still forms part of the estate for IHT purposes, so there could be tax to pay if the other joint tenant is not the wife or husband. If the joint tenants are married, there'll be no IHT on the first death, but the whole value of the house would be in the estate when the second partner died
- with a *tenancy in common,* each owns a completely separate share of the home which can be left to whoever they wish. So you could leave your share to your children rather than to your spouse: there would be a possible IHT liability on the value of your share, but the size of your partner's estate would be reduced.

If it's important to you to pass on the family home intact, take professional advice on the best way to organise it.

Make a will

Your will can be a very important step in planning to reduce your IHT (though it is currently possible to rearrange things after your death to reduce the bill – see

p. 359). Drawing up your will may also alert you to steps you need to take to minimise your tax bill, e.g. by making lifetime gifts.

Apart from any tax-saving, a will is also the best way to make sure that your worldly goods end up where you want after your death. If you don't leave a valid will, the intestacy rules distribute them in ways that might not be what you intended. For example, if you live with someone without being married to him or her, he or she might get nothing.

Here are some points to bear in mind:

- if you're married, make sure that you leave your spouse enough to live on. Remember that old age can be expensive and prolonged – so, if you can, leave a large safety margin. It's only when you've done this that you should look at ways of cutting the IHT bill
- consider making enough taxable gifts on death to use up your nil-rate band. You can do this by making gifts direct to your children or grandchildren
- unless you say that gifts are *subject to tax,* the tax on them will normally come out of the residue of your estate. If you've left the residue to your spouse, much (or all) of it could be swallowed up in paying the tax on other gifts
- if you are uncertain about what to do with the whole or part of your estate, you can set up a discretionary trust (see p. 356) in your will, giving the trustees two years to give away the property. You can discuss your wishes with the trustees so that they know what sorts of priorities you would set; and if they make the gifts within the two years, the tax is the same as if you had made the gifts yourself.

If there's a large asset you're hoping to pass on, such as a family home, business or farm, take professional advice about drawing up the will – there are various subtle tax points to be watched.

Trusts

Trusts are not only for the rich. Even if you're no more than comfortably off, one type of trust – the *accumulation and maintenance trust* – can be worth considering for your children, grandchildren or other younger people for whom you've got a soft spot. And many people who are not rich at all set up trusts in their wills. The following roles have to be defined for nearly all trusts:

- **a settlor** The person who sets up the trust, and puts money (or property) into it
- **trustees** The people who 'own' the trust property. But unlike a normal owner, they can't do what they like with it. They have to follow the instructions of the *instrument* – often a deed or a will – which sets up the trust. There are also legal rules about what they must (and must not) do
- **beneficiaries** The lucky people who will – or, in some cases, may – be given money, or property, or the use of property, from the trust. See Example 10.

EXAMPLE 10

Ned Settlor sets up a trust in his will. He wants his wife Gladys to have all his money, but he wants the house to go to the children after her death. So he leaves the money direct to Gladys, but he leaves the house to trustees 'in trust for my wife Gladys for her life and afterwards to my children in equal shares'. Gladys and the children are the beneficiaries.

Note: Ned is careful to take competent legal advice. As a result, the trust is worded so that:

- if Gladys is short of money, the trustees can 'advance' money to her – i.e. they can raise capital on the security of the house, and give it to Gladys. (If they do advance money in this way, the children will get less)
- if Gladys wants to move, she can sell the house and buy another.

Trusts with an interest in possession

The simplest type of trust is one with a life interest, e.g. a gift 'to Gladys for life, and then to my children in equal shares'. Gladys has an *interest in possession*, while the children have a *reversionary interest*, i.e. they are entitled to the trust property when the interest in possession comes to an end.

With gifts to an interest in possession trust made on or after 17 March 1986, there will be a possible IHT bill only if you die within seven years of making the gift. If you make the gift on death, the property forms part of your estate.

The property covered by the interest in possession is treated as being owned by the person who has the interest. If he or she dies or gives it away, IHT is charged as if it were his or her own property:

- if the person dies, the value is added to his or her estate
- if the person gives it away, tax is due only if he or she dies within seven years of the gift.

The only difference between an interest in possession and ordinary property is that the IHT is paid by the trustees, not by the person with the interest in possession.

If you have an interest in possession and the property becomes yours, you become 'absolutely entitled' to it – there is no IHT at this stage. There will, of course, be IHT when you die or give it away. There's also no IHT if the property goes back to the settlor (or to the settlor's wife or husband if she or he has not been dead for longer than two years).
IHTA 1984 s49–s54

Discretionary trusts

These are trusts where the trustees can decide who gets the money. For example, you could set up a trust under which the trustees could pay income (or capital) 'in such proportions as they in their absolute discretion shall decide, to all or any of my children, David, Maureen, Alison, any of their children, grandchildren or remoter issue, with any income or capital remaining on 1 August 2072 to be given to charitable purposes'.

Gifts to discretionary trusts on death, e.g. if you set one up in your will, count as part of your estate. In your lifetime, they count as chargeable transfers (see p. 334). But with gifts to the following types of discretionary trusts there will be no IHT unless you die within seven years of the gift (when there may be a tax bill):

- a trust for disabled people
- an accumulation and maintenance trust (see below).

Gifts from a discretionary trust of its capital are liable to IHT at a rate which depends on the amount given away. And the money or property in the trust may be liable to IHT even if it is not given to anyone else. Once every ten years, there will be a *periodic charge* on the trust which has the effect of collecting about the same amount of IHT as if the

trust's property belonged to an individual and were passed on at death once every 30 years.
IHTA 1984, s58–s69

Accumulation and maintenance trusts

This is a special type of discretionary trust. If you stick to the rules, there is no IHT to pay when the capital from the trust is paid to the beneficiaries, and there is no periodic charge.

Accumulation and maintenance trusts are commonly used to put money into trust for children:

- while your children are still young, you set up the trust and put some capital in it
- income made by the trust is accumulated (i.e. kept in the trust). Any income which isn't accumulated must be used for the 'maintenance, education or benefit' of your children
- some time after your children reach 18, and by the time they reach 25, the trust may come to an end and the property may be shared among them. If you don't want the trust to hand out the capital, you can give the children the right to the income instead. You can give the capital later (see Rule 2 below).

If you set up a trust for your children, you'll be taxed at your top rate of tax on any income paid out for them while they're under 18 (unless they're married) – see below for rules. The money will count as *your* income, not your children's.

If the trust *isn't* for your children, or they're over 18 or married, income paid out for them will count as *their* income. Any child, no matter how young, is entitled to the full single person's allowance of £3,765. So if, say, a child has no other income, and is paid income of £3,000 (gross), the trustees deduct tax at 34 per cent (£1,020), and hand over £1,980. The child can claim back the £1,020.

The rules in detail

Rule 1 At least one of the beneficiaries must be alive when the trust is set up. So a trust 'for my son Alan's children' is no good unless Alan already has a child. Any children of Alan's born later are added to the list of beneficiaries. If all the beneficiaries die, but others could be born, the trust still keeps going.

Rule 2 At least one of the beneficiaries must get an *interest in possession* in at least part of the trust property by the time he or she reaches the age of 25. A right to the income of part (or all) of the property is an interest in possession. So is the right to a share of the trust capital.

Rule 3 There can be no entitlement to trust property until a beneficiary has acquired an interest in possession. (This doesn't contradict Rule 2: to get an interest in possession you must have a *right* to income or capital. If trustees decide merely to hand out income or capital to you there's no right to it, and no interest in possession.)

Rule 4 The trust must come to an end within 25 years, unless Rule 5 applies.

Rule 5 The trust can last for more than 25 years if all the beneficiaries have one grandparent in common. Illegitimate and adopted children count in the same way as legitimate children. If one of the beneficiaries dies before getting an interest in possession, his or her share can go (if the trust deed says so) to his or her widow, widower, or children.
IHTA 1984 s71 Trustee Act 1925 s31, s32

Income paid to your children

Income paid from a trust set up by you to children of yours who are under 18 and unmarried is taxed as your income (and at your top rate of tax). You get a tax credit equal to the tax which the trustees have to deduct before they pay out the income.

Normally, the trustees have to deduct tax at the 24 per cent basic rate, *plus* an additional rate of 10 per cent – making 34 per cent in all. If you pay tax at the lower rate of 20 per cent or the basic rate of 24 per cent only, you can claim the extra 14 or 10 per cent back from the Revenue – but you must pay this to the trustees or your child.

If you have to pay tax at the higher rate of 40 per cent on the income, you will have to hand over an extra 40 − 34 = 6 per cent to the Revenue. You can claim back this extra tax from the trustees (or – though you probably wouldn't want to – from the child who receives the income).
ICTA 1988 s663, s667

After you've gone

Re-arrangement of your estate by agreement – the basics

After your death the gifts you made on death can currently be re-arranged – the revised gifts take effect for IHT just as if they had actually been made by you. (The same is true of arrangements made between your relatives if you die without leaving a will.) Various rules apply:

- the new arrangements must take effect within two years of your death
- the arrangements must have the consent of all beneficiaries under your will who are affected by them
- the parties to the arrangement must give their consent in return for what they get under the arrangements (or for no return at all) – not in return for anything else.

To reclaim any IHT paid, you must do so generally within six months of re-arrangement. The relief can be claimed even if:

- the effect is to make someone a beneficiary of your estate who was not one under your will
- the people concerned have already received their gifts.

If someone refuses a gift (or disclaims it within two years) your estate is taxed as if the gift to that person was never made. No claim needs to be made in this case.
IHTA 1984 s142

Re-arrangement – is it worth it?

A re-arrangement of your gifts is a good idea if you haven't left enough for your surviving spouse and have given more than enough to other members of your family. They can re-direct their gifts without a further IHT charge. (Such a re-arrangement could mean a *refund* of tax because more of the revised gift would be tax-free.)

Alternatively, if your surviving spouse has far more than will be needed, he or she can direct gifts to other members of your family. And if, for example, you have given property to your wife for life and after her death to your son, they could (if your son is over 18) agree to split the property between them now. This might reduce the tax when your wife dies. However:

- the arrangements can't alter retrospectively the income tax position. Someone who has been entitled to receive income from a gift which is subsequently given up is taxed on the income he or she was entitled to receive
- if a parent redirects a legacy producing income (of more than £100 a year) to his or her unmarried child under 18, the parent will be taxed on that income until the child reaches 18 or marries
- there is a similar rule for CGT. Variations and disclaimers within two years of your death can be treated as if you had made the revised gifts yourself and as if the original gifts had not been made. The CGT relief does not have to be claimed just because the IHT relief is.

TCGA 1992 s62

Paying IHT

Who has to pay

The Revenue looks first to the giver for tax on a chargeable transfer. So if you want the other person to pay the tax, get a promise that he or she will pay. If you don't pay the tax, the Revenue can get it from the other person anyway. If the person receiving the gift has given it away to someone else, the Revenue can recover the tax from that person.

If you die within seven years of making a potentially tax-free gift, the tax, if any, is due from the person you made the gift to. The same is true if you die within seven years of making a chargeable transfer on which further tax becomes due.

For tax on your death, your personal representatives – or the trustees of settled property if you died having an *interest in possession* in settled property – are liable for the tax. So are the beneficiaries if they have received the property.

IHTA 1984 s199–s205

When to tell the Revenue

When you make a chargeable gift you have to tell the Revenue if:

- your total of taxable gifts for the current tax year exceeds £10,000, or if
- your running total, including the current gift, exceeds £40,000.

You tell the Revenue about lifetime gifts on form IHT–100 which you get from the Capital Taxes Offices.*

Always keep accurate records of the gifts you've made, and the tax, if any, you've paid on them.

For IHT on your death, your personal representatives usually have to prepare an *Inland Revenue account* and submit it to the Probate Registry as part of seeking probate. This lists the value of every asset in your estate (shares, homes, valuables, etc.), including those which are jointly owned. They'll also have to give details of:

- gifts made in the seven years before death which aren't tax-free, including transfers of value (e.g. where you sold something for less than its market value)
- interests you had in trusts.

You give these details on form IHT200/200N available from the Capital Taxes Offices. If your estate counts as a *small estate*, meaning that its gross value is no more than twice the nil-rate band – i.e. twice £200,000 = £400,000 in 1996–7 – your representatives can instead send in simplified accounts using form IHT202/202N. And if your estate is valued at no more than £125,000 in 1996–7, your representatives do not have to submit accounts at all.

When to pay the tax

Tax on lifetime gifts is normally due six months after the end of the month in which you make the gift. But if you make the gift after 5 April and before 1 October, tax is due on 30 April in the following year.

Tax on your death is payable six months after the end of the month in which you die, but your personal representatives will usually want to get probate (or letters of administration) before then. To do so they will have to deliver the accounts and pay the tax first.

Interest is charged on unpaid tax from the time it was payable. The rate for IHT was 5 per cent when we went to press.

IHTA 1984 s226, s233

Payment by instalments

Sometimes IHT can be paid in instalments and in some cases the instalments do not attract interest. The instalment option is available for lifetime gifts (if the other person pays the tax) and for gifts on death of:

- land and buildings, wherever situated
- a business or an interest in a business
- timber, where a lifetime gift has triggered IHT deferred from a previous owner's death
- a controlling holding of shares or securities – whether quoted or unquoted – in a company
- a non-controlling holding of unquoted shares or securities in a company, if certain conditions are specified.

If you want to pay by instalments you should tell the Revenue by the normal due date for paying tax (see above). The tax has to be paid in ten equal yearly instalments. The first instalment is due on the normal due date for paying the tax. Normally interest is due on the outstanding tax. However, in the case of agricultural land, a business or an interest in a business, or many holdings of unquoted shares or securities, interest is due only if instalments are not paid on time.
IHTA 1984 s227–s229, s234

Quick succession relief

If you die within five years of receiving a gift on which IHT has been paid, some of that tax can be subtracted from the tax due on your estate. The amount subtracted is worked out by two simple calculations:

- divide the net value of the gift to you by the gross value of the gift, and multiply the result by the tax paid on the gift
- deduct 20 per cent of the answer for each *complete* year since the gift.

The tax credit is given whether or not you still own the gift at your death.

There is a similar relief for IHT on the termination of your interest in settled property, whether or not the termination takes place on your death.
IHTA 1984 s141

EXAMPLE 11

Joe Brown left Bruce White £30,000 free of tax in January 1995. Joe's estate paid the IHT on the gift, which came to £20,000. Bruce died 18 months later. His estate is given an IHT credit of:

$$\frac{30,000}{50,000} \times £20,000 \times 80 \text{ per cent} = £9,600$$

Life insurance

Life insurance policies provide a way of paying IHT (in addition to offering a simple way of setting up trusts – see p. 274):

- *term* insurance can provide money to pay IHT if you die within seven years of making a potentially tax-free gift (this would have helped Margaret and Brian Ferguson pay the tax on their gifts in Example 5 on p. 339)
- *whole life* insurance can pay out to cover the IHT when you die on an asset you don't want to sell, such as a family home or business.

For how to keep the proceeds out of your estate (and avoid paying IHT on them), see p. 274.

19 *TAX FACTS*

You can query your tax liability for up to six tax years before the current tax year – i.e. you can go back to the 1990–1 tax year if you claim before 6 April 1997. This chapter gives tax rates, allowances and taxable values for company cars and car fuel benefit for earlier years. We give the Retail Prices Index (RPI) figures you'll need for capital gains tax (CGT). There's a list of Inland Revenue leaflets and Revenue concessions.

Rates of tax charged on each slice of taxable income over seven tax years

1996–7	20 per cent up to £3,900 24 per cent on £3,901 to £25,500 40 per cent on £25,501 and over
1995–6	20 per cent up to £3,200 25 per cent on £3,201 to £24,300 40 per cent on £24,301 and over
1994–5	20 per cent up to £3,000 25 per cent on £3,001 to £23,700 40 per cent on £23,701 and over
1993–4	20 per cent up to £2,500 25 per cent on £2,501 to £23,700 40 per cent on £23,701 and over
1992–3	20 per cent up to £2,000 25 per cent on £2,001 to £23,700 40 per cent on £23,701 and over
1991–2	25 per cent on up to £23,700 40 per cent on £23,701 and over
1990–1	25 per cent on up to £20,700 40 per cent on £20,701 and over

Tax calendar for the 1996–7 tax year

Types of income or gain	Date tax due
wages or salary; most pensions from employers	deducted when you get the income (e.g. monthly, weekly) under PAYE
investment income already taxed; share dividends and unit trust distributions; bank and building society interest; interest on most local authority loans	tax at 20 per cent rate deducted (or deemed to have been deducted) before you get the income; no basic-rate tax to pay; any higher-rate tax is due as for 'other income' (see below)
other income investment income not taxed before you get it [1]; income from property [2]; profits from being self-employed [3]	two equal interim payments [4] on 31 January 1997 and 31 July 1997 with a final payment on 31 January 1998
capital gains	31 January 1998
deadline for sending in your tax return if you work out your own tax bill	31 January 1998
deadline for sending in your tax return if you want your tax office to work out your bill in time for you to meet the 31 January 1998 payment date and avoid penalties	30 September 1997

[1] Income on which tax is based depends on when income first started – see p. 244.
[2] For how rents from property are taxed, see p. 228.
[3] Profits on which tax is based depend on when business started – see p. 182.
[4] Based on previous year's tax bill. You can ask for your interim payments to be reduced, if you believe this year's tax bill will be lower.

Note: If most of your income comes from employment or an employer's pension, any tax due on income from other sources – provided it doesn't vary much from year to year – may in practice be deducted under Pay-As-You-Earn (PAYE) so you will not be paying tax at dates shown in *Date tax due* column.

Allowances for seven tax years

Type of allowance		1996–7	1995–6	1994–5	1993–4	1992–3	1991–2	1990–1
personal	£	3,765	3,525	3,445	3,445	3,445	3,295	3,005
higher personal 65–74 [1]	£	up to 4,910	up to 4,630	up to 4,200	up to 4,200	up to 4,200	up to 4,020	up to 3,670
higher personal 75+ [1]	£	up to 5,090	up to 4,800	up to 4,370	up to 4,370	up to 4,370	up to 4,180	up to 3,820
married couple's [2]	£	1,790	1,720	1,720	1,720	1,720	1,720	1,720
higher married couple's 65–74 [1] [2]	£	up to 3,115	up to 2,995	up to 2,665	up to 2,465	up to 2,465	up to 2,355	up to 2,145
higher married couple's 75+ [1] [2]	£	up to 3,155	up to 3,035	up to 2,705	up to 2,505	up to 2,505	up to 2,395	up to 2,185
additional personal [2]	£	1,790	1,720	1,720	1,720	1,720	1,720	1,720
blind person's	£	1,250	1,200	1,200	1,080	1,080	1,080	1,080
widow's bereavement [2]	£	1,790	1,720	1,720	1,720	1,720	1,720	1,720
total income limit – age-related allowances	£	15,200	14,600	14,200	14,200	14,200	13,500	12,300

[1] Your age on the birthday falling within the tax year – husband or wife in the case of the married couple's allowance.
[2] Relief restricted to 20 per cent in 1994–5 and to 15 per cent from 1995–6 onwards.

Capital gains tax rates for seven tax years

Tax year	Tax-free slice	Rate of tax on rest
1996–7	£6,300	20% or 24% or 40%
1995–6	£6,000	20% or 25% or 40%
1994–5	£5,800	20% or 25% or 40%
1993–4	£5,800	20% or 25% or 40%
1992–3	£5,800	20% or 25% or 40%
1991–2	£5,500	25% or 40%
1990–1	£5,000	25% or 40%

Car fuel benefit

The tables show the taxable values for car fuel benefit for average or low business mileage, i.e. up to 17,999 miles. For mileage of 18,000 and over, the values are halved.

The first table shows the taxable value for free petrol if you count as earning £8,500. The £8,500 limit has remained unchanged since 6 April 1979.

Size of engine	1996–7	1995–6	1994–5	1993–4
up to 1,400cc	£710	£670	£640	£600
1,401–2,000cc	£890	£850	£810	£760
2,000cc +	£1,320	£1,260	£1,200	£1,130

Size of engine	1992–3	1991–2	1990–1
up to 1,400cc	£500	£480	£480
1,401–2,000cc	£630	£600	£600
2,000cc +	£940	£900	£900

The taxable values for diesel fuel are as follows:

Size of engine	1996–7	1995–6	1994–5	1993–4	1992–3
up to 2,000cc	£640	£605	£580	£550	£460
2,000cc +	£820	£780	£750	£710	£590

Taxable value of company cars for tax years 1989–90 to 1993–4

These figures apply if you count as earning £8,500 – see pages 156 and 163 and do average business mileage, i.e. 2,501–17,999 miles. If you travel more than this, the value is halved; if less, multiply by 1.5.
For the system of company car taxation from 6 April 1994, see p. 163.

*Market value of car when new

Tax year	Size of engine	Age of car at the end of the tax year: Under 4 years	4 years or more	Under 4 years	4 years or more	Under 4 years	4 years or more
1993–4		*up to £19,250		*£19,251–£29,000		*more than £29,000	
	up to 1,400cc	£2,310	£1,580				
	1,401cc–2,000cc	£2,990	£2,030	£6,210	£4,180	£10,040	£6,660
	2,000cc+	£4,800	£3,220				
1992–3		*up to £19,250		*£19,251–£29,000		*more than £29,000	
	up to 1,400cc	£2,140	£1,465				
	1,401cc–2,000cc	£2,770	£1,880	£5,750	£3,870	£9,300	£6,170
	2,000cc+	£4,440	£2,980				
1991–2		*up to £19,250		*£19,251–£29,000		*more than £29,000	
	up to 1,400cc	£2,050	£1,400				
	1,401cc–2,000cc	£2,650	£1,800	£5,500	£3,700	£8,900	£5,900
	2,000cc+	£4,250	£2,850				
1990–1		*up to £19,250		*£19,251–£29,000		*more than £29,000	
	up to 1,400cc	£1,700	£1,150				
	1,401cc–2,000cc	£2,200	£1,500	£4,600	£3,100	£7,400	£4,900
	2,000cc+	£3,550	£2,350				
1989–90		*up to £19,250		*£19,251–£29,000		*more than £29,000	
	up to 1,400cc	£1,400	£950				
	1,401cc–2,000cc	£1,850	£1,250	£3,850	£2,600	£6,150	£4,100
	2,000cc+	£2,950	£1,950				

Retail Prices Index to work out your indexation allowances for capital gains tax

The RPI was rebased in January 1987 – in other words, it went back to 100. We've reworked the index figures for months before January 1987. You can find index figures for months after this book goes to press in the Department of Employment's *Monthly Gazette* (try your local reference library).

	Jan	Feb	Mar	Apr	May	Jun	Jul	Aug	Sept	Oct	Nov	Dec
1982	n/a	n/a	79.44	81.04	81.62	81.85	81.88	81.90	81.85	82.26	82.66	82.51
1983	82.61	82.97	83.12	84.28	84.64	84.84	85.30	85.68	86.06	86.36	86.67	86.89
1984	86.84	87.20	87.48	88.64	88.97	89.20	89.10	89.94	90.11	90.67	90.95	90.87
1985	91.20	91.94	92.80	94.78	95.21	95.41	95.23	95.49	95.44	95.59	95.92	96.05
1986	96.25	96.60	96.73	97.67	97.85	97.79	97.52	97.82	98.30	98.45	99.29	99.62
1987	100.0	100.4	100.6	101.8	101.9	101.9	101.8	102.1	102.4	102.9	103.4	103.3
1988	103.3	103.7	104.1	105.8	106.2	106.6	106.7	107.9	108.4	109.5	110.0	110.3
1989	111.0	111.8	112.3	114.3	115.0	115.4	115.5	115.8	116.6	117.5	118.5	118.8
1990	119.5	120.2	121.4	125.1	126.2	126.7	126.8	128.1	129.3	130.3	130.0	129.9
1991	130.2	130.9	131.4	133.1	133.5	134.1	133.8	134.1	134.6	135.1	135.6	135.7
1992	135.6	136.3	136.7	138.8	139.3	139.3	138.8	138.9	139.4	139.9	139.7	139.2
1993	137.9	138.8	139.3	140.6	141.1	141.0	140.7	141.3	141.9	141.8	141.6	141.9
1994	141.3	142.1	142.5	144.2	144.7	144.7	144.0	144.7	145.0	145.2	145.3	146.0
1995	146.0	146.9	147.5	149.0	149.6	149.8	149.1	149.9	150.6	149.8	149.8	150.7

Inheritance tax rates since 18 March 1986

The tax on gifts made between three and seven years of death is reduced on a sliding scale – see p. 340.

In this table, the first percentage gives the tax rate for chargeable gifts on death, or within three years of death. The percentage in brackets gives the tax rate for gifts chargeable while you are still alive.

6 April 1996 to 5 April 1997	up to £200,000	nil
	£200,001 and over	40% (20%)

6 April 1995 to 5 April 1996	up to £154,000	nil
	£154,001 and over	40% (20%)
10 March 1992 to 5 April 1995	up to £150,000	nil
	£150,001 and over	40% (20%)
6 April 1991 to 9 March 1992	up to £140,000	nil
	£140,001 and over	40% (20%)
6 April 1990 to 5 April 1991	up to £128,000	nil
	£128,001 and over	40% (20%)
6 April 1989 to 5 April 1990	up to £118,000	nil
	£118,001 and over	40% (20%)
15 March 1988 to 5 April 1989	up to £110,000	nil
	£110,001 and over	40% (20%)
17 March 1987 to 14 March 1988	up to £90,000	nil
	£90,001 to £140,000	30% (15%)
	£140,001 to £220,000	40% (20%)
	£220,001 to £330,000	50% (25%)
	£330,001 and over	60% (30%)
18 March 1986 to 16 March 1987	up to £71,000	nil
	£71,001 to £95,000	30% (15%)
	£95,001 to £129,000	35% (17½%)
	£129,001 to £164,000	40% (20%)
	£164,001 to £206,000	45% (22½%)
	£206,001 to £257,000	50% (25%)
	£257,001 to £317,000	55% (27½%)
	£317,001 and over	60% (30%)

Tax forms you might come across

In this section we list and explain briefly the more common Inland Revenue forms. **Note:** some of the forms will be replaced by new ones designed for the new system of self-assessment. Details were not available as we went to press.

Tax returns

P1 For people with fairly simple tax affairs

11P For people who earn at a rate of £8,500 or more a year and who work for an employer

11 Mainly for the self-employed

1 For partnerships, trustees, executors and personal representatives

Reclaiming tax

P50 If you're out of work for more than 4 weeks and are not claiming unemployment benefit or income support, use this form to claim back tax you've overpaid

PP120 Use this form to claim tax relief on pension contribution

R40 If you're a non-taxpayer, but tax has been deducted from any income you receive from certain investments, or alimony or maintenance payments, use this form to claim back tax

R185 Use this form to claim tax back on covenant payments you've received (for pre-15 March 1988 covenants)

Employment

P45 Your employer will give you this when you leave a job

P46 Your employer will give you this to fill in when you start your first job

P15 Coding claim – you should fill this form in at the same time as P46 and send it to the Revenue immediately to get your PAYE code

P38(s) For students who get holiday jobs, if their total income doesn't exceed the personal allowance (£3,765 in the 1996–7 tax year)

P60 Your employer gives you this (or an equivalent certificate) at the end of the tax year – it tells you how much you've earned during that year and how much tax has been deducted

P11D Your employer uses this form to declare to the Revenue how much you've been paid during the tax year in the way of expenses, fringe benefits, etc.

Payments you make

R185 Use this form to certify that you've deducted tax from a payment you're making

R190(SD) Complete this and give to a charity together with your donation under the Gift Aid scheme. Get the blank form from the charity

43 Use this form if you need to provide the Revenue with details of personal pension payments

IHT100 Use this form if you need to tell the Revenue about any chargeable transfers for inheritance tax purposes

Income

P2(T) This is the PAYE Coding Notice the Revenue will send you to tell you what your PAYE code is

Notices of assessment

300	**Schedule A or D notice of assessment** You'll get this form if you let property or are self-employed
P70(T)	**Schedule E notice of assessment** You may be sent this form if most of your income comes from a job
900	Notice of assessment for higher-rate taxpayers
CG4	Capital gains tax assessment

Inland Revenue leaflets

Here we list the main explanatory leaflets available from the Revenue. You can get them from your local tax office or tax enquiry centre (although some inheritance tax leaflets are available only from Capital Taxes Offices*). Some leaflets are updated regularly or have supplements added, so make sure you've got the newest edition.

IR1	Extra-statutory concessions
IR6	Double taxation relief for companies
IR9	The tax treatment of livestock – the herd basis
IR14/15	Construction industry tax deduction scheme
IR16/17	Income tax – share acquisitions by directors and employees
IR20	Residents and non-residents – liability to tax in the UK
IR24	Class 4 National Insurance contributions
IR26	Income tax assessments on business profits – changes of accounting date
IR28	Starting in business
IR33	Income tax and school leavers
IR34	Income tax – Pay-As-You-Earn
IR37	Income tax and capital gains tax – appeals
IR40	Income tax – conditions for getting a sub-contractor's tax certificate
IR41	Income tax and the unemployed
IR42	Lay-offs and short-time work
IR43	Income tax and strikes
IR45	What to do about tax when someone dies
IR46	Income tax and corporation tax – clubs, societies and associations
IR51	Business expansion scheme
IR53	Thinking of taking someone on? PAYE for employers
IR56	Employed or self-employed?
IR57	Thinking of working for yourself?
IR58	Going to work abroad

IR60	Income tax and students
IR64	Giving to charity (for businesses)
IR65	Giving to charity (for individuals)
IR68	Accrued income scheme
IR69	Expenses – Forms P11D
IR71	PAYE – inspection of employers' and contractors' records
IR72	Inland Revenue investigations – the examination of business accounts
IR73	Inland Revenue investigations – how settlements are negotiated
IR75	Tax reliefs for charities
IR78	Personal pensions
IR80	Income tax and married couples
IR85	Business expansion scheme – private rented housing
IR87	Rooms to let – income from letting property
IR89	Personal equity plans (PEPs)
IR90	Tax allowances and reliefs
IR91	A guide for widows and widowers
IR92	Income tax – a guide for one-parent families
IR93	Separation, divorce and maintenance payments
IR95	Shares for employees – profit-sharing schemes
IR97	Shares for employees – SAYE share options
IR99	Schemes for employees – executive share options
IR103	Private medical insurance
IR104	Tax and your business – simple tax accounts
IR105	How your profits are taxed
IR106	Capital allowances for vehicles and machinery
IR109	PAYE: Inspection of employers' and contractors' records – how settlements are negotiated
IR110	A guide for people with savings
IR113	Gift Aid – A guide for donors and charities
IR114	TESSA – tax-free interest for taxpayers
IR115	Tax and childcare
IR116	Guide for sub-contractors with tax certificates
IR117	A sub-contractor's guide to the deduction scheme
IR119	Tax relief for vocational training
IR120	You and the Inland Revenue
IR121	Income tax and pensioners
IR122	Volunteer drivers – treatment of mileage allowance
IR123	Mortgage interest relief: buying your home
IR127	Are you paying too much tax on your savings?
IR133	Income tax and company cars – employees' guide
IR134	Income tax and relocation packages
IR136	Income tax and company vans
IR137	The enterprise investment scheme
IR141	Open government
IR142	Self assessment – an introduction
IR146	Double taxation relief – admissible and inadmissible taxes

IR148	Guidance notes for contractors in the construction industry – are your workers employed or self-employed?
480	Expenses and benefits – a guide for tax
P7	Employer's guide to PAYE
CGT4	Capital gains tax – owner-occupied houses
CGT6	Capitals gains tax – retirement relief on disposal of a business
CGT11	Capital gains tax and small businesses
CGT13	Capital gains tax – the indexation allowance for quoted shares
CGT14	Capital gains tax – an introduction
CGT15	Capital gains tax – a guide for married couples
CGT16	Capital gains tax – indexation allowance – disposals after 5 April 1988
IHT1	Inheritance tax
IHT2	Inheritance tax on lifetime gifts
IHT3	An introduction to inheritance tax
IHT8	Inheritance tax – alterations to inheritance following a death
COP1	Mistakes by the Inland Revenue
COP2	Investigations
COP3	Inspection of employers' and contractors' records
COP6	Collection of tax
RAO	How to complain about the Inland Revenue
S01	Stamp duty on buying a freehold house (two versions – one is just for Scotland)
S02	The Stamp Office customer promise
S03	The Stamp Office adjudication customer promise
S04	How to get the most out of your Stamp Office
S05	Common stamp duty forms and how to complete them (two versions – one is just for Scotland)
S06	A short history of stamp duties
S07	Stamp duty on leasehold domestic property (not issued in Scotland)
S08	Stamp duty on agreements securing short tenancies
S09	A table of ad valorem stamp duties (two versions – one is just for Scotland)
S010	Penalties payable when documents are stamped late
SVD1	Shares Valuation Division – an introduction

For **inheritance tax leaflets**, write to Capital Taxes Offices* in Nottingham, Edinburgh or Belfast.

The Shares Valuation Division deals with valuing unquoted shares for capital gains tax and inheritance tax. Unquoted shares are those not listed, quoted or traded on the Stock Exchange.

In Scotland and Northern Ireland, you can contact the

Capital Taxes Offices* in Edinburgh or Belfast.

For England and Wales contact the Shares Valuation Division, Nottingham*.

Inland Revenue concessions

Concessions mean that you are let off paying tax that is technically due. For example, if you are a miner and opt for payment instead of the free coal you are entitled to, you won't have to pay tax on the money you receive instead.

Below we give a brief summary of the income tax concessions in Section A of Inland Revenue leaflet *IR1* (and new concessions awaiting inclusion) – this section deals with income tax and individuals. In some cases you'll need to look at the exact wording of the concession.

A1 **Flat rate allowance for cost of tools and special clothing** You can claim an allowance if you have to pay for the tools and clothing you need for work. For most kinds of trade, a flat rate is agreed with the relevant trade union(s). If you spend more than the flat rate, you can claim back more.

A2 **Meal vouchers** You won't be taxed on the first 15p per working day of meal vouchers given to you by your employer provided that the vouchers are non-transferable, and they are used for meals only.

A4 **Directors' travelling expenses** If you're a director of more than one company within the same parent company, you won't be taxed on travelling expenses you receive for business travel from one company to the other(s). This includes hotel expenses, provided they are reasonable and necessary. The same applies if you're an employee of one company and director of another.

A6 **Miners: free coal and allowances in lieu** Miners do not pay income tax on free coal or on cash they receive in lieu.

A7 **Business passing on the death of a trader** Special rules apply if a trader dies and the business passes to the trader's husband or wife who was living with him or her. This concession will be withdrawn from 6 April 1997 when new rules make it redundant.

A8 **Loss relief for capital allowances unused on the cessation of a business** Applying normal rules when a business ends could mean that some capital allowances are lost. A special rule allows losses which would otherwise be lost to be set against income in the final year of the business.

A9 **Doctors' and dentists' superannuation contributions**
This concession deals with tax relief on personal pension contributions paid by doctors and dentists who also are required to contribute to the NHS superannuation scheme.

A10 **Overseas provident fund and pension scheme**
No liability to income tax on lump sums received from an overseas provident fund (or anything similar) when employment overseas ends if certain conditions met.

A11 **Residence in the United Kingdom: year of commencement or cessation of residence** Normally, on arrival in the UK in any given tax year, your income for the *whole* of that year (whether or not it was earned in this country) will be subject to UK tax (the same applies if you leave the country). But if you intend to stay for at least three years or are coming to work for at least two years or if you leave the UK to go and live abroad (intending to live there permanently), you will be liable for tax for only that part of the tax year when you were actually here, provided that you have not been ordinarily resident in the UK prior to or after this stay. There are special rules for Ireland.

A12 **Double taxation relief: alimony, etc. under United Kingdom court order or agreement: payer resident abroad** If you pay alimony, even if you live abroad, the money you pay counts as income arising in the UK. But relief by way of credit is allowed provided that: you are resident abroad; the money you pay comes out of your income in the country where you are resident and is taxable there; any UK tax you deduct from the payments is accounted for; and the person who receives the money is resident in the UK and effectively bears the overseas tax.

A13 **Administration of estates: deficiencies of income allowed against income of another year** This concession allows relief for higher-rate tax to some beneficiaries of an estate if the income of the estate (during the administration period) is a minus figure for tax purposes.

A14 **Deceased person's estate: residuary income received during the administration period** Special rules may lower the tax liability of legatees who are not resident or ordinarily resident in the UK.

A16 Annual payments (other than interest) paid out of income not brought into charge to income tax If you make covenant payments, maintenance payments or other annual payments from which you deduct tax, you have to account to the Revenue for the tax you've deducted. If your taxable income is lower than the gross amount of the payments, you'll have to hand over extra tax. Concession A16 gives relief against this rule if you make payments late, but – if the payments had been made in the correct tax year – you would have had enough taxable income to cover the payments.

A17 Death of taxpayer before due date for payment of tax If this occurs and the executors cannot release the money to pay the tax, interest on the unpaid tax is waived until 30 days from the date on which probate is granted.

A19 Arrears of tax arising through official error Often partly or completely waived, according to your income, if you haven't been notified by the end of the tax year after the year in which the error occurred.

A22 Long service awards These are not taxable provided the employee has been working for the employer for at least 20 years and has received no other such reward within the previous 10 years, and the article doesn't cost the employer more than £20 per year of service. The award must either be a tangible article of reasonable cost or shares in the company you work for (or an affiliated company).

A24 Foreign social security benefits You don't have to pay tax on these provided they correspond to UK social security benefits which are exempt from tax.

A25 Crown servants engaged overseas Locally engaged unestablished staff engaged overseas as servants of the Crown won't be liable to UK income tax if they are not resident in the UK for tax purposes and if the maximum rate of pay for their grade is less than the maximum pay of an executive officer working in Inner London.

A27 Relief for mortgage interest: temporary absences from mortgaged property for up to a year These are ignored when determined if a property is a 'main residence'. Absences of four years are ignored if you have to live elsewhere because of your work. If you live in the property for a minimum of three months, a further four-year concession will be granted. Similarly, people working abroad can qualify for the same four-year concession if they return and live in a property for three months.

A28 **Relief for mortgage interest: residents of the Republic of Ireland** They qualify for UK income tax relief for interest paid on a loan from a lender in the Republic of Ireland, providing certain conditions are met.

A29 **Farming and market gardening: relief for fluctuating profits** For the purposes of the average provisions in Section 96, ICTA 1988, 'farming' includes the intensive rearing of livestock or fish on a commercial basis for the production of food for human consumption.

A30 **Interest on damages for personal injuries (foreign court awards)** No liability to UK income tax provided there would have been no liability to income tax on interest in the country where the award was made.

A34 **Ulster savings certificates: certificates encashed after death of registered holder** Interest paid after the death of the holder is exempt from income tax if the holder lived in Northern Ireland when the certificates were purchased.

A37 **Tax treatment of directors' fees received by partnerships and other companies** In certain circumstances, directors' fees will be assessed under Schedule D, rather than Schedule E.

A39 **Exemption for Hong Kong officials. Extension of ICTA 1988, Section 320** Some Hong Kong officials who work in the UK are not liable to UK income tax.

A40 **Adoption allowances payable under the Adoption Allowance Regulations 1991 and Section 51 of the Adoption (Scotland) Act 1978** These are not liable to income tax.

A41 **Qualifying life insurance policies: statutory conditions** The Revenue may count life insurance polices as qualifying policies even though they have minor infringements which, technically, means they aren't qualifying policies.

A43 **Interest relief: investment in partnerships and close companies** Tax relief on loans taken out to invest in or to lend money to a partnership, a co-operative, an employee-controlled company or close company won't be withdrawn when the organisation is restructured – e.g. a partnership becomes a co-operative or a close company, provided that the relief would have been allowed if the loan had been taken out to invest in the new organisation.

A44 Education allowances under Overseas Service Aid Scheme There won't be income tax to pay on certain education allowances payable to public servants from overseas under the Overseas Aid Scheme.

A45 Life insurance policies: variation of term assured policies A term assurance policy with a term of ten years or less continues to be a qualifying policy even if the rate of premium is reduced to less than half, following a reduction in the sum assured or an extension of the term (but the total term must still be less than ten years).

A46 Variable purchased life annuities: carry forward of deficit in capital element This refers to annuities where the amount of any annuity payment doesn't depend on the length of a person's life. If the tax-free part of the income – the capital element – comes to more than the annuity payment, the difference can be carried forward as an allowance in deciding the size of the capital element in the next payment.

A47 House purchase loans made by life offices to staffs of insurance associations A loan on a qualifying policy made by a life office to a full-time employee of certain insurance associations won't count as a surrender of rights under the policy.

A49 Widow's pension paid to widow of Singapore nationality, resident in the United Kingdom, whose husband was a United Kingdom national employed as a Public Officer by the Government of Singapore These widow's pensions are exempt from tax.

A55 Arrears of foreign pensions If you receive a foreign pension which is granted or increased retrospectively, tax due on it can be calculated as if the arrears arose in the years to which they relate.

A56 Benefits in kind: the tax treatment of accommodation in Scotland provided for employees The annual value of accommodation provided to employees is assessed for tax by reference to the property's rateable value. By concession, the annual value of accommodation in Scotland will not be assessed on the 1985 rates revaluation. Instead, the 1978 valuation will be used in assessing the annual value of accommodation for 1985–6 and 1986–7, and for subsequent years an annual value calculated by scaling back the 1985 rating value will be used.

A57 Suggestion schemes Certain awards (up to a maximum of £5,000) for ideas put forward through staff suggestions schemes at work will be free of tax.

A58 Travelling and subsistence allowance when public transport disrupted You won't be taxed on (reasonable) extra travel costs of getting to work or the cost of accommodation near work that your employer pays for or reimburses when public transport is disrupted by industrial action.

A59 Home-to-work travel of severely disabled employees Disabled people who cannot use public transport will not be taxed on the value of special travel facilities or on money provided by local authorities or the employment service to enable them to get to and from work.

A60 Agricultural workers' board and lodging Agricultural employees who receive free board and lodging but are entitled to higher cash wages in lieu may not be taxed on the value of the board and lodging, provided they don't count as earning £8,500 or more. They are paid net and no deduction is made from their wages to cover board and lodgings.

A61 Clergymen's heating and lighting, etc., expenses Clergy who do not count as earning £8,500 or more, and who perform their duties from accommodation provided by their employers, won't be taxed on heating, lighting, cleaning or gardening expenses that their employer meets for them.

A62 Pensions to disabled employees If you retire following an injury at work or because of a work-related illness or a war wound, any extra pension paid over and above the amount you would have got if retiring on grounds of ordinary ill heath is not taxed. The same applies to a pension awarded solely on one of these grounds.

A63* External training courses – expenses borne by employer The cost of books and fees your employer pays for you to attend certain external training courses won't be taxed if you are under 21 when the course starts. Provided you are not away for more than 12 months, extra travel expenses and living costs met by your employer while you are on the course may not be taxable either.

A64* External training courses – expenses borne by employee If your employer encourages or requires you to go on a full-time external training course of four weeks or more in the

UK and gives you time off work on full pay, you can get tax relief on the cost of books and fees for the course not met by your employer (unless the course is for re-sit examinations). Extra travel expenses or costs of living away from home also qualify for tax relief, unless you're away for over 12 months.

A65 **Workers on offshore oil and gas rigs or platforms – transfers from or to mainland** Workers on offshore oil and gas rigs won't be taxed on the value of travel to and from the mainland provided free by their employer, nor on reasonable overnight expenses at the point of departure from the mainland, which their employer pays or reimburses.

A66 **Employees' late-night journeys from work to home** If your employer pays for taxis to take you home after working late (i.e. 9 p.m. onwards) you won't be taxed on this benefit, provided that this does not happen regularly or frequently and provided that it would be unreasonable to expect you to travel home by public transport.

A67 **Payments made to employees moved to a higher-cost housing area** Payments made to you by your employer to cover increased accommodation costs which have been incurred due to a compulsory transfer from one area to another will not be taxed provided that the payments are regular, are for a limited period of time and taper as the years progress. The total payment must not exceed the maximum amount payable in the Civil Service.

A68 **Payments out of a discretionary trust which are emoluments taxable under Schedule E** Employee trusts are established to make discretionary payments to employees or their families. They pay a high rate of tax on the income they produce. Certain payments from such trusts are also taxed as income for the beneficiary. To prevent double taxation, trustees can claim back tax paid on all trust income which has been used to make payments on which the beneficiary has subsequently paid income tax.

A69 **Composite-rate tax: non-resident depositors** If a building society converts to company status, certain declarations which have been made to the building society will be treated as having been made to the successor company.

*Relief under concessions A63 and A64 will not be available when you get relief at source. Since 6 April 1992, most relief for vocational training has been given at source.

A70 **Small gifts to employees by third parties, and staff Christmas parties**
A Gifts (i.e. goods or gift vouchers) worth £150 or less given to an employee or members of his or her family by people unconnected with his or her employer will not be taxed.
B Christmas parties and similiar annual parties open to all staff will not be taxed provided annual expenditure on such events is no more than £75 a head.

A71 **Company cars for family members** If a relative receives a company car from your employer you will not be taxed on it provided that the relative is an employee of the company in his or her own right and provision of a car is normal for someone in his or her position.

A72 **Pension schemes and accident insurance policies**
You do not pay income tax on any payments made by your employer to members of your family or household on your death or retirement.

A74 **Meals provided for employees** Income tax is not charged on free or subsidised meals provided to employees on work premises or in any canteen where meals are provided for staff generally (or on the use of a voucher to obtain such meals) as long as the meals are on a reasonable scale and *either* are available to all staff *or* the employer provides free or subsidised vouchers for staff who don't receive the meals.

A76 **Business Expansion Scheme: subscriber shares** If, when a company is first incorporated, you own one of two subscriber shares (i.e. 50 per cent of the share capital), you might still be able to apply for tax relief under the Business Expansion Scheme. This applies until the company issues further shares, and provided the company does not enter into any other transactions.

A77 **Motor mileage allowances paid to volunteer drivers** If you're a volunteer driver, only a quarter of the amount by which your allowances exceed the cost of running and maintaining your car for voluntary service was taxed in 1992–3. Half the amount was taxed in 1993–4 and three-quarters in 1994–5. (The full amount has been taxed from 1995–6.) The concession does not apply to taxi and mini-cab drivers who drive on a voluntary basis.

A78 **Spouse travelling abroad** Special rules regarding 'residence' and 'ordinary residence' may apply if you are accompanying your husband or wife when he or she goes abroad to work full-time. This applies when your husband or wife is regarded for the period abroad as not resident and not ordinarily resident, and provided you will not be in full-time employment abroad as well.

A79 **Tax-exempt special savings accounts (TESSAs)** In Scotland, a curator bonis can open a TESSA account on behalf of an incapacitated person aged 18 or over, in addition to his or her own TESSA.

A80 **Blanket partnership continuation elections** Partners can elect for their partnership to continue, rather than for it to end each time a partner leaves or a new one joins. This concession means that one election can cover all future changes in the partnership until any of the partners withdraw from the arrangement. It applies to firms with at least 50 partners (or fewer than 50 if at least 20 partners are not resident in the UK immediately after the first change). All new partners must add their name to the election.

A81 **Termination payments and legal costs** If you take legal action against your former employer for dismissing you, you may succeed in recovering your legal costs from the former employer. The money you receive won't be liable to tax if the costs are paid as a result of a court order. There will be no tax on costs paid in an out of court settlement direct to your solicitor if the settlement requires costs to be paid.

A82 **Repayment supplement to individuals resident in EU member states** A repayment supplement is interest paid by the Revenue on tax rebates (see p. 60) to people resident in the UK. This concession allows repayment supplements to be made if you were resident in the European Union in the year of tax assessment to which the rebate relates. It applies to rebates dating back to 12 July 1987.

A83 **Benefits under permanent health insurance policies** You don't have to pay tax on income benefits during periods of sickness or disability paid in the first 12 months after 6 April 1994, provided that the benefits were first paid on or after that date. The concession does not apply to policies which have received tax relief as part of pension contributions.

A84 **Detached national experts** Civil servants and private-sector employees won't be taxed on daily subsistence allowances paid by the European Commission.

A85 **Transfer of assets by employees and directors to employers and others** From 6 April 1994, if you sell or transfer an asset to your employer – for example, you sell your home at a guaranteed price to your employer as part of a relocation package – normal transaction costs paid by the employer do not count as a taxable benefit to you.

A86 Blind person's tax allowance From 6 April 1994, if you become eligible for the blind person's allowance by being registered as blind, you can also get the allowance for the previous tax year if at the end of that tax year you had obtained evidence of blindness but had not completed the registration process.

A87/A88 Loss relief on accounts basis If you are self-employed or in a partnership and you make losses, strictly speaking the losses should be apportioned to the relevant tax years for the purpose of claiming relief. However, recognising long-standing practice, you can instead claim relief for the accounting year in which the loss occurred. Where a trade using the accounts basis for losses ceases, the Revenue will work out whether any further loss relief is due.

IR press release 19.12.94 Compensation by an overseas government for loss or confiscation of property A gain you make as a result of payments you receive on or after 19 December 1994 under the Foreign Compensation Act 1950 for property which was lost, confiscated or destroyed – e.g. as a result of war – is free of capital gains tax, provided you were the owner at the time of the loss.

IR press release 3.5.95 Interest relief on loan for home used partly for business Where you use part of your home exclusively for business, a mortgage on the home can be treated as if it were in two parts: you can claim mortgage interest relief on the part corresponding to residential use of the home, and you can treat the business part as an allowable expense in calculating your taxable profits.

IR press release 16.5.95 Jobmatch scheme Allowances and vouchers received under the government's pilot Jobmatch scheme for the long-term unemployed are exempt from income tax.

IR press release 28.11.95 Accommodation provided by reason of employment Where a property is provided for the use of more than one employee (or director) at the same time, the total tax they pay on the benefit will be no more than the tax which would have been due if the property had been provided to just one employee. There will no longer be an extra tax bill, where the property costs your employer more than £75,000 to provide, if tax is based on the open-market rent the property could fetch.

ADDRESSES

Adjudicator's Office
3rd Floor
Haymarket House
28 Haymarket
London SW1Y 4SP
Tel 0171-930 2292

Capital Taxes Office
Ferrers House
P.O. Box 38
Castle Meadow Road
Nottingham NG2 1BB
Tel 0115-974 2424

Capital Taxes Office
16 Picardy Place
Edinburgh EH1 3NB
Tel 0131-556 8511

Capital Taxes Office
52–58 Great Victoria Street
Belfast BT2 7QL
Tel (01232) 236633

Financial Intermediaries and
Claims Office
St John's House
Merton Road
Bootle L69 9BB
Tel 0151-472 6000

Financial Intermediaries and
Claims Office International
Fitzroy House
P.O. Box 46
Nottingham NG2 1BD.
Tel 0115-974 2000

Shares Valuation Division
Fitzroy House
P.O. Box 46
Nottingham NG2 1BD
Tel 0115-974 2374

Stamp Offices
Belfast (01232) 314614
Birmingham 0121-200 2616
Bristol 0117-922 5549
Edinburgh 0131-556 8511
Manchester 0161-833 0413
Newcastle 0191-245 0200
Worthing (01903) 701280

INDEX